Date Due

Date Due			
Nov 11 '60			
Jan3 6 3			
Oct 19'62			
Oct 15'64			
Feb 13'65			
Jul 9 '65			
Sep 27'66			
Oct 10 66			
Oct 25 66			
Dec 7'66			
Jan 4'67			
Jan 19'67			
Feb 7'67			
Oct 22 68			
Mar 16'71			

PATTERNS

OF

ENGLISH

by Paul Roberts

Professor of English, San Jose State Teachers College
San Jose, California

HARCOURT, BRACE

AND COMPANY

New York · Chicago

Copyright, © 1956, by Harcourt, Brace and Company, Inc.

PRINTED IN THE UNITED STATES OF AMERICA

[b · 5 · 56]

July, 1959

Contents

Part One

THE FOUR

FORM CLASSES

1 : The English language

The language we speak is in some ways the most important language in the world. It is spoken by close to three hundred million people. Nearly everyone who lives in the United States speaks English, and also nearly all the people in Canada, England, Australia, and New Zealand. Besides this, English is spoken as a second language by many people in many countries. Probably there is no large town or city in the world in which we could not find at least a few people who speak English.

Now, an interesting thing is that among all these speakers of English there are no two people who speak it exactly alike. We have all noticed how we can recognize our friends' voices on the telephone, even before they tell us who is speaking. Obviously, if everyone spoke alike, we couldn't do this. Voices are like fingerprints. Some fingerprints are very much like others, but each one has some special loops and whorls. In the same way, some voices are very similar, but each one has its special personality.

But it is not only in the sound of the voice that the way in which each of us speaks English differs. We differ also in the words we know and use, in the meanings we give to our words, and sometimes in the forms that the words have. Some of these differences separate large groups of people. If you have ever heard an Englishman speak, you know that the English speak quite differently than Americans do. Our "elevator" is to the English a "lift"; our automobile "hood" is a "bonnet"; our "subway" is a "tube." Where an American will say "I didn't have any," the Englishman will say "I hadn't got any."

Even in our own country there are many differences between the speech of peoples in different parts of the country. What some people call a "frying pan" others call a "skillet." What is a "sofa" to some people is a "couch" to others, a "lounge" to others, and a "chesterfield" to still others. When the time is 1:45, some people would say it's "a quarter to two," others "a quarter of two," and still others "a quarter till two."

English differs, then, according to the country (or the part of a country) in which it is spoken.

But English also differs in many other ways. Men don't speak it the way women do; boys don't speak it the way girls do. We would not expect to hear the following conversation between two boys:

JOSEPH. Hi, Edward. Where've you been?

EDWARD. Oh, Joseph! I've been shopping, and do you know, I found the most darling pair of slacks.

JOSEPH. Kid! Did you really!

EDWARD. Yes, and kid you'll just die when I tell you what I paid for them.

No, boys would be more likely to say this:

JOSEPH. Hey, Ed. Where ya been?

EDWARD. What's doin', Joe? Downtown. I bought me some pants.

JOSEPH. Uh.

EDWARD. They really soaked me for 'em too.

Thus language differs according to sex. It also differs according to age. If we hear a little child say, "I heard the dearest little bird singing the merriest little song," we think it rather sweet. But if we were to hear the same sentence from a man of forty, we would be inclined to call a doctor. We simply do not expect people of different ages to talk alike. Our fathers and mothers use words and phrases that we never use; on the other hand, we use words and phrases that our parents never use and perhaps do not even know about.

English differs from place to place, from one age group to another, from one sex to another, from person to person. No two people speak English exactly alike.

And that's not all. This whole complicated mass of English is steadily changing. It isn't today what it was yesterday, nor what it will be tomorrow. The change is rather slow, for the most part, so that we perhaps cannot even notice it going on, but over the centuries it mounts up. Here is what has happened to the first line of the Lord's Prayer in the last fifteen hundred years or so:

1600: Our Father, which art in heaven, hallowed be thy name.
1300: Fader oure thet art ine hevenes, yhalyed bi thi name.
 900: Faeder ure thu the eart on heofenum, si thin nama gehalgod.
 600: Atta unsar, thu in himinam, weihnai namo thein.

Who can tell what it will look like in the year 3500?

English is something different, then, to every person who speaks it, and the whole mass of English is steadily changing, every minute that it is used. You may wonder how we can study anything so complicated. Several facts make it possible. For one thing, the writing system we use when we study the language hides a good many of the differences that occur in speech. This has its bad points, but it does help us to ignore these differences while we concentrate on other matters.

We should remember that speech and writing are quite different things. Writing is not really language at all. It is just marks we make on paper to suggest sounds we make in our mouths when we talk. Sometimes the written marks don't suggest the speech sounds very accurately, because the speech has drifted away from the marks used to indicate it. Suppose I write

"Cha doon." You probably won't understand it. But if I were to say "Cha doon" in the right situation with the proper tone of voice, you would understand immediately. And if you were asked to write down what had been said, you would write "What are you doing?" Actually nobody pronounces all the letters contained in "What are you doing?" Each of us pronounces the sentence in his own way, and in different ways on different occasions, but we all write it in the general way.

This is what makes it rather hard to learn to spell English. We can't always use the pronunciation as a guide. But it makes it easy to read one another's writing. No matter how you and I pronounce a word, we both write it in the same way. When we see it, you think of it in your pronunciation and I think of it in mine, and there's no trouble. This shared system of writing helps us to leave differences of sound out of account and focus our attention on something else we share: basic sentence patterns.

Remember that, in spite of our many differences, everyone who speaks English can — to a certain extent at least — understand everyone else who speaks English. Boys can understand girls, old people can understand young people, New Yorkers can understand Californians. Sometimes, to be sure, understanding is difficult. A person from London and a person from Seattle, talking together, may have moments when each one wonders what in the world the other one is trying to say. But still, if both are patient and if both speak slowly, they can get along and have their conversation. For there will be one respect in which their different brands of English will be very much alike: they will both use pretty much the same basic sentence patterns. That is the part of English that we shall study here — the basic sentence patterns shared by all speakers of English.

Do not jump to the conclusion that our study will be simple and well ordered, like the multiplication table. These basic sentence patterns, even if we keep to the more obvious of them, have much complexity and variety. But their variety is finite — which means that it has limits. Given a certain collection of words, there are certain different ways in which we can arrange them to make sentences, but only a limited number of different ways. Suppose we have the following words: *pigeons, worms, eat.* There are just two ways in which these can be put together to make an English sentence:

Pigeons eat worms.   Worms eat pigeons.

The second sentence isn't true, but it's a good English sentence. However, the other possible arrangements would not give us English sentences. We don't say either of the following:

Eat worms pigeons.   Eat pigeons worms.

And we don't normally say:

Worms pigeons eat.   Pigeons worms eat.

Or suppose we have these words: *the, the, bit, beautiful, dog, man, quickly.* We might get several different patterns or arrangements out of these:

The beautiful dog quickly bit the man.
The beautiful dog bit the man quickly.
Quickly the beautiful dog bit the man.
The dog quickly bit the beautiful man.
The beautiful man quickly bit the dog.
The beautiful man bit the dog quickly.

We might even find a few odd arrangements that we could call English:

The quickly beautiful dog bit the man.
The man the beautiful dog bit quickly. (The woman he took his time about.)

But most other arrangements would not be possible. The following are not English sentences:

The man dog beautiful the quickly bit.
Beautiful dog the bit man the quickly.
The quickly man beautiful bit the dog.

Thus we can say that English consists of a limited number of patterns which form the basis of what we call sentences. Furthermore, we have a limited number of *kinds* of words which, being arranged in various ways, make up these patterns. That is what we shall study — the patterns of English sentences and the kinds of words which compose them. Even so, we shall have to put limits to this study. We shall not have time to explore all the little ways in which the patterns of American speakers differ from the patterns of British speakers, or those in which the patterns of the past differ from the patterns of the present. We shall not be able to say much about another interesting and complicated variety of English — the English used by people without much education.

Even if we limit ourselves to the English of educated Americans of the twentieth century, we shall have to stick pretty much to broad lines and basic patterns, leaving many corners unexplored. But still we shall see a picture varied enough to justify the remark that man never invented a machine more interesting and delicate and complicated than the English language.

● EXERCISE 1

A. See if you can think of half a dozen objects for which different people have different names. One example would be the piece of living-room furniture which some people call a *couch*, others a *sofa* or *lounge* or *chesterfield*. Another would be the piece of bedroom furniture with drawers for clothes. What do you call that? Think of names for furniture, parts of the house, clothes, foods, and things like that. List them and compare your list with those prepared by your classmates.

B. Make a list of words or phrases which girls use regularly but which boys seldom or never use.

C. Make a list of words or phrases which boys use regularly but which girls seldom or never use.

D. Find out what these words mean in England. A good dictionary will tell you.

1. pram	**3.** petrol	**5.** braces	**7.** boot
2. bobby	**4.** chemist	**6.** spanner	**8.** lorry

E. How do you pronounce the sentence "Are you going to go?" Do you pronounce it differently on some occasions than on others? Do you ever shorten it? If so, what do you leave out?

F. Do you pronounce *either* with the vowel of *sky* or the vowel of *ski?* Suppose your ordinary pronunciation uses the vowel of *ski*. You're talking to someone who pronounces it with the vowel of *sky*, and you use the word just after he has used it. Suppose that you want to be especially polite, what do you do?

G. Make four different English sentences by arranging these words in different ways.

a   the   man   tiger   chased

H. Make as many English sentences as you can by arranging these words in different ways.

our   anxiously   watched   the   cat   parrot   large   very

---

2 : How we learn the patterns of English

If you were born and raised in America and if the language that you have heard mostly during your life is the language of people with some education, then you already know the standard patterns of English. You will learn in this book various ways to describe and name these patterns and their parts. But the patterns themselves you already know. You learned most of them before you were three, a few more between three and six. By six, your equipment for speaking English — so far as patterns go — was complete. By six you were an expert speaker of English — much more skillful at it, for example, than the average French boy who has studied English for six years in high school or college. He might know more large words than you do, but he would in general envy you your ability to speak English — to manage its complicated structures effortlessly, as if it were as easy as breathing. As it is — for you.

How do we learn the patterns of English? We learn them by hearing them over and over, and by trying over and over to repeat what we hear. When we are babies, we babble, making the most of the fact that we can make noises come out of our mouths. By the time we are two, however, our babbling has begun to give place to form. We begin to make not just any sound but those particular sounds that are used in English, as we hear them from our fathers and mothers and brothers and sisters. The sounds go together to form words, and the words fall into patterns. At the age of two we have begun to speak and understand English sentences. Soon we have a very clear idea of the difference between "The bear ate the man" and "The man ate the bear." If someone reads us a story which includes the sentence "The bear ate the man," we know perfectly well who got eaten and who had dinner.

By this time, too, we can tell the difference between sentences which are statements and sentences which are questions. If a lady comes to the door and says "Is your mother home?" we do not just smile amiably, as we might if she said "This is a pretty house." Instead, we answer. We even know the difference between different kinds of questions. If someone asks us "Do you live in a pretty house?" we know we're not supposed to say "On Maple Street." We're supposed to say "Yes" or "No." But if someone asks "Where do you live?" we know that "On Maple Street" is a better answer than "Yes" or "No."

We know a great many words by the time we're four or five,

and we know more than what they mean. We also know how they are supposed to behave. For instance, we may feel that *desk* means "a big thing in Papa's study" or "what Mama writes on." We also know that *desk* fits in certain places in sentences:

> He sat at his **desk.**   It's in the **desk** drawer.
> That **desk** is dusty.   Where is the **desk?**

And it will not fit in certain other places, like these:

> Let's **desk** awhile.   That's certainly very **desk.**
> You **desk** while I dust.   Later we ate rather **desk.**

Some of the things we learn about words are very complicated — much more complicated than the meanings given in the dictionary. Consider what we know about the word *the* by the time we're four or five. We know that we can put it before a word like *desk:*

> I saw **the** desk.

But not before a word like *Charlie* or a word like *ate* or a word like *quickly:*

> I saw **the** Charlie.
> I saw **the** ate.
> I saw **the** quickly.

We learn that we cannot ordinarily put it before a word like *tall:*

> I saw **the** tall.

But if a word like *desk* follows a word like *tall*, we can use *the:*

> I saw **the** tall desk.

We learn that *the* will not come before *poor* if *goes* follows *poor:*

> **The** poor goes away.

But it will come before *poor* if *go* follows *poor:*

> **The** poor go away.

Or if *went* follows *poor:*

> **The** poor went away.

We learn that we often have *the* before *house:*

He's in the house.

But we often leave it out before *school:*

He's in school.

All these and many other things we learn about *the* when we're three or four or five years old. At the same time we learn that most of the things that are true for *the* are also true for *this* and *these*, that quite a few of them are true for *a* or *every*, and that none of them are true for *very* or *because*.

The word *grammar* can mean several different things. It can mean the difference between "I seen him" and "I saw him." Or it can mean a set of terms, like *noun, subject, sentence.* But *grammar* can also mean simply the way a language works and expresses its meanings. In this sense you already know English grammar. If you didn't, you couldn't speak English and couldn't read this book.

What you will do now is learn to observe and describe and talk about the things that happen when you use English. We will try to get a conscious knowledge of the patterns you already use naturally in your speech. When you have that knowledge, you will be able to apply it to sentence building and punctuation and other matters that come up in writing English.

● **EXERCISE 2**

A. The word *desk* occurs in the pattern "Where is the ——?" That is, we can say "Where is the desk?" But it does not occur in the pattern "Let's —— awhile." Nobody says "Let's desk awhile." Write down ten other words of which this is true — words which occur in the pattern "Where is the ——?" but do not occur in the pattern "Let's —— awhile." (You may think of some words which occur in both patterns. Save those for Exercise D.)

B. Some words occur in a pattern like "Let's —— it" but not in a pattern like "Where is the ——?" Such a word is *remember*. We say "Let's remember it," but we do not say "Where is the remember?" Other examples are *bring* and *write*. Can you think of ten more?

C. As we learn the language, some of the distinctions we learn to make between groups of words are rather small. For instance, we learn that one set of words occurs in the pattern "Let's ——" but does not occur in the pattern "Let's —— it." We say "Let's sleep" and "Let's agree," but we do not say "Let's sleep it" and "Let's agree it." See if you can think of five other words like *sleep* and *agree*.

D. Some words have very wide occurrence. The word *watch* occurs in both "Where is the ——" and "Let's —— it." We say "Where is the watch?" and we also say "Let's watch it." This is also true of *roll, paper, tree, dress*. Write down ten more such words.

E. The words *beautiful* and *honest* belong in one class of words, and the words *beauty* and *girl* belong in another. One difference between them is that *beautiful* and *honest* occur in the pattern "She's very ——." We say "She's very beautiful" and "She's very honest." But we do not say "She's very beauty" or "She's very girl." On the other hand, *beauty* and *girl* occur in the pattern "She's a ——," but *beautiful* and *honest* do not. Using these patterns to help you decide, list ten more words like *beautiful* and *honest*. List ten more like *beauty* and *girl*.

F. The words *beautifully* and *around* have something in common. For instance, both of them occur in the pattern "We walked ——." We say "We walked beautifully" and "We walked around." But they are not alike in all ways. Write one sentence in which *beautifully* occurs but *around* cannot replace it. Then write a sentence in which *around* occurs and *beautifully* cannot replace it.

G. The words *the* and *a* are very much alike. In many sentences in which *the* occurs, *a* also occurs. We say "I bought a watch" or "I bought the watch" and "A man came to the door" or "The man came to the door" or "The man came to a door." But *a* and *the* are not exactly alike. In some sentences in which *the* occurs, *a* cannot replace it. See if you can think of some sentences in which *the* cannot be replaced by *a*.

3 : Nouns and verbs

Understanding an English sentence is not just a matter of recognizing the words and knowing what they mean. We must also be able to recognize the patterns in which the words occur and know what these patterns mean. For instance, we may know the meaning of the words *the, he, trains,* and *seals.* But we don't get a sentence meaning from these words until we have them arranged in some pattern:

He trains the seals.

If we arrange them in a different pattern, we get a different meaning:

He seals the trains.

Trains in the first sentence is not the same kind of word as *trains* in the second; *seals* in the first is not the same kind of word as *seals* in the second. We know they are different words because we know they occur differently in the patterns. We are able to understand what the sentences mean chiefly because we are able to recognize the patterns.

If words occur regularly in the same patterns — the same positions in sentences — we say that they belong to the same **form class** or to the same group of **structure words.** In English there are four form classes. We call them **nouns, verbs, adjectives,** and **adverbs.** These are called **form classes** because many of them have special forms — endings and the like — which mark them off one from another. We'll go into this in more detail later on.

In addition to the four form classes, English has more than a dozen groups of **structure words** — words whose main duty is to make the structure of our sentences clear. They tie the form classes together in various ways and permit us to express more complicated meanings than we could without them.

The form classes are very large, containing many thousands of words. The groups of structure words are very small; none of them contains more than a hundred words, and some contain only one or two words. We shall begin by identifying the form classes. Later on we shall identify the structure words as they appear in the sentence patterns that we study.

A **noun** is a word like *apple, beauty,* or *desk.* That is, it is a word that patterns as *apple, beauty,* or *desk* do. It is a word that occurs in positions like those in which *apple, beauty,* and *desk* occur. Let us notice some of these positions:

I saw the **apple.** I was disappointed in the **apple.**
I saw the **beauty.** I was disappointed in the **beauty.**
I saw the **desk.** I was disappointed in the **desk.**
I saw the ——. I was disappointed in the ——.

Her **apple** is gone. **Apples** are plentiful in Washington.
Her **beauty** is gone. **Beauties** are plentiful in Washington.
Her **desk** is gone. **Desks** are plentiful in Washington.
Her —— is gone. ——s are plentiful in Washington.

If we try to fit other words into these positions in which *apple, beauty,* and *desk* occur, we find that some will fit and some will not. *Peach, joy, pitcher, locomotive, tomato, lawn, gardener, idea, thing* all pattern like *apple, beauty,* and *desk:*

I saw the **peach.** I was disappointed in the **pitcher.**
Her **happiness** is gone. **Locomotives** are plentiful in Washington.

We say that these are therefore all nouns. But *come, honest, without, usually* will not fit in these patterns. We do not say "I saw the come" or "Her honest is gone" or "I was disappointed in the usually" or "Withouts are plentiful in Washington." *Come, honest, without, usually* are therefore not nouns, or at least are not in ordinary use.

There are some nouns that occur in slightly different patterns. These are words like *Charlie, Spain,* or *Mr. McGuire.* We'll talk about them later on (pp. 34–39).

A **verb** is a word that patterns like *sing, beautify,* or *arrive.* That is, it is a word which occurs in positions like those in which *sing, beautify,* and *arrive* occur. Here are some such positions:

They will **sing** later.   They **sing** when they can.
They will **beautify** later.   They **beautify** when they can.
They will **arrive** later.   They **arrive** when they can.
They will —— later.   They —— when they can.

Please **sing**.   He **sing**s once in awhile.
Please **beautify**.   He **beautifi**es once in awhile.
Please **arrive**.   He **arrive**s once in awhile.
Please ——.   He ——s once in awhile.

Many other words pattern like *sing, beautify,* and *arrive.* Examples are *see, drive, come, think, continue, replace, believe.*

They **see** once in awhile.
Please **drive**.
They will **come** later.

And so on. These are therefore verbs. But *apple, beauty, happy, usually, without* do not fit in these patterns. We do not say "They will apple later," "Please beauty," "They happy when they can," "He usuallies once in awhile." So these are not verbs.

Some verbs occur in slightly different patterns. For example, *find* rarely occurs in "Please ——." But it does occur in "Please —— it."

NOTE

It may have struck you as you read this chapter that we're being a little too positive when we say "This word occurs in this pattern, but this other word does not." You may very likely think of particular expressions which disprove what has been said. If so, don't worry about it at this point. What we want to see now are the main lines of English structure. We can take up the special points, or some of them, later.

It is worth noting now, however, that any English word can be forced into any English pattern. For instance, we might say, "Comes are plentiful in Washington." It's hard to see what this would mean, but whatever it means, *comes* is certainly a noun there, because it is in a noun position. So we don't say that *come, honest, without* can *never* be used as nouns. What we say is that they aren't usually. We'll go into this in more detail in another chapter.

Another point that might bother you is that whenever we talk about a word we use it as a noun. If we say *"Come* is a verb," we have used *come* as a noun, just like *Charlie* in "Charlie is a boy." But this is obviously a special thing, and we'll ignore it from here on.

● **EXERCISE 3**

A. If we wanted to make a list of all the words that are used as nouns in English, we could do it by taking patterns like "I saw a ——" and "He hasn't any ——" and "The —— was interesting" and finding the words that would fit in the blanks. Nobody has time to list them all, but it shouldn't take you long to list fifty. Remember that any word that will fit in one of these blanks is a noun. It's more fun if you think of odd ones, like "He hasn't any dimples" or "The scoop was interesting."

B. There are several kinds of verbs. One kind occurs in patterns like "Please ——" or "Let's ——." Another kind occurs in patterns like "Please —— it" or "Let's —— it." Many verbs occur in both patterns. Make a list of twenty-five words that can occur in "Please ——" or "Let's ——"; for example, "Please stop" or "Let's wrestle."

C. Now make a list of twenty-five words that can occur in "Please —— it" or "Let's —— it"; for example, "Please stop it" or "Let's oil it."

D. Any position in a sentence in which *desk, beauty,* or *apple* may occur is a noun position, though, as we'll see later, occasionally two word classes can occur in the same position. Find some more noun positions by making up five different sentences using the noun *desk.* Under each one list five other words that could replace *desk.*

EXAMPLE   That's a very nice desk, isn't it?

hammer   torpedo   vegetable   bug   idea

E. Any position in a sentence where *sing*, *beautify*, or *arrive* occurs is a verb position. Find some more verb positions by making up five different sentences using *sing*. Under each one list five other words that could replace *sing*.

EXAMPLE   **Why do you want to sing that?**

do   say   believe   peel   enlarge

4: Adjectives and adverbs

An **adjective** is a word that patterns like *happy*, *beautiful*, *good*. It is a word which occurs in positions like those in which *happy*, *beautiful*, or *good* occurs. Such positions are these:

She was **happy.**
She was **beautiful.**
She was **good.**
She was ——.

A very **happy** girl came in.
A very **beautiful** girl came in.
A very **good** girl came in.
A very —— girl came in.

The girl seemed **happy.**
The girl seemed **beautiful.**
The girl seemed **good.**
The girl seemed ——.

Other words that pattern like *happy*, *beautiful*, and *good* are *new*, *young*, *lively*, *quick*, *sincere*, *honest*, *hopeless*, *continuous*, *wooden:*

It was **new.**
A very **young** girl came in.
She seemed **lively.**

But *apple, beauty, beautify, quickly, with* will not fit very easily in these patterns. We do not say "A very apple girl came in"; "She looked beauty"; "It was beautify"; "She was quickly"; "She seemed with." *Apple, beauty, beautify, quickly, with* are therefore not adjectives.

An **adverb** is a word that patterns like *in, beautifully, often:*

> She walked **in.**
> She walked **beautifully.**
> She walked **often.**
> She walked ——.

Other words that pattern like *in, beautifully,* and *often* are *up, over, by, slowly, happily, purposefully, then, sometimes, seldom:*

> She walked **up.**   She walked **purposefully.**
> She walked **over.**   She walked **then.**
> She walked **by.**   She walked **sometimes.**
> She walked **slowly.**   She walked **seldom.**
> She walked **happily.**

But *apple, beauty, beautify, beautiful, until* do not occur in this pattern. We do not say "She walked apple," "She walked beauty," etc. These words are therefore not adverbs.

SUMMARY OF THE FORM CLASSES

These are the four form classes: noun, verb, adjective, adverb. They make up most of the English vocabulary, and they are quite different in several ways from the various little structure words that go along with them. The reason we call them form classes is that many of them have special features of form that mark them for what they are.

For instance, many adverbs end in *ly;* many adjectives end in *ful;* many verbs end in *fy;* many nouns end in *ness* or *tion.* These forms are very complicated. No one form runs through any one class. We couldn't say that an adverb is a word that ends in *ly*, because many adverbs don't end in *ly* and some words that do end in *ly* are not adverbs. Nevertheless, the forms are important. As we speak and hear English, we have to be able to recognize the form classes. If we actually can't tell whether a word in a sentence is a noun or a verb, then we usually can't understand the sentence. The various endings are one of several kinds of markers that keep our sentences straightened out.

You may have noticed that many of our words occur in pairs: one a noun and the other a verb; or one an adjective and the other a noun. One example of such pairs is *beauty* and *beautify*. We have several other pairs in English that use the same form:

NOUN	VERB
beauty	beautify
glory	glorify
horror	horrify
peace	pacify

But this is only one of many form relationships between nouns and verbs. Here is another:

NOUN	VERB
separation	separate
relation	relate
invitation	invite
investigation	investigate

But not every noun that ends in *tion* has a related verb. We have no verb related to *indignation,* for instance.

There are form relationships between other classes. Here is one between nouns and adjectives:

NOUN	ADJECTIVE
goodness	good
softness	soft
friendliness	friendly
readiness	ready

Sometimes we have relationships that run through all the form classes:

NOUN	VERB	ADJECTIVE	ADVERB
beauty	beautify	beautiful	beautifully
continuation	continue	continual	continually
stupidity	stupefy	stupid	stupidly

As you see, we can often put a word into a different form class by adding or taking away or changing an ending. This is one of the points that make form classes different from the other word groups in English, the structure groups.

● EXERCISE 4

A. This exercise will help you become aware of the pairs of words that occur in the noun and verb classes — like *beauty* (noun) and *beautify* (verb), or *arrival* (noun) and *arrive* (verb). Remember that a noun is the form that fits a pattern like "His —— was interesting" or "We need some ——." A verb is the form that fits a pattern like "Let's ——" or "Let's —— it."

Here you are given a list of nouns; for each one try to think of the verb that is related to it.

1. beauty	**4.** loss	**7.** sale	**10.** insistence
2. arrival	**5.** inducement	**8.** suspicion	**11.** preacher
3. decision	**6.** relief	**9.** trial	**12.** fright

B. Now here are some verbs. Try to think of related nouns. For some you may think of more than one.

1. beautify	**5.** reduce	**9.** marry	**12.** starve
2. arrive	**6.** give	**10.** bedevil	**13.** conquer
3. depart	**7.** propose	**11.** breathe	**14.** think
4. rely	**8.** defend		

C. We have many pairs of words of which one is a noun and the other is an adjective — like *goodness* (noun) and *good* (adjective) or *hope* (noun) and *hopeful* (adjective). Remember that the noun will fit a pattern like "His —— surprised us" and "They were people of great ——." The adjective will fit a pattern like "He seemed ——" and "They were very ——."

Here you are given a group of nouns. Try to think of the related adjectives.

1. goodness	**6.** nose	**11.** dream	**16.** strength
2. hope	**7.** friend	**12.** sin	**17.** wood
3. courage	**8.** value	**13.** beauty	**18.** dirt
4. decency	**9.** faith	**14.** happiness	**19.** element
5. gold	**10.** artist	**15.** pepper	**20.** fear

D. Now here are some adjectives. Try to think of the related nouns.

1. good	**4.** reckless	**7.** anxious	**10.** marvelous
2. hopeful	**5.** dangerous	**8.** collegiate	**11.** lovely
3. hard	**6.** intelligent	**9.** long	**12.** tragic

E. Some words occur in series of four: *beauty* (noun), *beautify* (verb), *beautiful* (adjective), *beautifully* (adverb). Below you are given a list of words. Decide what form class each word usually belongs to. Then think of the related forms that occur in the other three form classes. For instance, if you were given *continue*, you would note that it is a verb and recall that the noun form is *continuation*, the adjective *continuous* or *continual*, and the adverb *continuously* or *continually*.

If you are in doubt, test with these patterns.

NOUN	We saw the ———.
	His ——— was surprising.
VERB	Let's ———.
	Let's ——— it.
ADJECTIVE	It seemed ———.
	They were very ———.
ADVERB	He walked ———.
	They did it very ———.

1. beauty	**4.** resentful	**7.** glory	**10.** purify
2. continuous	**5.** sadly	**8.** stupidly	**11.** depend
3. endanger	**6.** decisive	**9.** helper	**12.** reliable

5 : Words which belong to two form classes

Most of the words we have noticed so far belong to some single form class. For example, *beauty* and *apple* are always nouns. We always use them in patterns like "I have an apple" or "Her beauty was wonderful" and never in patterns like "Let's apple" or "She is very beauty." But some words occur in two form classes. For instance, *change* occurs in patterns in which *beauty* occurs:

She hasn't any **beauty**.	Her **beauty** is gone.
She hasn't any **change**.	Her **change** is gone.

In these sentences *change* is therefore a noun. But it also occurs in patterns in which *beautify* occurs:

Let's **beautify** it.	It ought to be **beautified**.
Let's **change** it.	It ought to be **changed**.

In these sentences *change* is a verb. The best way to describe this situation is to say that *change* is a word that belongs to two form classes. In one case it is a noun, and in the other it is a verb.

Many English words — especially common ones — are like *change:* the same form is used both as noun and as verb. Such words pattern sometimes like *beauty* and sometimes like *beautify*. When they occur in noun positions they are nouns; when they occur in verb positions they are verbs. Here are some examples:

comb	NOUN	They bought a **comb**.
	VERB	They should **comb** their hair.
fence	NOUN	He built a **fence**.
	VERB	Don't **fence** him in.
hurry	NOUN	I'm in a **hurry**.
	VERB	Please **hurry**.

walk	NOUN	Let's go for a **walk**.
	VERB	Let's **walk** for awhile.
mother	NOUN	Where's your **mother?**
	VERB	She **mothers** him too much.
table	NOUN	They laid the motion on the **table**.
	VERB	They **tabled** the motion.
mop	NOUN	We need a new **mop**.
	VERB	We'd better **mop** the floor.
barbecue	NOUN	Let's have a **barbecue**.
	VERB	Let's **barbecue** the meat.

You will notice that some of these uses are very special. For instance, *table* is usually a noun; it occurs as a verb just in the special pattern "to table the motion." On the other hand, *try* is usually a verb, but it occurs as a noun in the special pattern "That was a good try."

Some words occur both as nouns and as adjectives. For example, *criminal* patterns like *beauty* and also like *beautiful:*

NOUN	She's a **beauty**.
	She's a **criminal**.
ADJECTIVE	That's a very **beautiful** thing to do.
	That's a very **criminal** thing to do.

Here are some other examples:

unfortunate	NOUN	He's an **unfortunate**.
	ADJECTIVE	He's **unfortunate**.
silly	NOUN	She's a **silly**.
	ADJECTIVE	She's **silly**.
sweet	NOUN	She eats a **sweet**.
	ADJECTIVE	She is **sweet**.
brave	NOUN	He's an Indian **brave**.
	ADJECTIVE	He's a very **brave** Indian.
American	NOUN	He's an **American**.
	ADJECTIVE	He's an **American** soldier.

Some words occur both as adjectives and as adverbs. That is, they occur in patterns like those in which *beautiful* occurs and also in patterns like those in which *beautifully* occurs. Such a word is *hard:*

ADJECTIVE   He's a **beautiful** worker.
He's a **hard** worker.

ADVERB   He works **beautifully**.
He works **hard**.

Here are some more examples:

high   ADJECTIVE   That's a **high** building.
ADVERB   He leaped **high** into the air.

early   ADJECTIVE   **Early** birds get the worms.
ADVERB   Please come **early**.

long   ADJECTIVE   It's a **long** story.
ADVERB   We searched **long** and patiently.

fast   ADJECTIVE   He's a **fast** runner.
ADVERB   He runs **fast**.

● EXERCISE 5

A. Below is a list of words. On the basis of your experience with them, decide which are used as nouns, which as verbs, and which as both nouns and verbs. First try them in these patterns:

NOUN   Let's have a ———.
His ——— was surprising.
The ——— was good.

VERB   Let's ———.
Let's ——— it.

Then write other short sentences to show their use. For instance, for *smoke* you might write "There was some smoke in the room" to show it as a noun and "They smoke all the time" to show it as a verb. For *pretend* you might write "He pretended to like it" to show its use as a verb; probably you can't illustrate *pretend* as a noun, since it doesn't usually occur as a noun.

1. smoke	6. turkey	11. water	16. eye
2. pretend	7. park	12. chair	17. rug
3. strike	8. map	13. trip	18. raise
4. car	9. temper	14. insist	19. imagine
5. fish	10. speak	15. floor	20. plan

B. Now try these. Some occur in common use as both noun and adjective; some as noun but not adjective; some as adjective but not noun. Here are some test patterns:

NOUN   He's a ——.
          The —— is good.

ADJECTIVE   He's ——.
             It's very ——.

1. sincere	4. general	7. college	9. heavy
2. brave	5. busy	8. commercial	10. stingy
3. hopeful	6. welcome		

You may notice that a couple of these also occur as verbs sometimes.

Part Two

THREE

IMPORTANT

STRUCTURE

GROUPS

6 : How we recognize the form classes

In order to speak or understand English, we must be able to tell one form class from another. Of course we don't have to know the technical names for the different classes. We may never have heard the terms _noun_ and _verb_. But just the same we must be able to tell these two kinds of words apart so that we grasp or convey meaning, and this is one of the first things we learn when we learn to speak English. If we hear the sentence "Sam seals trains," we know that Sam works on the railroad. If we hear "Sam trains seals," we know that he works in a circus. We know because we are able to make out which words are nouns and which are verbs.

If we hear or read a sentence in which we can't tell whether some word is a noun (like _beauty_ or _desk_) or a verb (like _beautify_ or _see_), then the sentence will be ambiguous. That means that it will have at least two possible meanings and that we can't tell which meaning it is supposed to have. This doesn't happen very often, because the language provides many safeguards to keep it from happening. It is most likely to happen in a telegram or a newspaper headline, where some parts of the pattern are left out. Suppose you saw a headline with these words:

ARMY DEMANDS CHANGE

This sentence has two possible meanings. It can mean (1) that the Army wants to have a change or (2) that the demands of the Army have changed. The trouble is that *demands* can be either a verb or a noun, and *change* can also be either a verb or a noun, and in this sentence we have no way of knowing which is the verb and which the noun.

But usually words in our sentences are marked in some way as one class or another. They may be marked *by something in the word itself*, or *by structure words* that accompany it, or *by the position* in the sentence. We will examine some of these markers carefully as we go along, but it won't be necessary to describe all of them. The important thing is to recognize that our sentences are full of them and that as speakers of English we react to them properly without any particular trouble.

Here is the headline again with a few small changes made. Notice that each version has only one possible meaning; each one has something in it that marks the form classes:

ARMY ASKS CHANGE

ARMY DEMANDS A CHANGE

ARMY WILL DEMAND CHANGE

ARMY DEMANDS WILL CHANGE

ARMY DEMANDED CHANGE

ARMY DEMANDS CHANGED

ARMY DEMANDS CHANGES

Each of the form classes — nouns, verbs, adjectives, and adverbs — has a general meaning of some sort that applies to its class. For example, nouns have the general meaning of naming in some way or other; adjectives suggest some kind of quality. But it is not the meaning that tells us which class a word is in. It is the other way around. In a good sentence the pattern marks out the different word classes sharply and clearly. The pattern tells us what meaning the words are supposed to have, what class they belong in.

We can't tell the class meaning of the words *man* and *pump* just by looking at the words themselves. Are they names or actions? In order to know, we must see them in some pattern:

Man the pump.

Now the sentence pattern tells us that *man* is a verb and *pump* is a noun. But it could be different:

Pump the man.

Here the pattern shows that *pump* is a verb and *man* is a noun.

One sign which shows that meaning does not tell us what form class a word is in is that we can often classify nonsense words if we hear them in well-marked sentences. Look at this sentence:

Bool that gloob over there.

We don't know the meaning of *bool* and *gloob*, but if we heard the sentence we would recognize *bool* as a verb and *gloob* as a noun and know that someone wanted us to bool a gloob.

Or suppose we hear somebody say:

Let's buy some steekers.

We don't know what a *steeker* is, but in this sentence it is clearly marked as a noun, and in fact the sentence tells us a lot about it. We know from the sentence that a *steeker* is a thing, that it's a thing you can buy, and that there are more than one of them.

Or suppose somebody says:

Let's steeker those peanuts.

We know that here *steeker* is a verb, because it occurs after *let's*, just as *plant* and *eat* and *grab* and *beautify* may. Again we know a good deal about *steekering:* it is something you can do, and specifically something you can do to peanuts.

Or, instead, we might have:

He was a rather steekerful fellow.

Steekerful is clearly marked as an adjective by the *ful*, by the *rather*, and by the position. It indicates a quality that a fellow might have.

Finally, we might hear "She plays very steekerfully." *Steekerfully* is obviously an adverb, like *beautifully*, marked by the *ly*, the *very*, and the position after the verb *play*. It is clearly a way one can play.

In the next few chapters we shall examine some of these form-class markers in more detail. Remember as we go along that when we ask whether a word is a noun, a verb, an adjective, or an adverb, we are not asking what it means or what it modifies or anything like that; we are asking simply whether it is a word like *beauty* or a word like *beautify* or a word like *beautiful* or a word like *beautifully*.

NOTE ON WRITING AND SPEECH

At this point in our study we are concerned mostly with written sentences. We are examining some of the signals that mark the different word classes in the patterns that we write. You may notice that many of the ambiguous (two-meaning) sentences that we study would not be ambiguous at all if they were spoken. This is because speech has many more signals than writing does to keep the routes of meaning clear. In the second half of this book we shall examine these speech signals in detail and see how they relate to our writing system. Right now it's simpler to consider the words just as they appear on the page.

But it's a good idea to keep in mind from the start the true connection between speech and writing. We are likely to think that speech is a kind of careless and corrupt way of communicating as compared to writing. This isn't true. People learn to speak long before they learn to write, and mankind itself learned to speak hundreds of thousands of years before writing was invented. Writing is based on speech, and it tries to indicate the sounds that occur in speech. But it never is able to show them completely or very exactly. It cannot convey the elaborate signaling system that speech possesses. For this reason writing is more likely to be misunderstood than speech is.

● EXERCISE 6

A. Each of the sentences given below is ambiguous; that is, it can have either of two quite different meanings. Point out the words that could be either noun or verb. Then change the sentence in some way so as to make clear first one meaning and then the other. You won't have to change much in order to mark the form classes clearly. Sometimes other words can be substituted to give the clear meaning.

For example, suppose the sentence were "Plan moves slowly." This is ambiguous because both *plan* and *moves* may be either noun or verb, and there is no marker to tell which is which. We could express one meaning with any of these: "The plan moves slowly," "Plan moved slowly," "Plan is moving slowly," "Plan goes slowly." In all of these, *plan* is marked as the noun and the second word as the verb. We could express the other meaning with any of these: "Plan the moves slowly," "Plan your moves slowly," "Plan campaign slowly."

Now, following the example, write two clear sentences expressing the two meanings of each of these ambiguous sentences.

EXAMPLE　Plan moves slowly.　　(1) Plan is moving slowly.
　　　　　　　　　　　　　　　　(2) Plan your moves slowly.

1. Time flies. **2.** Man pumps quickly. **3.** Mail slips out. **4.** School requests mount. **5.** Beauty marks blossom. **6.** Navy witnesses smoke. **7.** Batter flies out.

B. We're not likely to write ambiguous sentences like those above, unless we have occasion to write headlines or telegrams. Neither are we likely to write nonsense sentences. But studying both ambiguous sentences and nonsense sentences helps us to see the structure in our language.

In the sentences below see if you can pick out the nouns, verbs, adjectives, and adverbs. Then for each sentence write another, substituting other nonsense words.

> EXAMPLE   **The grobe was bickling its bompers.**
> **The murgin was stuming its rallofledge.**

1. His parklip seemed rather stacious. **2.** There were no cribbins in the squanch. **3.** You tribble the rimbits while I speen the dallylags. **4.** A very lobeful blint was fendously loofing the strogs. **5.** A dirty little moggen bloored the strene. **6.** You didn't flench that kabe very spoothly, Andrews. **7.** Some billyflaps were clining a somewhat dorgy snule.

7: Determiners:
Markers of nouns

We have seen that the form classes can be marked in several different ways. They can be marked by some feature in the words themselves or by something distinctive in the positions in which the words occur. Or they can be marked by certain accompanying words which we call **structure words.** It won't be necessary to go into all the features that mark the form classes in our sentences, but it is necessary to examine some of the groups of structure words.

Any speaker of English over twelve years old has many thousands of words in his vocabulary. All but about two hundred of these pattern in one or another of the four large form classes: noun, verb, adjective, adverb. These two hundred are the structure words. They are mostly very common words, like *the, might, very, let's, if, because, therefore, who, that,* and so on. These pattern in very special ways, quite different from the patterning of the words in the form classes. In our study we shall examine about a dozen varieties of structure words.

The first group is made up of words that pattern like *the.* These are called **determiners.** Determiners have many different meanings, but they have one thing in common: they pattern with nouns. They operate as a signal which warns us that a noun is coming.

We can see how they work by putting them into patterns that are ambiguous without them. We saw that the sentence "Plan moves slowly" has two meanings: it might be a statement about a slow-moving plan or it might be an order. Now look at this:

The plan moves slowly.

This is no longer ambiguous. The determiner *the* now marks *plan* as a noun, and the sentence is clearly a statement. Or we could do it this way:

Plan the moves slowly.

Now the determiner marks *moves* as the noun, and the sentence is clearly an order.

Determiners make up a rather large group of words by comparison with other structure groups. If you speak English, there is no need to memorize the list, since you already know how to use them, but here they are anyway. As we'll see later, some of them have other uses too, but they can all occur as determiners, patterning with nouns. The ones most frequently used are:

the	these	her	few	either
a	those	its	several	neither
an	my	no	any	one
every	our	both	all	two
each	your	some	most	three
this	their	many	more	four
that	his	much		

Here are some of them in use. Notice that they pattern just as *the* patterns, and notice the nouns that come after them.

The men shot **the** wolf.   **Few** men shot **several** wolves.
This man shot **that** wolf.   **Your** man shot **my** wolf.
Each man shot **every** wolf.   **No** man shot **both** wolves.

The grass holds **the** water.
Some grass holds **much** water.
This grass holds **some** water.

Now notice how they clarify sentences that are otherwise ambiguous:

Plan moves slowly.   Ship sails today.
This plan moves slowly.   **Neither** ship sails today.
Plan **your** moves slowly.   Ship **some** sails today.

Fence ends there.
My fence ends there.
Fence **those** ends there.

Determiners pattern with nouns and occur in front of nouns, but not always right in front. Sometimes other words come between. Look at these sentences:

The cat purred happily.
The great big ugly-looking alley cat purred happily.

The determiner *the* patterns with *cat* in both sentences, although in the second sentence other words come between. But in both sentences *the* works as a signal to the eye or ear that a word like *cat* is going to fall, sooner or later, in that part of the sentence pattern.

It may have struck you that adjectives (*beautiful, sincere, honest*) also pattern with nouns: *the cats* or *beautiful cats*. And you may wonder why we don't say that adjectives and determiners are the same thing. They are similar in function, to be sure, and in written sentences sometimes occur in identical positions: "He liked the cats." "He liked beautiful cats."

But if we examine their over-all behavior, we find that *the* and *beautiful* are very different. For instance, we say "Cats are very beautiful," but we don't say "Cats are very the." If a determiner and an adjective are used in the same pattern, the determiner always comes first: we say "Some small cats came in," but we don't say "Small some cats came in."

In English structure what we have called adjectives (*honest, beautiful, sincere*) and what we have called determiners (*the, some, every*) are quite different things.

● **EXERCISE 7**

A. Copy these sentences, using determiners where the blanks occur. Try to use at least once each of the determiners listed on page 31. Notice that some determiners can't be used in some blanks, and see if you can say what it is about the noun that rules them out.

EXAMPLE

—— men shot —— wolf.   I saw —— father in —— bank.
The men shot **a** wolf.   I saw **his** father in **that** bank.

1. —— boys had —— elephant. **2.** —— girls had forgotten —— notebooks. **3.** —— people like —— movies. **4.** —— men said they needed —— money. **5.** He left —— car in —— garage. **6.** She has to clean —— room —— morning. **7.** —— cat was washing —— face. **8.** —— trees had shed —— leaves. **9.** Who put —— oysters in —— gravy? **10.** —— people go swimming —— day. **11.** —— clerk sold —— ladies —— earrings. **12.** —— morning —— father found —— dollars. **13.** —— teeth were examined by —— dentist. **14.** —— people had seen —— comet. **15.** —— cement had been left by —— builders. **16.** Not —— boys can repair —— own bicycles. **17.** —— young lady left —— purse in —— car. **18.** —— men have ever climbed —— mountain.

B. This time the determiners have been put in and the nouns left out. Copy the sentences using nouns where the blanks occur. Be sure that the noun you choose sounds all right with the determiner you put it with.

1. The —— smiled at his ——. **2.** A small —— lives in that ——.
3. Both —— had forgotten their ——. **4.** Much —— will be needed
every ——. **5.** The —— gave his —— a ——. **6.** Several —— have
examined that ——. **7.** These —— need more ——. **8.** Not all ——
will like your ——. **9.** Some —— brings me a —— every ——. **10.** No
real —— needs any ——. **11.** Few —— understand these ——.
12. We don't want any —— under the ——. **13.** Three —— were
waiting in that ——. **14.** Your —— needs a new —— on its ——.
15. I broke my —— on an —— this ——. **16.** Neither —— has
much ——. **17.** Each —— will be given seventeen ——. **18.** No ——
ever saw any —— in these ——. **19.** Our —— lost their ——.
20. Their —— won't accept either ——.

C. Here are three other ambiguous sentences. By putting in determiners, show first one meaning and then the other.

EXAMPLE   Plan moves slowly.
           This plan moves slowly.
           Plan **your** moves slowly.

1. Herd crowds together. **2.** Seal sinks quickly. **3.** Guard watches
carefully.

---

8 : Proper nouns and pronouns

The patterning of nouns and determiners is very complicated.
Some nouns go with some determiners but do not go with others:
we say "The blood flowed" and "Much blood flowed" but not
"A blood flowed" or "Many bloods flowed." Some determiners
go with all forms of a noun: *the apple* or *the apples*. Some go with
only one form or another: *an apple*, but not *an apples; several
apples*, but not *several apple*.

These differences divide the big noun class into several sub-

classes. Some of these subclasses have names — like **concrete
noun, abstract noun, noun of material.** It would be possible
to explore these subclasses and see how the determiners mark
them out. We would see that many words occur in more than
one subclass. *Paper*, for instance, is one kind of noun in "We
bought a paper" but another kind in "We bought some paper."
We would see that a noun may be in one subclass for some
speakers and not for others. A scientist studying blood, for example, might speak of "a blood" or "several bloods," whereas
the ordinary speaker would not.

In general a detailed study of the way determiners pattern
with nouns in English would explain a great deal about the way
a speaker of English looks at the world. The determiners he has
learned to use in his childhood sort the things of the world for
him and help teach him how to see them.

Most of this we must here pass over lightly, but there is one
subclass of nouns that we need to notice particularly. This is the
group called **proper nouns.**

Proper nouns are nouns that do not ordinarily pattern with
determiners. These are mostly names of people and places:
*Charlie, Agnes, Mrs. Goobser, Germany, St. Louis, Juno, Mt. McKin-
ley, Washington.* When we write such nouns, we always capitalize
the first letter.

The feature that singles out this sublcass of nouns and makes
them different from other nouns is that we do not use determiners
with them. In ordinary use we do not say "a Charlie," "the
Agnes," "every Mrs. Goobser," "several Germanies." Sometimes you may hear sentences like "I know a Charlie" or
"There were several Charlies in the room." When that happens,
Charlie has slipped out of the proper-noun subclass and become
a common noun, though it is still capitalized. It is patterning
just like *boy*, and it obviously means "boy named Charlie."

We have another set of proper nouns with a different feature.
These are words like *the United States, the Netherlands, the Hague,
the Queen Mary, the Sahara Desert.* Their feature is that they *always*

occur with the determiner *the* — never with any other determiner and never without *the*.

Here are some proper nouns in sentences. Compare them with the common nouns in the same patterns.

COMMON   Your **son** is very handsome.
PROPER   **Charlie** is very handsome.

COMMON   We all admired the young **lady.**
PROPER   We all admired **Agnes.**

COMMON   Some **states** have no speed limit.
PROPER   **Nevada** has no speed limit.

We also have about sixty structure words which pattern almost exactly as proper nouns do: that is, they do not occur with a determiner. These are the words called **pronouns** — words like *he, them, something, mine, this.* These words are like nouns in that they occur in noun positions in sentences. They are like proper nouns in that they do not pattern with determiners. Compare these:

COMMON NOUN   Your **son** is very handsome.
PROPER NOUN   **Charlie** is very handsome.
PRONOUN   **He** is very handsome.

COMMON NOUN   That **country** is a long way off.
PROPER NOUN   **Germany** is a long way off.
PRONOUN   **Something** is a long way off.

In fact, the most important distinction between pronouns and proper nouns seems to be that we do not usually begin conversations with pronouns and we do with proper nouns. If we meet a friend on the street, we might begin the conversation by saying "Charlie broke his ankle last week." But we would not begin by saying "He broke his ankle last week." *He* will not ordinarily occur except when *Charlie* (or some such word) has already occurred: "Charlie broke his ankle last week. He is in the hospital."

Here is a list of the words that are commonly used as pronouns in English. Notice that they can be divided into several little subgroups:

I	you	he	she	it	we	they
me	yours	him	her	its	us	them
mine	yourself	his	hers	itself	ours	theirs
myself	yourselves	himself	herself		ourselves	themselves

this	each	few	all	each other
that	either	many	any	one another
these	neither	much	most	
those	both	none		
such	some	several		

anybody	somebody	everybody	nobody	one
anyone	someone	everyone	no one	two
anything	something	everything	nothing	three

All of these can occur in some of the noun positions, though not all can occur in all noun positions. Here are some examples:

NOUN	The **boy** is here.
PRONOUNS	**He** is here.
	This is here.
	Someone is here.
	Each is here.
	Mine is here.
	Most is here.
NOUN	I saw the **men.**
PRONOUNS	I saw **him.**
	I saw **them.**
	I saw **yours.**
	I saw **both.**
	I saw **some.**
	I saw **nothing.**

You may have noticed that some of the words on the pronoun list also appear on the determiner list on page 31. These words are *his, her, its, this, that, these, those, such, each, either, both, some, few, many, much, several, all, any, one, two, three.* Just as some words, like *change*, occur as both noun and verb, so some words can occur as both determiner and pronoun. These words are determiners when they pattern with following nouns; they are pronouns when they do not:

DETERMINER	**His** car broke down.
PRONOUN	**His** broke down.
DETERMINER	I saw **her** mother.
PRONOUN	I saw **her**.
DETERMINER	**This** water is polluted.
PRONOUN	**This** is polluted.
DETERMINER	Where shall I put **those** blankets?
PRONOUN	Where shall I put **those**?
DETERMINER	**All** hope was lost.
PRONOUN	**All** was lost.

We saw earlier that proper nouns sometimes slip out of the proper noun group and become common nouns:

PROPER	I used to know **Charlie**.
COMMON	I used to know a **Charlie**.

In a similar way some pronouns sometimes cease to be pronouns and become nouns. They become nouns whenever they start patterning with determiners in the noun way:

PRONOUN	She married **nobody**.
NOUN	She married a **nobody**.
PRONOUN	**Something** moved in the woods.
NOUN	A noisy **something** moved in the woods.

Another thing that may trouble you is the fact that pairs like *my* and *mine*, *your* and *yours* are split up — *my* and *your* being called determiners and *mine* and *yours* pronouns. The words are obviously related, and it would be quite possible to treat them together, as most books do. But despite their relationship, *my* and *mine* pattern quite differently. *My* patterns like *the; mine* patterns like *I* or *me* or *Jack:*

DETERMINERS   **The** cat died.   PRONOUNS   **I** was here.
            My cat died.   **Mine** was here.

                          NOUN   **Jack** was here.

Since we are particularly interested here in the patterns of English, we must keep these differently patterning words separate. In such a word as *his* we have really two words, one patterning like *my* (determiner) and one like *mine* (pronoun).

● **EXERCISE 8**

A. In each of these sentences two nouns are italicized. Rewrite the sentences, using any proper noun or pronoun in place of each noun. Try to get as much variety as possible. Notice what else drops out along with the noun.

EXAMPLE   **An elderly *gentleman* caught several *fish*.**
           Nobody caught Alice.

1. My *mother* was washing the *dishes*. **2.** Every *youngster* played a little *tune*. **3.** The *lawn* needed *water* badly. **4.** Several *antelopes* were standing in the *yard*. **5.** Your *brother* needs a *shave*. **6.** Her *child* had the *measles* last week. **7.** No *mountain* ever stopped his *brother-in-law*. **8.** The *principal* was always shocked by such *behavior*. **9.** Some *senators* wanted to investigate the *company*. **10.** His *sister* married a young *salesman* from Toledo. **11.** Few *explorers* ever survived in that *jungle*. **12.** The younger *lad* ordered a *bottle* of ginger ale. **13.** The *head* of the company expressed his *disapproval*. **14.** These *ladies* know all about this sad *business*.

B. Rewrite each of these sentences twice. Use a proper noun in place of the italicized noun the first time. Use a pronoun the second time. Notice what words drop out.

EXAMPLE

He saw a handsome *lad* in the mirror.   He saw **himself** in the mirror.
                                          He saw **Charlie** in the mirror.

1. A dirty little *child* came in. **2.** We needed some willing *helpers*.

3. He says he saw a green *cat*. **4.** Every young *fellow* gets lonesome sometimes.

C. Write two sentences using each of the following words. Use the word as a determiner the first time and as a pronoun the second time.

EXAMPLE   **This** story is rather dull.   **This** is rather dull.

1. this   **3.** several   **5.** some
2. that   **4.** both   **6.** five

---

9 : Auxiliaries: Markers of verbs

Our next structure group is a set of words that pattern with verbs. These are called **auxiliaries.** They are words like *can* in *can go*, or like *is* in *is going*, or like *have* in *have gone*. *Auxiliary* means "helping" or "supporting." Auxiliaries have many different meanings, and they change the meaning of the verbs they pattern with in many different ways. For instance, they may give the time of the action or indicate whether it is going on or completed. They make up a very important part of our system of asking questions. But apart from all this, they have this important feature in common: they all pattern with verbs.

In a way, auxiliaries are to verbs what determiners are to nouns. Just as a determiner acts as a signal that a noun is coming, so an auxiliary acts as a signal that a verb is coming. Determiners help to mark off nouns from the other form classes, and auxiliaries help to mark off verbs.

There are about twenty auxiliaries in common use. Most of them pattern with the simple form of the verb — like *go, sing, wait, think, remember:*

They **can** go.	He **may** go.	We **must** go.
They **do** go.	I **could** go.	They **ought to** go.
He **does** go.	He **will** go.	They **have to** go.
He **did** go.	He **would** go.	He **has to** go.
We **shall** go.	You **should** go.	He **had to** go.
They **might** go.		

One auxiliary patterns with verbs that end in *ing*, like *going*, *waiting*, *speaking*, *remembering*. This auxiliary has five forms:

I **am** going.	I **was** going.
You **are** going.	They **were** going.
He **is** going.	

This auxiliary is generally called the word *be*. It is a word of great importance in English structure. As we shall see, it is used not only as an auxiliary but also as a verb.

There are only two auxiliaries which can pattern with past forms of the verb — like *gone, waited, remembered, seen. Be* is one of the auxiliaries, and *have* is the other. *Have* has three forms.

I **am** gone.	She **was** gone.	They **have** gone.
They **are** gone.	You **were** gone.	He **has** gone.
She **is** gone.		He **had** gone.

Because auxiliaries pattern with verbs, they serve to mark verbs in sentences. Recall the ambiguous sentence "Army demands change," in which we can't tell whether *demands* is a noun and *change* a verb or whether *demands* is a verb and *change* a noun. Suppose now we add the auxiliary *may:*

Army demands may change.

This is no longer ambiguous. The auxiliary *may* marks *change* as a verb. We could also do it the other way:

Army may demand change.

Now *demand* is marked as the verb.

Most of the forms on the list of auxiliaries occur only as auxiliaries. But *do* (*does, did*), *be* (*am, is, are, was, were*), *have* (*has, had*), and *can* also occur commonly as verbs. They are auxiliaries when they occur before verbs:

AUXILIARY	VERB			AUXILIARY	VERB
He	does	multiply.	They	have	left.
We	are	waiting.	He	can	think.

But when these words occur before some other form class, they are not auxiliaries but verbs:

VERB	NOUN			VERB		NOUN
He	does	multiplication.	They	have	a	complaint.
We	are	friends.	He	cans		tomatoes.

Occasionally it happens that we have two words together in such a way that we can't tell whether the first is an auxiliary and the second a verb or whether the first is a verb and the second a noun or adjective. When that happens, the sentence has two possible meanings:

They can fish.

This may mean either (1) "They are able to fish" (auxiliary–verb) or (2) "They put fish into cans" (verb–noun). But this is most unusual. One or the other of the words is nearly always marked:

AUXILIARY	VERB			VERB		NOUN
They	may	fish.	He	cans		fish.
They	are	fishing.	They	can		tomatoes.
He	can	fish.	They	can	the	fish.

● **EXERCISE 9**

A. Copy the following sentences, putting auxiliaries in the blank spaces. Try to use all the auxiliaries mentioned in this chapter.

1. They —— go home tonight. **2.** You —— see a doctor. **3.** They —— seeing what they —— do about it. **4.** He —— already left when we got there. **5.** They —— think we —— blaming them.

6. Charlie —— show you around the plant. **7.** We —— need some banana oil. **8.** I —— hoping that you —— come. **9.** —— you think he —— agree? **10.** I'm sure he —— invited. **11.** I —— eaten better soup. **12.** We —— just moseying around. **13.** If he —— accused, no one —— defend him. **14.** —— we dance? **15.** —— I have another tamale? **16.** He —— inspecting the goldfish that we —— bought. **17.** I —— say they —— pack the stuff more carefully. **18.** What —— you want to do about it? **19.** We —— clean up the place. **20.** —— anybody get in the game?

B. Copy these sentences, putting verbs in the blanks. Notice the auxiliaries that come before the blanks, and be sure that you get the right verb form.

EXAMPLE   He was —— it in his hand.   I did —— the letter.
           He was **holding** it in his hand.   I did **mail** the letter.

1. We might —— an answer by Monday. **2.** He was —— me the same old story. **3.** He would often —— the trail to the cabin. **4.** He could —— the other one if he wanted to. **5.** He had —— a strange thing behind the stairs. **6.** They must —— pretty old by now. **7.** We'll —— better later on. **8.** They were —— from behind. **9.** I think you should —— that boil. **10.** She was quietly —— the zebra. **11.** Can I —— an answer by Monday? **12.** What will they —— about it? **13.** They ought to —— it in warm gravy. **14.** Has he ever —— the smaller pool? **15.** May I —— to your parents? **16.** I was just —— there minding my own business. **17.** I am —— a package by parcel post. **18.** He has to —— the other goat.

C. The following sentences are ambiguous because either of two words might be a verb. Copy the sentences and rewrite each one twice, using auxiliaries to mark first one word and then the other as the verb.

EXAMPLE   Army demands change.   (1) Army demands **are** changing.
                                   (2) Army **may** demand change.

In (1) the auxiliary *are* marks the word *change* as the verb. In (2) the auxiliary *may* marks *demands* as the verb.

1. Navy witnesses smoke. **2.** Varsity reserves date. **3.** Swiss watches crash. **4.** Baby swallows fly. **5.** Company ships sink.

10 : Linking verbs

Just as there are several different kinds of **nouns**, so there are several different kinds of verbs. Most of the differences we won't need to bother about, but one distinction is very important in the structure of English sentences. This is the distinction between **linking verbs** and **non-linking verbs**. This distinction marks off some of the half-dozen basic sentence patterns in English.

You may have noticed that many verbs in English are followed by an adverb or by nothing at all:

> Birds sing.
> Birds sing sweetly.
> Boys play.
> Boys play noisily.
> Boys stand around.

Verbs which occur in patterns like these are **non-linking verbs**. On the other hand, some verbs are followed by adjectives:

> Boys are noisy.
> Men grow old.
> Birds sound silly.

Verbs like these are **linking verbs**.

Both linking verbs and non-linking verbs occur in other patterns too, as we'll see presently. But first study them in these patterns. If the verb is followed by an adverb or by nothing, it's a non-linking verb. If it's followed by an adjective, it's a linking verb:

NON-LINKING	LINKING
The girls **sulked**.	The girls **were** sulky.
The cat **miaowed** constantly.	The cat **seemed** cheerful.
He **looked** up.	He **looks** thin.
They **grew** rapidly.	They **grew** tall.
They **sleep** soundly.	They **are** sleepy.
The cake **fell**.	The cake **tasted** good.

Sometimes these two patterns are very close in form but very far apart in meaning. If you say "The bloodhound smells well," you mean that he's a skillful smeller; *well* is here an adverb, and it marks *smells* as a non-linking verb. If you say "The bloodhound smells good," you mean you don't mind sniffing him; *good* is an adjective, and it marks *smells* as a linking verb.

If you can't tell whether the verb is a linking verb or a non-linking verb, you can't understand the sentence. Here is one in which you can't tell:

The detective looked hard.

Looked is sometimes a linking verb and sometimes a non-linking verb, and *hard* is sometimes an adjective and sometimes an adverb, so there's nothing here to mark the pattern. It could mean that he's a tough-looking detective (linking verb–adjective) or that he made a careful search (non-linking verb–adverb). Usually a sentence is marked one way or another:

> **The detective looked quick.**   (linking)
> **The detective looked quickly.**   (non-linking)
> **The detective looked inside.**   (non-linking)
> **The detective seemed hard.**   (linking)
> **The detective searched hard.**   (non-linking)

Most of the thousands of verbs that we use are non-linking verbs. Only about sixty forms occur as linking verbs, and only about a dozen of these occur commonly. The verb most commonly used as a linking verb is *be* (*am, is, are, was, were*). Other common ones are *become, appear, feel, seem, look, taste, smell, sound, grow, remain*. Here they are, used as linking verbs:

> **The girl is** beautiful.   **The cake tastes** good.
> **The girl became** sick.   **The cake smells** good.
> **The boss appeared** calm.   **His story sounds** reasonable.
> **The sun feels** good.   **The child grew** tall.
> **Father seems** thoughtful.   **The room remained** quiet.
> **The kid looked** foolish.

Some other verbs appear before adjectives in special expressions. They are linking verbs when they do. Here are a few examples:

> His story **rang** true.
> The danger **loomed** large.
> The cow **ran** dry.

Most of the forms on the list of linking verbs can also appear as non-linking verbs. Even *be* can occur before adverbs instead of adjectives; when it does, it is a non-linking verb.

NON-LINKING
VERB

The girl	is	here.
The boss	appeared	suddenly.
The boys	remained	unwillingly.
His story	smells.	

We have said that linking verbs pattern with adjectives and non-linking verbs pattern with adverbs. Both of them pattern with nouns. Compare these:

> That man **is** my father.
> That man **shot** my father.

These sentences are different, quite apart from what happened to Father. They are different kinds of sentences, and the difference is that in the first sentence *man* and *father* refer to the same person, whereas in the second they refer to different people. When a verb stands between two nouns or pronouns, it is a linking verb if it makes the nouns or pronouns refer to the same person or the same thing; it is a non-linking verb if it makes the nouns or pronouns refer to different people or different things.

In American English the linking verbs that occur most often in this pattern are *be* (*am, is, are, was, were*) and *become. Be* occurs much more commonly than *become:*

That man **is** my father.	The dogs **were** poodles.
The principal **was** my hero.	He **became** my best friend.
You **are** an expert.	It **was** he.
I **am** the boss.	

Almost all of the other verbs that occur between two nouns or pronouns will make the nouns or pronouns refer to different people or things. They are non-linking verbs:

That man **made** a million dollars.	I **saw** the boss.
The principal **broke** his watch.	The dogs **drank** the ginger ale.
You **need** a vacation.	He **married** my best friend.

All verbs, whether linking or non-linking, can occur with auxiliaries. Here are some linking verbs with auxiliaries.

That girl **will be** sorry.	His story **did ring** true.
His sister **had been** beautiful.	We **could be** good friends.
You **should feel** ashamed.	He **may become** a banker.

Here are some non-linking verbs with auxiliaries:

He **can sing** very well.
You **ought to give** up.
He **was tasting** the cake.
The boss **had appeared** suddenly.
She **should be** here.
The dogs **were slurping** the ginger ale.

● **EXERCISE 10**

A. Copy the following sentences, filling the blanks with linking verbs. Any word you put in the blank will be a linking verb, because the blanks are all followed by adjectives. But try to pick verbs that sound right. Try to use as many different verbs as you can.

1. Her brother —— handsome. **2.** My mother —— angry. **3.** The hill —— steep. **4.** The grass —— brown. **5.** His sister always —— silly. **6.** The milk —— sour. **7.** His suitcase —— heavy. **8.** Everybody —— uncomfortable. **9.** We'll all —— old. **10.** The idea —— good. **11.** The weather —— cold. **12.** He had —— warm. **13.** The soup —— salty. **14.** I understand that his doctor —— insane. **15.** Since we —— thirsty, we asked for some milk.

B. Fill these blanks with non-linking verbs as you copy the sentences. You have a wider choice here.

1. He —— beautifully. **2.** Somebody —— here. **3.** He —— up. **4.** The men —— outside. **5.** His mother —— constantly. **6.** The lawyer —— angrily. **7.** The dishes —— noisily. **8.** The road —— endlessly. **9.** The children —— around. **10.** The monkeys —— sadly. **11.** The crowd —— away. **12.** His car —— sometimes. **13.** A good pen never ——. **14.** Everything ——. **15.** The horse —— up the hill. **16.** An old friend —— by for dinner.

C. Copy these sentences twice. The first time use a non-linking verb in the blank; the second time use a linking verb. All of these blanks stand between nouns or pronouns. Remember that only two verbs occur very often to make nouns refer to the same person or the same thing.

1. He —— my friend. **2.** The lawyer —— a judge. **3.** His father —— a teacher. **4.** I —— an outfielder. **5.** The horse —— a colt. **6.** You —— the boss. **7.** They —— Indians. **8.** The culprit —— a policeman. **9.** The train —— the St. Louis Eagle. **10.** We —— the cooks.

II : Intensifiers: Markers of adjectives and adverbs

Nouns pattern with the structure words called determiners. Verbs pattern with the structure words called auxiliaries. Adjectives and adverbs pattern with a group of structure words called **intensifiers.**

An intensifier is a word which patterns like *very* — that is, which occurs in positions like those in which *very* occurs. Notice the positions of *very* in these sentences:

That's a **very** good idea.   He spoke **very** quickly.
Some **very** beautiful girls came in.   He did his work **very** thoroughly.
He was **very** unhappy.

You observe that *very* patterns with adjectives — *good, beautiful, unhappy*. It also patterns with adverbs — *quickly, thoroughly*. But it doesn't pattern with nouns: we don't say "Some very girls came in" or "He lives in a very house." And it doesn't pattern with verbs: we don't say "She was very singing" or "She was singing very."

(*Very* used to be an adjective, with the meaning "true," and it still is an adjective sometimes, as in expressions like "the very idea" or "He's the very man I met." Except for these usages, *very* is always an intensifier, patterning with adverbs and adjectives.)

English has several words which pattern like *very*, though some of them have other uses too. Here are some common ones:

He was **very** unhappy.   He spoke **very** quickly.
He was **rather** unhappy.   He spoke **rather** quickly.
He was **pretty** unhappy.   He spoke **quite** quickly.
He was **somewhat** unhappy.   He spoke **more** quickly.
He was **awfully** unhappy.   He spoke **most** quickly.
He was **really** unhappy.   He spoke **too** quickly.

We use the term **intensifiers** for all of these because they pattern like *very*, though some of them don't "intensify" as much as *very* does. Speakers of English differ a good deal in the words they use as intensifiers. It may be that you don't use all the forms on the list above. On the other hand, you probably use as intensifiers some words which are not on the list.

Intensifiers express different degrees or shades of meaning. But in addition to this they all work to keep the structure of our sentences clear by separating the form classes. Since they pattern with both adjectives and adverbs, they do not serve to distinguish adjectives from adverbs. But they do distinguish adjectives from nouns, since they pattern with adjectives and not with nouns; and they also distinguish adjectives from verbs, since they pattern with adjectives and not with verbs.

Let us have an example. This is a little complicated, but it's very important, so hang on.

We said that nouns are words like *beauty* and adjectives are words like *beautiful*. In many of their uses *beauty* and *beautiful* are kept well apart by the structure of the sentences. Most sentence positions in which they occur are positions for one or the other but not both. We say "She's a beauty" but not "She's a beautiful"; we say "She's beautiful" but not "She's beauty."

However there is one position in which both *beauty* and *beautiful* — both nouns and adjectives — do occur. This is a position between determiners and nouns. Both nouns and adjectives are used to modify nouns:

> That's a **beautiful** shop.
> That's a **beauty** shop.
>
> That's a **nose** specialist.
> That's a **nosey** specialist.
>
> We had a **house** guest.
> We had an **interesting** guest.

Obviously, these sentences illustrate two different kinds of meaning. A nose specialist is not the same sort of thing as a nosey specialist. A nose specialist specializes in noses; but a nosey specialist does not specialize in noseys. On the other hand, a nosey specialist is a specialist who is nosey, but a nose specialist is not a specialist who is nose. The only way we can describe this situation is to say that nouns can be modified by adjectives (*beautiful, nosey, interesting*) and that they can also be modified by other nouns (*beauty, nose, house.*)

But the question is more important than just figuring out a way to describe the sentences. When we read or hear a sentence in which a noun is preceded by another word, we have to know, one way or another, whether that other word is a noun or an adjective. Otherwise we can't understand the sentence.

Here is a written sentence in which you can't tell the meaning, at least without some further clue from the situation:

He's a criminal lawyer.

It happens that *criminal* patterns like *beautiful* and is an adjective in some sentences:

That was criminal.

But it also patterns like *beauty* and is a noun in some sentences:

They arrested some criminals.

Now in the sentence "He's a criminal lawyer" you can't tell which *criminal* is being used. If it's the adjective, the sentence means that the lawyer is criminal. But if it's the noun, the sentence means that the lawyer defends criminals.

If we add an intensifier to this sentence, the intensifier will mark *criminal* as an adjective, since intensifiers pattern with adjectives and not with nouns:

He's a very criminal lawyer.

Or take this sentence:

He's a sweet salesman.

Does it mean that he's sweet or that he sells candy? An intensifier will mark the adjective:

He's a rather sweet salesman.

You may notice that none of these sentences would be ambiguous if they were spoken instead of written. Say this aloud: "He's a sweet salesman." Your voice will mark *sweet* as either adjective or noun, depending on which you mean. This is possible, as we shall see later (pp. 227–33), because speech has so many more signals in it than writing does.

Intensifiers may also distinguish adjectives from verbs. We have some forms, ending in *ing* or *ed*, which pattern both as adjectives and as verbs. An example is the word *entertaining*. It is a verb in the sentence "She was entertaining some guests," but it is an adjective in "She was an entertaining speaker." But what is it in this sentence:

She was entertaining.

Does the sentence mean that she was giving a party or that she was witty? Any intensifier will mark the adjective:

She was very entertaining.
She was quite entertaining.
She was awfully entertaining.
She was most entertaining.

We don't show you these ambiguous sentences because they are dangers which you have to be warned against. Of course an ambiguous sentence is a bad sentence; a sentence must be understandable above all things. But you are not very likely to write ambiguous sentences of this type, because there are a great many signals operating in the language to keep the word classes sorted out.

You are given examples of ambiguous sentences simply to demonstrate that the word classes *are* sorted out in our actual use of language. You do actually have to know whether a word is a noun, a verb, an adjective, or an adverb. And among the important markers of these classes are the various structure words, like determiners, auxiliaries, and intensifiers.

TERMINOLOGY

It may be that you are used to calling words like *very, rather,* and *somewhat* adverbs, putting them in with *beautifully* and *often.* They are certainly similar. But the general behavior of *very* is considerably different from that of *beautifully*, and we get a clearer view of the patterns of the language if we keep the two groups separate. The difference isn't important enough, however, to spend much time worrying about borderline words, or words which seem to be borderline, like *remarkably*. You'll get along all right if you notice just the intensifiers listed on page 49.

SUMMARY

We have now taken up three important structure groups: determiners, auxiliaries, and intensifiers. We have seen their relationships with the four great form classes:

Determiners (*the*, *a*, *every*, *my*, etc.) pattern with nouns.

Auxiliaries (*may*, *should*, *have*, *is*, etc.) pattern with verbs.

Intensifiers (*very*, *rather*, *somewhat*, etc.) pattern with adjectives and adverbs.

None of these word classes are entirely stable. That is, some items are not always in the same word class. Words are always slipping out of one class and into another. We have seen that nouns often become verbs, adjectives become nouns, proper nouns become common nouns, pronouns become nouns, determiners become pronouns, intensifiers sometimes occur as adjectives or adverbs. This slipperiness of the words in the classes is what makes analysis of language hard. It is the reason that people have been so long in learning how to analyze it.

The fact is that language has so many signals in it that we can make some parts of our language do double or triple duty and still be understood. Speech has many more signals than writing, but even writing has more than it absolutely has to have. So *pretty* can occur as intensifier or adjective, *both* as pronoun or determiner, *is* as auxiliary or verb, *criminal* as noun or adjective — *provided there is some signal in the sentence to tell which class or subclass is meant.* If there is no signal, then you have a two-meaning sentence, like these:

She's a pretty little girl.   It was moving.

In speech even these would probably be signaled, so that only one meaning would be conveyed.

● **EXERCISE 11**

A. Each of the sentences following contains one adverb or one adjective. Copy the sentences, using an intensifier before the adjective or adverb. Try to use all of the intensifiers listed in this chapter.

EXAMPLE   That was a silly remark.
That was a **rather** silly remark.

1. She had a beautiful mouth. **2.** The youngsters worked quietly. **3.** A young lady opened the door. **4.** He told us a funny story. **5.** I'm afraid I answered rudely. **6.** Father puffed briskly on his pipe. **7.** Sylvia was charming. **8.** Miss Benson hasn't been well since September. **9.** We had a good time at the school picnic. **10.** Where can we rent a small tiger? **11.** We liked to dine with Georgia because she ate elegantly. **12.** He was accompanied by a sloppily dressed apprentice. **13.** I think this one might be good. **14.** He seemed to be uncertain about what to do. **15.** Charlie did well in civics.

B. If you have trouble knowing whether a word patterning with a noun is an adjective or another noun, you can usually tell by trying to use an intensifier with it. If an intensifier will pattern with it, it's an adjective. If it won't, it's probably a noun. For instance, in *a college student, college* is a noun; we wouldn't say "a very college student" or "a rather college student." But in *a sad student, sad* is an adjective; we could say "a very sad student" or "a rather sad student." No test of this kind works all the time, but this one works almost all the time.

Here are some phrases to practice on. Determine whether the middle word is an adjective or a noun, and prove it by showing that it will pattern with *very* or *rather* or that it will not.

1. an old truck 2. his foolish sister 3. a brick wall 4. a handsome actor 5. a police court 6. a tree surgeon 7. every staff sergeant 8. some basketball players 9. these rotten tomatoes 10. his girl friend 11. those boyish scouts 12. a surly expression 13. a greedy eater 14. several house painters 15. a pork sandwich

C. Fashions in language change, and fashions in intensifiers change rather fast. When the author of this book, who is now old, was young, few educated people used *real* as an intensifier. Now many educated people do, though not the author of this book. How many intensifiers can you think of in addition to the ones listed in this chapter? Take the sentence "That's very good" and think of what might substitute for *very*. Don't count words that end in *ly;* some of them are intensifiers, but most of them are adverbs.

D. Each of the following sentences is ambiguous because one word may be either an adjective or a noun, or it may be either an adjective or a verb. Describe the two meanings. Then add an intensifier and see what form class it selects for the ambiguous word.

1. A radical hunter spoke to us. 2. You might call her an unfortunate helper. 3. He's a light specialist. 4. He was entertaining. 5. It was moving.

Notice that in speech the meaning is likely to be clear even without the intensifier. This is because of the greater number of signals in the speech pattern.

Part Three

SENTENCE

PATTERNS

12 : Symbols and sentences

In order to discuss more easily the words that make up English sentences, it will be useful to have a shorthand method of referring to them. If you have studied science, you know that a chemist does not always write out the words *hydrogen, oxygen, chlorine, sodium*. Instead, he gives these elements letters: H, O, Cl, Na. Then he can easily show the component parts of water by writing H_2O, of table salt by writing NaCl.

In a similar way we shall give numbers and letters to the word classes that we have studied, and, using these, we can easily indicate various sentence patterns. A little time spent in memorizing these symbols will save much time later on.

We shall use the figures **1, 2, 3, 4** for the following classes:

1	noun or pronoun	**3**	adjective
2	verb	**4**	adverb

In studying sentence patterns we usually don't need to distinguish pronouns from nouns. Sometimes, however, it is useful to distinguish linking verbs from non-linking verbs. When it is, we will use the symbol **2L** to mean "linking verb."

We shall use various letters to refer to the larger groups of structure words. Sometimes we shall take the letter from the name of the structure group; sometimes it will be more convenient to take it from the first letter of some prominent word in the group. The structure words that we have so far studied will be symbolized in this way:

D   determiner   **A**   auxiliary   **V**   intensifier *

Symbols for other structure groups will be given when these groups are studied. Some groups consist of only one word; for these it will be simplest just to write the word in our formula.

Here, then, is the list of symbols for all the classes so far studied:

FORM-CLASS WORDS

1	any noun or pronoun
2	any verb
2L	linking verb
3	adjective
4	adverb

STRUCTURE WORDS

D   determiner   (patterning with nouns)
A   auxiliary   (patterning with verbs)
V   intensifier   (patterning with adjectives and adverbs)

Now suppose we want to write a formula for the sentence pattern of "The boy replied politely." If we had no symbols, we would have to write: "determiner noun verb adverb." But with symbols we can write it this way: **D 1 2 4.**

WHAT SENTENCES ARE

All of our talk and all of our writing is made up of particular arrangements of form classes and structure words. We call these arrangements sentences. In speech we mark off sentences, one from another, by complicated adjustments in the pitch of the

---

* This is from the word *very*, which occurs prominently in this group; if we used I — for *intensifier* — it would be too easily confused with 1, the symbol for *noun*.

voice. In writing we mark them off by beginning them with a capital letter and closing them with a period.

We sometimes think of sentences as being "complete thoughts." They are complete, in a way, but in another way they aren't complete at all. Most sentences are closely connected in form and meaning with sentences that go before and sentences that come after. A sentence is usually not complete in meaning. It is complete in the sense that it consists of one of a number of word patterns, and the sentence is complete when the pattern has been completed.

For instance, one arrangement is the pattern **1 2L 3**: "Brides are beautiful." If it is our intention to express a thought like this, we can't do it by writing just "Brides" or "Brides are." We must continue to the end of the pattern: "Brides are beautiful."

We need not define "sentences" any further. If you do not already know what an English sentence is, you will when you have studied sentence patterns for a month or so.

KINDS OF SENTENCES

There are three main kinds of sentences in English. The differences among them are seen in the different effects they have on hearers.

Some sentences tend to make people do things. These are called **request sentences.**

> Get out of the way. (Hearer gets out of the way.)
> Hurry up. (Hearer hurries.)
> Turn on the light. (Hearer turns on the light.)
> Put up or shut up. (Hearer puts up or shuts up.)

Some sentences tend to make people say things in answer to the sentences. These are called **question sentences.**

> Are you going? (Hearer answers "Yes" or "No.")
> Did he bring the cash? (Hearer answers "Yes" or "No.")
> Where is he? (Hearer answers "In the bathtub.")
> Who's there? (Hearer answers "It's Charlie.")

Some sentences tend not to make us say something or do something but simply to keep on listening. These are called **statement sentences.**

> I saw Charlie the other day.
> There's a new show at the Majestic.
> He's very fond of spiders.
> The earth is round.

Remember that sentences are classified according to the *tendency* they have to make people behave in certain ways — according to the effect they *generally* have on people. Sometimes a request sentence may not produce any action. Someone may say "Turn on the light," and the hearer, instead of acting, may reply "Turn it on yourself." But still we would call "Turn on the light" a request sentence, because this pattern usually produces action.

We are going to begin by studying the basic patterns of statements. Later on we shall see how these can be turned into requests and questions (pp. 272–85). Remember, these patterns are *basic*. We shall see that all of them can be enlarged in many ways by modification and combination. But nearly every English sentence, even the most complicated, will turn out to be based on one of a relatively few basic patterns.

● **EXERCISE 12**

A. Learning a set of symbols is a matter of practice. Here is something to practice on. Turn each of the sentences below into a formula by writing the proper symbol for each word. For instance, the sentence "All brides are beautiful" would give the formula **D 1 2L 3:** D for the determiner *all*, 1 for the noun *brides*, 2L for the linking verb *are*, 3 for the adjective *beautiful*. The sentence "She is a bride" would give the formula **1 2L D 1.**

   1. He shouted loudly. **2.** My brother coughed. **3.** His money came.

1—noun   2—verb   3—adjective   4—adverb
A—auxiliary   D—determiner   V—intensifier

4. Each boy brought a dog. **5.** We saw Charlie. **6.** The girls stayed away. **7.** His sister was unhappy. **8.** Those dentists are my brothers. **9.** Your hands are dirty. **10.** We were building a garage. **11.** My uncle can play the piano. **12.** Nobody had any money. **13.** A beautiful cat came in. **14.** We needed a small tiger. **15.** He is an attorney. **16.** This milk is sour. **17.** This is sour milk. **18.** The little boys had gone. **19.** I think he was a farmer. **20.** A very handsome nose specialist spoke up.

B. Now try turning some formulas into sentences. For each formula below write a sentence. For instance, for the formula **D 1 2 4** you might write "The men came in" or "Some cats howl horribly" or any of a number of other sentences. Some patterns give you more leeway than others. For example, if **2L** stands before **3**, you may be able to use *is* or *looked* or *appeared* or *tasted* or any of a number of other verbs: "The pie is good," "The pie looked good," "The pie tasted good," and so on. But if **2L** stands before **1** or **D 1**, you will probably use only *is* (*am, are, was, were*) or *become:* "That man is my uncle," "He became my friend."

1. D 1 2L 3	**5.** D 1 2L D 1	**8.** D 1 A 2 D 1
2. 1 2L D 1	**6.** D 3 1 2 4	**9.** D 1 2L V 3
3. D 1 2 4	**7.** D 1 A 2	**10.** D V 3 1 A 2 D 1
4. D 1 2 D 1		

C. It isn't hard to distinguish statements, questions, and requests. If we couldn't tell them apart, we wouldn't know when to answer, when to act, and when simply to look intelligent. Here are some sentences. Write their numbers on a piece of paper, and for each number tell whether the corresponding sentence is a statement, a question, or a request. If it is a question, write a suitable answer. The end punctuation is left out to confuse you.

1. Has anybody seen Ralph **2.** Pick up your clothes **3.** Where do you live **4.** His aunt died last week **5.** Who is she going with **6.** I'm not afraid of you or your whole family **7.** Watch out for that truck **8.** Do you know where he keeps his shirts **9.** What are you going to do this week end **10.** Texas is the largest state in the Union

---

1–noun   2–verb   3–adjective   4–adverb
A–auxiliary   D–determiner   V–intensifier

D. Questions tend to make people answer, and requests tend to make them act. Statements simply call for people to pay attention. But paying attention isn't just a matter of being quiet. We must signal to the statement maker that we're there and taking in his statements. When two people are talking face to face, the hearer can signal his attention by nodding his head or beaming. But how do we do it on the telephone? Have you ever taken part in a telephone conversation when one person is doing nearly all the talking? What does the other person do or say? He isn't perfectly quiet; if he were, the talker would think he had hung up. What signals do we use on the telephone to show that we are paying attention to statements that are being made?

---

13 : The heart of statements

English statements occur in several different basic patterns. But all these basic patterns have one feature in common: they show a particular connection in form between two parts of the sentence. More exactly, they show a connection between a word in one part of the sentence and a word in the other part. One of these words is always a verb or an auxiliary. The other is usually a noun or pronoun, though it may be other things as well. We will begin with sentences in which one of the connecting words is a verb and the other is a noun.

NOUN FORMS

One of the characteristics of English nouns is that most of them have two forms — a form meaning "one" and a form meaning "more than one." For instance, *boy* means "one boy," whereas *boys* means "more than one boy." The same is true of the following examples: *desk, desks; fence, fences; class, classes;*

man, *men*. The form meaning "one" is called the **singular** form, and the form meaning "more than one" is called the **plural** form.

The great majority of English nouns have plurals that end in an "s" sound, a "z" sound, or an "iz" sound. For instance, we have an "s" sound in *cats, rats, cliffs, cops, sticks;* we have a "z" sound in *guns, trees, toes, dogs, lads;* we have an "iz" sound in *classes, witches, fences, roses, garages.* As you see, we spell all of these by adding either *s* or *es* to the singular form of the noun. This is the regular way of forming the plural of English nouns.

In addition to this, a few nouns form the plural in irregular ways. Seven common nouns form the plural by changing the sound without adding anything: *man, men; woman, women; foot, feet; goose, geese; tooth, teeth; mouse, mice; louse, lice.* A couple of nouns have *en* in the plural: *ox, oxen; child, children.* A few nouns add a "z" sound (the letter *s* in writing), as regular nouns do, but make other changes too: *loaf, loaves; wife, wives; knife, knives; lady, ladies.* Some nouns do not change at all: *deer, deer; quail, quail.* Some nouns that have come to us from foreign languages have kept their foreign forms for the plural: *memorandum, memoranda; alumnus, alumni; criterion, criteria.*

All of this adds up to one central fact: English nouns have singular and plural forms — various ways, regular or irregular, of expressing the meaning "one" and the meaning "more than one." These forms are called **number** forms.

VERB FORMS

Verbs do not have singular-plural forms in quite the same way. The verb *drink*, for example, does not have one form which means "drink once" and another form which means "drink several times." But verbs do have forms which vary according to whether certain nouns in their sentences are singular or plural. Let us suppose that the verb *drink* occurs in the sentence pattern *determiner noun verb adverb.* We will use the form *drink* if the noun is plural; but we will use the form *drinks* if the noun is singular.

D	1	2	4
The	boys	drink	slowly.
The	boy	drinks	slowly.
Those	girls	sing	constantly.
That	girl	sings	constantly.
Some	men	sleep	late.
That	man	sleeps	late.

When the form of a verb depends in this way on the singular or plural form of a noun in the sentence, we say that the noun and the verb **agree** with each other, or that they are **tied.** We also say that any noun that is tied to a verb is the **subject** of that verb. In our formulas we show this feature by drawing a double arrow ($\leftrightarrow$) between the two words that are tied, like this:

D	1 $\longleftrightarrow$ 2		4
The	boys	drink	slowly.
That	girl	sings	constantly.
Some	men	sleep	late.

Most verbs add *s* for singular noun subjects and pronouns that can substitute for them and occur without *s* for plural subjects. (Notice that the forms of tied verbs and nouns are in a way reversed, since plural nouns have *s* and singular nouns do not.) The verb *be* is special, but here again the form of the verb obviously depends on the noun to which it is tied:

D	1 $\longleftrightarrow$ 2L		3
The	boy	is	hungry.
The	boys	are	hungry.

In the first sentence, we use the form *is* because the form *boy* occurs. We say that *boy* and *is* are tied and that *boy* is the subject of *is*. In the second sentence we use the form *are* because the form *boys* occurs. *Boys* and *are* are tied, and *boys* is the subject of *are*.

Here are some more examples of subjects and verbs. Notice how the form of the verb varies with the form of the noun:

	SUBJECT ↔ VERB		
The	fence	needs	paint.
The	fences	need	paint.
The	mouse	was	pretty cute.
The	mice	were	pretty cute.
The	mailman	arrives	early.
The	mailmen	arrive	early.
The	desk	has	papers on it.
The	desks	have	papers on them.
The	paper	is	on the desk.
The	papers	are	on the desk.

Pronouns may also be tied to verbs. When they are, they are the subjects of the verbs, as in these examples:

SUBJECT↔VERB				SUBJECT↔VERB		
I	am	ready.		We	are	ready.
You	are	ready.		They	are	ready.
He	is	ready.		This	is	pretty good.
It	is	ready.		These	are	pretty good.

● **EXERCISE 13**

A. Copy the following sentences, but change the number of the first noun. If it is singular, make it plural; if it is plural, make it singular. Notice what must happen to the form of the verb. For instance, if the sentence were "The fence needs paint," you would write "The fences need paint." Changing *fence* to *fences* makes it necessary to change *needs* to *need*. If the sentence were "The boys have a dog," you would write "The boy has a dog."

1. The house was old. **2.** The dogs bark angrily. **3.** His reasons were good. **4.** My brother has bad manners. **5.** The mouse was dizzy. **6.** The walls were painted pink. **7.** The river goes dry in the summer.

8. The men do their work happily. **9.** His tooth aches in cold weather.
10. The pen was leaky. **11.** The child was crying. **12.** His sister was
scatterbrained.

B. In an English sentence the number of the subject controls the
form of the verb. The number of any other noun in the sentence has
no effect on the verb. Show that this is so by rewriting the following
sentences, changing the number of the noun that comes *after* the verb:
make it singular if it is plural and plural if it is singular. Notice that
the form of the verb does not need to change, though you may have
to change the determiner before the noun. In some sentences you may
drop the determiner altogether.

1. The school needs the building. **2.** The boys own the parrots.
3. He has a baseball. **4.** They want your address. **5.** We know some
policemen.

C. Write the plurals of the following nouns. If you don't know
what they are, look them up in the dictionary. Some of them have two
possibilities.

1. shelf	**6.** life	**11.** tenderfoot
2. louse	**7.** half	**12.** hero
3. moose	**8.** stratum	**13.** terminus
4. cherub	**9.** fish	**14.** phenomenon
5. pair	**10.** hippopotamus	**15.** stadium

14: Tied forms: Past tenses and auxiliaries

English verbs have forms which express the meaning "past time."
These are called **past tense** forms. For example, in addition to
the forms *come* and *comes*, which are used in sentences like "He
comes today" and "He comes every Tuesday," we have the
form *came*, which is used when the coming took place in the past.

We say "He came yesterday." Similarly, the past of *walk, walks* is *walked;* of *teach, teaches* is *taught;* of *hurry, hurries* is *hurried.*

Forms like *come, comes; walk, walks;* and *teach, teaches* are often called **present tense** forms to distinguish them from the past tense — *came, walked, taught.* These forms do not always express present time, however, and perhaps it is a little simpler to call them **non-past** forms. The past tense expresses past time pretty regularly.

Most English verbs form the past tense by adding a "d" sound, a "t" sound, or an "id" sound to the non-past form. Nearly all of these are spelled *ed.* Examples of verbs with a "d" sound in the past tense are *seemed, hurried, teased, flowed, skinned.* Verbs with a "t" sound are *walked, loafed, missed, popped, faced.* Verbs with an "id" sound are *ended, hated, skidded, petted.*

In addition to these we have quite a variety of irregular past tenses. These are verb forms that we just have to learn one by one as we learn English, but you've probably learned most of them by now. Examples are *ate, fell, bent, built, sang, began, got, put, taught, made, drove.*

The verb *be* has two forms for the past tense: *was* and *were. Was* occurs when the subject is singular and *were* when the subject is plural:

		SUBJECT	VERB	
	D	**1 ←——→ 2**		**3**
NON-PAST	The	boy	is	ready.
	The	boys	are	ready.
PAST	The	boy	was	ready.
	The	boys	were	ready.

For other verbs — like *come, make, continue* — the past tense has only one form, no matter what the subject is. However, when past tenses of such verbs occur in positions in which the non-past tense would be tied to a noun, we say that the past tense is also tied to the noun and that the noun is the subject of the verb.

	D	**SUBJECT** 1 ⟵——⟶ 2	**VERB**	
NON-PAST	The	boy	comes	late.
	The	boys	come	late.
PAST	The	boy	came	late.
	The	boys	came	late.
NON-PAST	The	fence	needs	paint.
	The	fences	need	paint.
PAST	The	fence	needed	paint.
	The	fences	needed	paint.

WHICH FORMS ARE TIED

We have said that the subject of a verb is whatever noun in the sentence is tied to the verb and agrees with it in form. But, we may ask, how do we know in any given sentence in which these forms occur which noun should agree with the verb and therefore be the subject?

If we are native speakers of English, we know because as small children we learned the complicated rules which govern the matter. We learned them painlessly because we learned them early. All we have to do now is become conscious of what we already know subconsciously. For example, it is a rule in English that a noun patterning with a preposition, like *with*, will not be the subject of a following verb. This sounds very complicated. Actually we already know it, because we know how to say "The boy with the goats is Charlie." As speakers of English, we know that the tie is between *boy* and the verb, not between *goats* and the verb. It would be nearly impossible for us to say "The boy with the goats are Charlie."

STATEMENTS WITH AUXILIARIES

In all the examples we have had so far the tie has been a simple one between the subject — noun or pronoun — and the verb. When an auxiliary is used, however, it is the auxiliary and not the verb itself that is tied to the subject as in these examples:

	SUBJECT	AUXILIARY	VERB	
D	**1** ←———→ **A**		**2**	**4**
The	farmer	was	thinking	hard.
The	farmers	were	thinking	hard.
	Sam	is	eating.	
The	youngsters	are	eating.	

	SUBJECT	AUXILIARY	VERB
D	**1** ←———→ **A**		**2**
My	friend	has	arrived.
My	friends	have	arrived.
My	friend	had	arrived.
My	friends	had	arrived.

	SUBJECT	AUXILIARY	VERB	
D	**1** ←———→ **A**		**2**	**3**
	Charlie	is	looking	better.
	They	are	looking	better.
His	sister	was	being	silly.
His	sisters	were	being	silly.

	SUBJECT	AUXILIARY	VERB	D	1
D	**1** ←———→ **A**		**2**	**D**	**1**
That	fellow	has	seen	a	ghost.
Those	fellows	have	seen	a	ghost.
	Charlie	was	watching	the	ghost.
	They	were	watching	the	ghost.

Some auxiliaries — like *may, might, could* — do not have variable forms. We say *he may, they may*, not *he mays, they may*. Even so, we say that these auxiliaries are tied to the subject whenever they are in positions in which there is a tie between the subject and other auxiliaries.

SUBJECT	AUXILIARY	VERB	D	1
1 ←———→ **A**		**2**	**D**	**1**
He	has	seen	a	ghost.
They	have	seen	a	ghost.
He	may	see	a	ghost.
They	may	see	a	ghost.

● **EXERCISE 14**

A. For each of the formulas given below write two sentences that will show the tie. For instance, if the formula were **D 1↔2 D 1**, you might write "My brother has the job" for the first sentence. Then, changing *brother* to *brothers*, you would have "My brothers have the job" for the second sentence. Use a singular subject in one and a plural subject in the other, and don't use past tenses.

1. D 1↔2 3   4. D 1↔A 2 (use a verb ending in *ing*)
2. 1↔2 4   5. D 1↔A 2 3 (use a verb ending in *ing*)
3. 1↔2 V 4

B. Most English verbs form their past tenses regularly, adding a "d" sound, a "t" sound, or an "id" sound, all spelled *ed: walked, started, hoped, stopped, leaned.* About two hundred verbs form the past tense irregularly. Write the past tense forms of the following verbs. You probably know them, but if you don't, look them up.

1. see	6. send	11. dig	16. wear	21. go
2. hold	7. steal	12. bleed	17. seek	22. swear
3. catch	8. hit	13. bind	18. sink	23. meet
4. ride	9. choose	14. fly	19. forget	24. shake
5. build	10. sting	15. swim	20. break	25. stand

C. Even the irregular verbs in English have some short stretches of regularity in them. There are small groups of words whose tense formations are similar in sound. For instance, these forms are similar: *freeze, froze; speak, spoke; steal, stole; weave, wove.* See how many other similar verbs you can list for each of the lists started below.

1. rise, rose; smite, smote   6. sing, sang; shrink, shrank
2. tear, tore   7. bind, bound
3. bend, bent   8. fling, flung
4. put, put; set, set; cost, cost   9. bleed, bled
5. know, knew   10. beseech, besought; think, thought

1–noun   2–verb   3–adjective   4–adverb
A–auxiliary   D–determiner   V–intensifier   ↔–tie

15 : Four basic statement patterns

English sentences show a good deal of variety. If we look at a long stretch of English writing, it may seem that no two sentences are exactly alike, and in a way this is true. But it is also true that if we look at the structure of the sentences, we see much similarity. In fact, practically all the sentences we speak and write can be seen to be built on just a handful of basic patterns. These patterns can be modified and combined in almost endless ways, but at the base our sentences are just these few patterns repeated over and over.

Just how many basic patterns there are in English can be argued. It depends on what one means by "basic." We'll begin with four very common ones. Later on we'll notice a few more.

PATTERN ONE

NOUN VERB $1 \leftrightarrow 2$ Birds sing.

The first basic statement pattern consists simply of a noun tied to a following verb. In our symbols this would be represented by a 1, a double arrow, and a 2: $1 \leftrightarrow 2$.

Here are some examples:

1 ←————→	2
Birds	sing.
Canaries	twitter.
He	left.
Something	happened.
It	works.

This — and all the basic patterns — can be expanded and modified in many ways. In this chapter we shall observe a few of the obvious changes that may be made. For instance, the noun may have a determiner in front of it:

D	1 ←——→ 2	
	Birds	sing.
The	birds	sing.
The	bird	sings.
A	ghost	walked.
My	horse	died.
The	teacher	quit.

Or the verb may have an auxiliary. When it does, the noun is tied to the auxiliary rather than to the verb:

D	1 ←——→ A		2
	Birds	**can**	sing.
The	birds	**are**	singing.
This	bird	**is**	singing.
Each	bird	**had**	sung.
His	ghost	**was**	walking.
	Charlie	**might**	object.

Or the pattern may contain an adverb:

D	1 ←——→ 2		4
	Birds	sing	**noisily.**
	Charlie	came	**in.**
The	team	played	**well.**
A	student	spoke	**up.**

D	1 ←——→ A		2	4
Every	bird	was	singing	**noisily.**
The	ghost	had	walked	**silently.**
	Charlie	might	come	**in.**
The	girls	were	screaming	**horribly.**

PATTERN TWO

NOUN VERB ADJECTIVE   **1↔2 3**   Birds are beautiful.

The second basic pattern consists of a noun tied to a verb with an adjective following: 1↔2 3. The verb in this pattern is always a linking verb. *Be* (*am, is, are, was, were*) is the most common verb in this pattern, but *seem, appear, look, taste, feel, grow* and several others also occur. Here are some examples:

D	1 ⟷ 2		3
	Birds	are	beautiful.
The	birds	are	beautiful.
That	bird	is	beautiful.
All	birds	look	beautiful.
	She	looks	sad.
	Everyone	seemed	sad.
The	pie	tastes	awful.

The verb may be preceded by an auxiliary, of course:

D	1 ⟷ A		2	3
	She	**was**	being	silly.
	Charlie	**is**	looking	better.
The	culprits	**were**	feeling	foolish.
My	horse	**had**	grown	old.
His	story	**may**	sound	plausible.

Or the pattern may contain an adverb:

D	1 ⟷ 2		3	4
	Birds	are	beautiful	**sometimes.**
	He	grew	old	**gracefully.**
Her	pies	taste	good	**sometimes.**

We shall see in later chapters that the adverb can appear in many places besides the end. But wherever the adverb comes, the basic pattern is still the same.

PATTERN THREE

NOUN LINKING VERB NOUN   **1⟷2L 1**   Canaries are birds.

The third pattern consists of a noun or pronoun tied to a linking verb and followed by another noun: 1⟷2L 1. The only verbs that occur commonly in this pattern are *be* (*am, is, are, was, were*) and *become*. These verbs standing between two nouns make the nouns refer to the same person or the same thing. They identify the two nouns. That is what sets this pattern apart from other similar patterns. Here are examples:

1 ⟷ 2L		1
Canaries	are	birds.
That	was	Charlie.
Cages	are	prisons.

Usually one of the nouns or both of them have determiners:

D	1 ⟷ 2L		D	1
	Canaries	are		birds.
Those	canaries	are	**my**	birds.
	Charlie	was	**the**	culprit.
The	culprit	was		Charlie.
Every	house	is	**a**	fortress.

In this pattern, too, we may also have an auxiliary or an adverb or both. If there is an auxiliary, the first noun is tied to the auxiliary.

D	1 ⟷ A		2L	D	1	4
	Canaries		are		birds.	
Those	canaries		are	my	birds.	
Those	canaries	**might**	be	my	birds.	
Those	canaries	**had**	been	my	birds.	
	He	**should**	be	the	boss	**actually.**
	He	**may**	become	the	boss	**later.**

PATTERN FOUR

NOUN VERB NOUN   1⟷2 1   Canaries eat worms.

The fourth basic pattern consists of a noun tied to a non-linking verb and followed by another noun: 1⟷2 1. A great many verbs occur in this pattern: *eat, see, like, have, reform, assist, manage,* and many others. When these verbs stand between two nouns, they make the nouns refer to different people or different things. That is what makes this pattern different from Pattern Three, in which *be* and *become* make the nouns refer to the same person or the same thing.

Here are some examples of Pattern Four:

1 ⟷	2	1
Canaries	eat	worms.
Charlie	drinks	milk.
Carpenters	build	houses.
Everybody	hated	school.
He	has	pneumonia.

Like the other patterns, Pattern Four can be expanded by such additions as determiners, auxiliaries, adverbs:

D	1 ⟷ A		2	D	1	4
	Canaries		eat		worms.	
My	canaries		ate	those	worms.	
My	canaries	were	eating	their	worms.	
The	canaries	had	eaten	the	worms	greedily.
The	boys	had	had	a	gun.	
	Charlie		needed	a	job.	
	Everybody		noticed	the	sign	later.
Our	minister	had	organized	a	club.	
	We	might	prune	the	roses.	

As we shall see presently, all of these basic patterns can be built up and expanded in many other ways too. As a kind of preview, here is a considerable expansion of "Canaries eat worms":

All the pretty little South American **canaries** that we kept in the cages in the front part of the house had been happily **eating** some especially appetizing **worms** which my brother Tom had picked up at a feed store on Post Street.

But it's still basically Pattern Four — "Canaries eat worms" — 1⟷2 1.

SUMMARY

Once again, these are the four basic sentence patterns:

PATTERN ONE	1↔2	Birds sing.
PATTERN TWO	1↔2 3	Birds are beautiful.
PATTERN THREE	1↔2L 1	Canaries are birds.
PATTERN FOUR	1↔2 1	Canaries eat worms.

Quite a bit later (pp. 169–73) we'll take up a few more basic patterns. But we'll work these four over pretty thoroughly first.

● **EXERCISE 15**

A. The best way to get a feeling for the basic sentence patterns is to produce a lot of them. To begin with, write ten sentences to illustrate Pattern One: 1↔2. Use a determiner with the noun, if you wish, and an auxiliary or an adverb with the verb; but don't make it any more elaborate than that.

EXAMPLE   Babies cry. (1↔2)
                  He quit. (1↔2)
                  My brother came. (D 1↔2)
                  My brother came in. (D 1↔2 4)
                  The girl was crying. (D 1↔A 2)
                  The girl was crying quietly. (D 1↔A 2 4)

After each of your sentences, write its formula in parentheses, as in the examples above.

B. Now write ten sentences to illustrate Pattern Two: 1↔2 3. Write the formula for each sentence in parentheses.

EXAMPLE   Turtles are slow. (1↔2 3)
                  His shirt was dirty. (D 1↔2 3)
                  My uncle felt sick. (D 1↔2 3)
                  His story had sounded true. (D 1↔A 2 3)
                  The milk turned sour later. (D 1↔2 3 4)

Use as many different verbs as you can.

C. Write ten sentences to illustrate Pattern Three: 1↔2L 1. Write the formula for each sentence in parentheses.

EXAMPLE   His car is a sedan.   **(D 1↔2L D 1)**
Charlie is my brother.   **(1↔2L D 1)**
He became an actor.   **(1↔2L D 1)**
He had been an actor.   **(1↔A 2L D 1)**

Here the verbs you use will probably be some form of *be* or *become*.

D. Write ten sentences to illustrate Pattern Four: 1↔2 1. Write the formula for each sentence in parentheses.

EXAMPLE   His car hit a sedan.   **(D 1↔2 D 1)**
Ed helped Charlie.   **(1↔2 1)**
The house needed some paint badly.   **(D 1↔2 D 1 4)**
He needed a shave.   **(1↔2 D 1)**

Part Four

CLUSTERS

16 : Noun clusters: The headword

What we want to do now is to see how the various parts of the basic sentence patterns can be expanded to make more complicated sentences and thus, through the patterns, to convey more precise and complicated meanings. We'll begin with the nouns. We'll see that in place of a simple noun in the pattern we can have what we call a **noun cluster.** A noun cluster is a noun with other words or groups of words clustering around it and modifying it in various ways. Later on we shall examine verb clusters and other kinds of expansion.

NOUN POSITIONS

First of all, we need to notice that each noun position in the four basic patterns has a special name. Here are the patterns again:

PATTERN ONE	1↔2	Birds sing.
PATTERN TWO	1↔2 3	Birds are beautiful.
PATTERN THREE	1↔2L 1	Canaries are birds.
PATTERN FOUR	1↔2 1	Birds eat worms.

We have already seen that the noun in each pattern which is tied to the verb is called the **subject.** The second noun in Pattern Three is called the **linking-verb complement.** This very clumsy term is the one commonly used, but instead of saying it all, you can just say the **complement.** You don't have to worry about what complement means, if anything. All you have to remember is that a complement is the noun after the linking verb in Pattern Three. The second noun in Pattern Four is called an **object,** or sometimes a **direct object.** Again, for our purposes, all object means is the noun after the non-linking verb in Pattern Four.

So we have three different positions for nouns: subject, linking-verb complement, and object. The subject is the noun that is tied to the verb. The complement is the noun after the linking verb of Pattern Three. The object is the noun after the non-linking verb of Pattern Four. Later on we shall see some other basic patterns and some other noun positions.

NOUN CLUSTERS

Now, in any one of these three positions — subject, complement, object — we may have a **noun cluster** in place of a simple noun. Let's take a simple example of Pattern One:

$$\mathbf{1} \longleftrightarrow \mathbf{2}$$
Dogs   bark   loudly.

In place of the simple noun *dogs*, we might have a noun cluster, like *those big dogs on our block*, as the subject of Pattern One:

Those big dogs on our block bark loudly.

Or we might have a noun cluster in place of the subject in Pattern Two:

$$\mathbf{1} \longleftrightarrow \mathbf{2} \qquad \mathbf{3}$$
Dogs   are   playful.
Those big dogs on our block are playful.

Or as subject in Pattern Three:

$$\mathbf{1} \qquad \mathbf{2L} \qquad \mathbf{1}$$
Dogs   are   pests.
Those big dogs on our block are pests.

Or as subject in Pattern Four:

1   2   1
Dogs   chase   cars.
Those big dogs on our block chase cars.

The word *dogs* can occur as the complement in Pattern Three:

1   2L   1
His   pets   are   dogs.

So can the noun cluster:

His pets are **those big dogs on our block.**

Dogs can occur as object in Pattern Four:

1   2   1
I   hate   dogs.

And so can the cluster:

I hate **those big dogs on our block.**

In general, *dogs* can be replaced in any position by a cluster of words with *dogs* as its center. A noun can be replaced by a noun cluster.

A **noun cluster** always consists of at least two parts: the noun itself and the word or words accompanying it. The noun is called the **headword** of the cluster. In our example — *those big dogs in our block* — *dogs* is the headword of the cluster.

Other parts of the cluster are called **modifiers.** *Some, big,* and *in our block* are modifiers in the example we used.

Modifiers in noun clusters have a great deal of variety. A noun headword may be modified by an adjective, a verb, an adverb, or another noun. Or it may be modified by a determiner or by any of several groups of words.

In the next few chapters we shall examine in detail the ways in which noun clusters are built: the particular modifiers that can be used, the order in which they are used, and the different meanings that they have.

● EXERCISE 16

A. Here are some noun clusters. These are not sentences but clusters of words in which the headword is a noun. Pick out the headword in each cluster.

1. the man inside **2.** some old houses **3.** a dog that wandered by **4.** a sleeping beauty **5.** the boys in the back room **6.** a policeman looking on **7.** a very lively little girl with ribbons in her hair **8.** every sophomore who came in late **9.** a reasonable excuse **10.** the angry little carnival man in the truck who had been waving his arms

B. Now, following the directions given, place each of these clusters in a noun position in one of the basic sentence patterns. For example, if you were directed to use cluster 1 (*the man inside*) as subject in Pattern Three, you might write: "The man inside is my brother." Perhaps you should first review the four basic patterns (p. 75).

1. Use cluster 2 (*some old houses*) as object in Pattern Four. **2.** Use cluster 3 as subject in Pattern One. **3.** Use cluster 4 as complement in Pattern Three. **4.** Use cluster 5 as subject in Pattern Three. **5.** Use cluster 6 as subject in Pattern Four. **6.** Use cluster 7 as subject in Pattern One. **7.** Use cluster 8 as object in Pattern Four. **8.** Use cluster 9 as complement in Pattern Three. **9.** Use cluster 10 as subject in Pattern One. **10.** Write a Pattern Four sentence with cluster 8 as subject and cluster 9 as object.

17: Noun clusters: Modifiers before the headword

A noun may be modified by a determiner, an adjective, a verb, an adverb, or another noun, or by a word group. If the modifier is a determiner, an adjective, a verb, or another noun, the modifier generally comes before the headword. If the modifier is an adverb or a word group, it comes after the headword.

The simplest and most common kind of noun cluster is that in which the modifier is a determiner:

MODIFIER	HEADWORD	MODIFIER	HEADWORD
D	**1**	**D**	**1**
the	house	every	plant
my	cat	some	difficulties
an	angel	no	home
a	sink	any	idea

Or the headword may have an adjective as a modifier:

MODIFIER	HEADWORD	MODIFIER	HEADWORD
3	**1**	**3**	**1**
small	house	red	ink
beautiful	cat	dirty	hands
new	sink	nosey	brother
serious	troubles	greedy	puppy

Frequently a noun cluster will contain two modifiers. We may have a determiner and an adjective at the same time. Then the determiner comes first and the adjective second:

MODIFIER	MODIFIER	HEADWORD
D	**3**	**1**
the	small	house
my	beautiful	cat
a	new	sink
some	serious	difficulties
his	dirty	hands
our	handsome	principal
any	good	idea
these	ripe	tomatoes

A noun may be modified by two or more adjectives at the same time:

MODIFIER	MODIFIER	MODIFIER	HEADWORD
D	**3**	**3**	**1**
that	cute	little	girl
a	foolish	old	dog

NOUNS AS MODIFIERS

A noun may be modified by another noun. That is to say, a noun cluster may consist of one noun as headword and another as modifier. This is a very important feature of the language:

MODIFIER	HEADWORD		MODIFIER	HEADWORD
1	1		1	1
town	house		India	ink
alley	cat		school	principal
kitchen	sink		paper	boy
money	troubles		athletics	committee

You may have forgotten how to tell an adjective from a noun in this position, that is, before another noun. Remember that you can usually put an intensifier, like *very* or *rather*, in front of the modifier if it is an adjective. You say "very small house," "very beautiful cat," "very new sink." But you can't ordinarily put *very* in front of a noun modifier. We wouldn't say "very town house," "very alley cat," "very kitchen sink."

Another difference is that a 3 1 cluster can usually be changed into a 1 2 3 sentence pattern. "The small house" equals "The house is small." "Beautiful cat" equals "The cat is beautiful." But a 1 1 construction cannot be turned around so. "Town house" doesn't equal "The house is town." "Kitchen sink" doesn't equal "The sink is kitchen."

Often a determiner and a noun both modify another noun:

MODIFIER	MODIFIER	HEADWORD
D	1	1
the	town	house
that	alley	cat
every	kitchen	sink
a	school	principal

We might also have all these modifiers together: a determiner, an adjective, and another noun as modifiers of the headword. When that happens, the regular order is D 3 1 1:

MODIFIER	MODIFIER	MODIFIER	HEADWORD
D	**3**	**1**	**1**
the	small	town	house
that	beautiful	alley	cat
this	new	kitchen	sink
a	handsome	school	principal
his	serious	money	troubles
an	industrious	paper	boy

VERBS AS MODIFIERS

Sometimes nouns are modified by verbs. These verbs may be of two types. They may be verbs ending in *ing: bleeding, singing, helping, fighting, poking.* Or they may be a past form like *broken, invited, stunned, written.* In our formulas we will give verbs of the *ing* type the symbol **2-ing**. We will give verbs of the past form the symbol **2-ed** (because most of them end in *ed*).

Here are examples of clusters in which the modifier is a **2-ing**:

MODIFIER	HEADWORD		MODIFIER	HEADWORD
2-ing	**1**		**2-ing**	**1**
purring	cat		fighting	man
singing	seaman		shrieking	aunt
helping	hand		running	water

You can probably see easily the difference in meaning between these clusters and those we had earlier. A purring cat is a cat that purrs. (But a beautiful cat is not a cat that beautifuls; an alley cat is not a cat that alleys.)

Here are examples in which the modifier is a **2-ed**:

MODIFIER	MODIFIER	HEADWORD
D	**2-ed**	**1**
a	stunned	cat
this	broken	bottle
our	invited	guests
no	written	invitation
some	cemented	bricks

These, too, have a special meaning. A stunned cat is a cat that something (or someone) stunned, not a cat that stuns. On the other hand, a purring cat is a cat that purrs, not a cat that something purred.

Not all words ending in *ing* or *ed* are verbs. Some have become adjectives. Compare these clusters; they look alike, but they are really different:

MODIFIER	MODIFIER	HEADWORD
2-ing	**1**	**1**
purring	alley	cat
3	**1**	**1**
interesting	alley	cat

Purring is a verb (like *crying, talking, smoking*), but *interesting* is an adjective (like *beautiful, attractive, talkative*). Usually you can tell the difference by trying an intensifier in front of the modifier. *Very* will pattern with adjectives, but not with verbs. We can say "a very interesting alley cat," but not "a very purring alley cat."

The same is true of words ending in *ed*. Some are verbs, but some are adjectives:

MODIFIER	HEADWORD		MODIFIER	HEADWORD
2-ed	**1**		**3**	**1**
cemented	wall		dilapidated	wall

We would say "a rather dilapidated wall," but not "a rather cemented wall."

WHAT MODIFIERS DO

You may have noticed something that modifiers do: they pin down, or narrow down, the meaning of the headword. A word like *dogs*, all by itself, has so many possibilities of meaning that one might say it has almost no meaning at all. We can't even tell what form class it belongs to until we see it in a pattern:

NOUN   **He likes dogs.**

VERB   **He dogs my footsteps.**

If we have it in a pattern such as "He likes dogs," we can identify it as a noun, but it is a noun of very general meaning. There's nothing wrong with this; sometimes we want to use words of very general meaning.

But sometimes we don't. Often we want to narrow down and specify. One way we do this is by using modifiers. The modifiers don't change the relation of the headword to the rest of the basic pattern, but they do change and restrict its meaning in a variety of ways. In all of the following sentences *dogs* is an object, but notice how its meaning changes:

I like dogs.

I like little dogs.

I like your dogs.

I like ranch dogs.

I like barking dogs.

I like these ranch dogs.

I like some little barking ranch dogs.

● EXERCISE 17

A. Write ten clusters that have a noun as headword and a determiner as modifier.

EXAMPLE   the cat   every tree   our town

B. Take the same nouns you used in Exercise A and modify them with adjectives.

EXAMPLE   beautiful cat   tall tree   sleepy town

C. Now see if you can modify each of your nouns with another noun. You may have to think hard with some of them.

EXAMPLE   alley cat   elm tree   home town

D. Now put all of the modifiers together on the same headword.

EXAMPLE   the beautiful alley cat   every tall elm tree
                     our sleepy home town.

E. Use each of the noun clusters in one of the noun positions of the four basic patterns and tell how you've used it.

EXAMPLE   The beautiful alley cat is unhappy.   (subject in Pattern Two)
               Every tall elm tree toppled over.   (subject in Pattern One)
               I hated our sleepy home town.   (object in Pattern Four)

F. Write ten clusters with a noun as headword and a **2-ing** verb as modifier.

G. Write ten clusters with a noun as headword and a **2-ed** verb as modifier.

---

18 : Noun clusters: Modifiers after the headword

In the last chapter we examined noun modifiers that come before the noun. Now we must look at some that come after the noun.

ADVERBS AS MODIFIERS

The simplest kind of noun modifier occurring after the noun that it modifies is an adverb. Not all adverbs modify nouns. The most common kind of adverbs that do are adverbs of the *there* type, with some kind of place meaning:

The men there went away.

In this sentence *the men there* is a noun cluster. *There* is an adverb modifying the headword *men*. Here are some more examples:

MODIFIER	HEADWORD	MODIFIER
D	**1**	**4**
some	people	upstairs
the	pavement	below
a	helper	inside
these	papers	here
the	paragraph	above
a	party	afterward

Naturally such headwords can have the other modifiers too:

MODIFIER	MODIFIER	MODIFIER	HEADWORD	MODIFIER
D	**3**	**1**	**1**	**4**
the	handsome	carnival	man	there
those	young	Colorado	people	upstairs

And remember that these are just noun clusters, not sentences. Here they are as parts of sentence patterns:

> The handsome carnival man there is my brother.
> I don't like those young Colorado people upstairs.

PREPOSITION GROUPS

In place of the adverb modifier after the noun, we may have a word group modifying the headword:

MODIFIER	HEADWORD	MODIFIER
the	man	in the truck
some	people	with the money
the	top	of the mountain

The words *in, with, of* in these clusters are called **prepositions.** In our formulas we will give them the symbol **P**. The characteristic of prepositions is that they pattern with a following noun with which they form a tight unit. The preposition plus its noun form a **preposition group** or **P-group**. Preposition groups are very common in English sentences. They have several possible functions. As we see, one of them is to modify a noun and thus be part of a noun cluster. They always follow the noun they modify:

MODIFIER	HEADWORD	MODIFIER		
D	1	P	D	1
the	man	in	the	truck
a	pail	under	the	sink
a	book	about	a	flier
some	maps	on	the	wall
his	cousin	from		Toledo
a	handful	of		dust
some	mice	in	the	piano
the	child	by	his	side

English has about fifty words which may occur as prepositions. The most common one is the word *of*, but you will also see *in, on, by, to, at, from,* and others cropping up in a great many sentences. Here is a fairly complete list of the words that may occur as prepositions:

aboard	at	despite	off	to
about	before	down	on	toward
above	behind	during	onto	under
across	below	for	over	until
after	beneath	from	per	unto
against	beside	in	round	up
along	besides	inside	since	upon
alongside	between	into	through	via
amid	beyond	like	throughout	with
among	by	near	till	within
around	concerning	of		

In addition to these we have several combinations, like *ahead of, contrary to, in spite of*. We still spell these as separate words, but we use them as units, and it is simplest to consider them as single prepositions. Here are some others:

according to	because of	in view of	out of
apart from	in front of	on account of	up to
back of	in place of		

Notice that we said these words *may* occur as prepositions. Some of them are regularly prepositions: *of, during, among, with,* and others. But many of them have other common possibilities, too. Quite a number of the words on the preposition list occur as adverbs on occasion. They are adverbs when they are used in positions like those in which *beautifully* occurs:

> She walked **beautifully.**
> She walked **in.**

They are prepositions when they form a unit with a following noun:

> She walked **in the yard.**

Notice that here *beautifully* does not fit in the position in which *in* occurs. We would not say this:

> She walked **beautifully the yard.**

Here are some more examples:

4		**P**	
He walked	by.	He walked	by the house.
He climbed	over.	He climbed	over the fence.
He looked	up.	He looked	up the road.
He stayed	aboard.	He stayed	aboard the ship.
He was	behind.	He was	behind the gun.
It fell	between.	It fell	between the acrobats.
He came	inside.	He came	inside the yard.

You remember we said a noun cluster can occur anywhere a noun can occur. Well, a noun can occur as part of a preposition group, so a noun cluster can also occur within a preposition group. As an example, we'll start with a P-group that is part of a noun cluster and then show that another cluster can occur inside the P-group:

NOUN CLUSTER

MODIFIER	HEADWORD	MODIFIER
D	**1**	**P-group**
the	man	with the dog
the	man	with the police dog
the	man	with the large police dog
the	man	with the large police dog on a leash

Now we have two noun clusters. One is the whole thing: *the man with the large police dog on a leash.* The other is the noun cluster inside the P-group: *the large police dog on a leash.*

In the last cluster we have another P-group: *on a leash.* This of course has a noun in it, and this noun could be built into still another cluster, and theoretically we could go on and on:

the man with the large police dog on a thin leash of brown leather with small silver rivets of considerable money value

But in actual practice we try to call a halt before the construction grows too complicated to be understood.

● **EXERCISE 18**

A. Write five noun clusters with the formula **D 3 1 4.**

EXAMPLE **the thin men there   an angry crowd outside**

B. Rewrite the clusters and this time substitute a preposition group for each adverb.

EXAMPLE **the thin men in my family   an angry crowd on the road**

C. Use each of your second set of clusters in one of the basic sentence patterns and indicate how you have used it:

EXAMPLE **The thin men in my family drink milk.   (subject in Pattern Four)**
We saw an angry crowd on the road.   (object in Pattern Four)

D. Using different prepositions, write five more clusters with the formula **D 1 P-group**.

EXAMPLE   **a shack behind the barn   a hike down the road**

E. Now expand this last set by developing the noun in the preposition group into another noun cluster.

EXAMPLE   **a shack behind the red barn on my uncle's ranch**
a hike down a country road with many turns

---

19 : Noun clusters: S-groups

Preposition groups (P-groups) are the most common of the noun modifiers that come after the headword. However there is another similar modifier of some importance. This is a construction that we will call an **S-group.** An S-group looks like a sentence pattern, except that it contains the word *who, which,* or *that* (or sometimes *whom* or *whose*) in front of it or in place of the subject.

MODIFIER	HEADWORD	MODIFIER
D	**1**	**S-group**
the	man	who was here
the	dog	that I bought
a	carpenter	who was on the roof
a	principal	who was smiling
a	stain	which wouldn't come out

Notice that these S-groups are just like ordinary sentences except for the *who, which,* or *that* and the position after the noun headword. All of the basic sentence patterns occur in S-groups as shown at the top of the next page:

	PATTERN ONE		PATTERN THREE
	(1↔2)		**(1↔2L 1)**
SENTENCE	Charlie sings.	SENTENCE	Gus is my enemy.
S-GROUP	who sings	S-GROUP	who is my enemy

	PATTERN TWO		PATTERN FOUR
	(1↔2 3)		**(1↔2 1)**
SENTENCE	The girl was beautiful.	SENTENCE	It ruined the picture.
S-GROUP	who was beautiful	S-GROUP	which ruined the picture

Who, which, and *that* in these positions are called **subordinators.** We give them this name because their effect is to take what would otherwise be a complete sentence and subordinate it to a larger pattern — make it part of a larger pattern. We give subordinators the symbol **S**, and this is why we call the group of words containing the subordinator an S-group. In other constructions we shall encounter other subordinators and different kinds of S-groups.

We make a notable distinction in our use of *who* and *which. Who* occurs when the headword in the noun cluster refers to a person:

MODIFIER	HEADWORD	MODIFIER
D	**1**	**S-group**
the	man	who just came in
the	waiter	who took our order
the	people	who couldn't wait
a	girl	who loved him

Which occurs when the headword in the noun cluster refers to something other than a person:

MODIFIER	HEADWORD	MODIFIER
D	**1**	**S-group**
the	cat	which sat on the fence
the	birds	which were chirping
a	stain	which wouldn't come out
the	reasons	which he gave

That occurs with any headword, in place of *who* or *which:*

MODIFIER	HEADWORD	MODIFIER
D	**1**	**S-group**
the	man	that just came in
the	people	that couldn't wait
the	cat	that sat on the fence
a	stain	that wouldn't come out

You may observe that all of the S-groups illustrated above could be turned into sentences if we replaced the subordinator with the headword of the cluster:

S-GROUP	the man who just came in
SENTENCE	The man just came in.

S-GROUP	the people that couldn't wait
SENTENCE	The people couldn't wait.

Sometimes S-groups occur without any **S** word at all. In these, the position of the group, after the noun headword, shows that it is an S-group and not a sentence. This happens only in constructions where the headword of the cluster would appear as an object if the S-group were turned into a sentence:

MODIFIER	HEADWORD	MODIFIER
D	**1**	**S-group**
the	reasons	he gave
a	man	we knew
a	letter	somebody sent
a	mouse	the cat dragged in

Compare these S-groups with sentences in which the headword has become the object:

He gave the reasons.   Somebody sent a letter.

We knew a man.   The cat dragged in a mouse.

It is possible to have a P-group and an S-group both modifying the same headword. When this happens, the P-group always comes first and the S-group second.

MODIFIER	HEADWORD	MODIFIER	MODIFIER
D	**1**	**P-group**	**S-group**
the	man	at the back	who was smiling
some	friends	from Toledo	who were wealthy

However, as will be explained later, it's easy to get mixed up in this construction so that the hearer or reader doesn't know what is modifying what.

SUMMARY

We have seen most of the different kinds of modifiers that occur in noun clusters — not quite all, but enough for now. We have seen that a noun may be modified in the following ways: By a determiner:

> those dogs **(D 1)**

By an adjective:

> enormous dogs **(3 1)**

By another noun:

> ranch dogs **(1 1)**

By a verb:

> yapping dogs **(2-ing 1)**

By a P-group:

> dogs in the yard **(1 P-group)**

By an S-group:

> dogs that were driving me crazy **(1 S-group)**

If we put these all together, the correct order is **D 3 2-ing 1 1 P-group S-group**:

D	**3**	**2-ing**	**1**	**1**	**P-group**	**S-group**

those enormous yapping ranch dogs in the yard that were driving me crazy

This is not a sentence, just a noun cluster. It can go in any noun position in a sentence pattern:

Those enormous yapping ranch dogs in the yard that were driving me crazy love meat.

Though we don't often have occasion to string as many modifiers as this on one headword, we can if we want to. But notice that we don't have much choice about the order in which the modifiers come. If we start mixing them up, we get something that isn't English, like this:

those ranch in the yard yapping that were driving me crazy dogs enormous

In some ways the English language gives us lots of leeway. In others it doesn't give us any. One respect in which the language will put up with no nonsense is the order of noun modifiers. It ordinarily won't tolerate even a very little shifting. "Enormous ranch dogs love meat" is an excellent English sentence. "Ranch enormous dogs love meat" isn't an English sentence at all.

● **EXERCISE 19**

A. Write five noun clusters with the formulae **D 1 S-group**. Use all the subordinators — *who, which, that* — remembering the distinction between *who* and *which*.

EXAMPLE   **a man who was wealthy**
           the money which we needed
           a fellow I know

B. Use each of your five clusters in one of the basic sentence patterns and indicate how you've used it.

EXAMPLE   **I met a man who was wealthy.   (object in Pattern Four)**
           The money which we needed just came.   (subject in Pattern One)
           He's a fellow I know.   (complement in Pattern Three)

C. Write five noun clusters with the formula **D 1 P-group S-group.** Make sure that the P-group and the S-group both modify the same headword.

EXAMPLE   **a man in my home town who was wealthy**
                 the cats on the fence which were fighting

D. Write four noun clusters with the formula **D 3 1 1 P-group S-group.**

EXAMPLE   **a handsome carnival man in my home town who was wealthy**
                 some silly choir girls in the back row that were always giggling

E. Use each of the last set of noun clusters in one of the basic sentence patterns.

---

20 : Verb clusters: Adverbs

Like nouns, verbs most commonly occur not all by themselves but in the company of other words that pattern with them and modify their meaning. In other words, they occur as the headwords of clusters.

Some of these clusters we have already seen in the basic sentence patterns. For example, in "Birds are beautiful," Pattern Two, *are beautiful* is a kind of unit — a cluster in which the headword is the verb *are*. In "He painted the fence," Pattern Four, *painted the fence* is a cluster in which the headword is the verb *painted*. But now we need to examine other verb clusters, in which the verbs of these basic patterns are modified in various ways.

We sometimes think that verbs are modified only by adverbs. They aren't always, as we shall see, but adverbs are probably the most common kind of verb modifiers.

Here are some clusters with verb as headword and adverb as modifier:

HEADWORD	MODIFIER	HEADWORD	MODIFIER
2	**4**	**2**	**4**
speak	slowly	went	away
answered	angrily	lived	there
thought	hard	sang	horribly
looked	up	stayed	late

KINDS OF ADVERBS

These adverbs, however, are of three distinct types. Some are adverbs of place or position:

HEADWORD	MODIFIER	HEADWORD	MODIFIER
2	**4**	**2**	**4**
lived	there	sat	down
went	away	stalked	out
looked	up	dropped	in

Some are adverbs of manner:

HEADWORD	MODIFIER	HEADWORD	MODIFIER
2	**4**	**2**	**4**
lived	thus	looked	carefully
sang	horribly	sat	uncomfortably
went	quickly	ate	greedily

Some are adverbs of time:

HEADWORD	MODIFIER	HEADWORD	MODIFIER
2	**4**	**2**	**4**
lived	then	stopped	often
went	later	refused	sometimes
looked	usually		

If you want to tell these different kinds of adverbs apart, notice that the most general words in each group are *there* (for place), *thus* (for manner), and *then* (for time). See which of these can most easily take the place of the word you're in doubt about. If *there* can be substituted, the adverb is a place adverb; if *thus*, it is a manner adverb; if *then*, it is a time adverb.

ORDER OF ADVERBS

The reason that we say that adverbs are divided into these groups is not that they have three different meanings. Any adverb has a different meaning from another adverb. The reason is rather that adverbs behave differently in sentences according to which group they belong to. Notice that we can use an adverb from each group in the same pattern.

HEADWORD	MODIFIER	MODIFIER	MODIFIER
2	**4**	**4**	**4**
went	away	quickly	later
looked	up	suspiciously	often
sat	down	unhappily	sometimes
stalked	out	angrily	usually
lived	there	thus	then

In other words, a quite common order is first the verb headword, then the adverb of place (*there*), then the adverb of manner (*thus*), then the adverb of time (*then*). To be sure, this isn't the only possibility. The order of adverbs is really rather flexible, and we'll see some other arrangements in a moment. But we can't scramble the three groups any way we want to. The following patterns wouldn't be used by native speakers:

> went later away quickly
> away went quickly later
> looked often suspiciously up

Neither do we ordinarily use two adverbs from the same group to modify the same headword (unless a word like *and* comes between them). We wouldn't say "looked up out" or "stopped usually often" or "ate quickly greedily."

We do, however, have many other possibilities. Sometimes we put the *then* adverb before the headword:

MODIFIER	HEADWORD	MODIFIER	MODIFIER
4	**2**	**4**	**4**
later	went	away	quickly
often	looked	up	suspiciously
sometimes	stalked	out	angrily
then	lived	there	thus

Sometimes, but not so often, the *thus* adverb comes before the headword. When it does, we usually have just a *there* adverb after the headword, or no modifier at all after it:

MODIFIER	HEADWORD	MODIFIER
4	**2**	**4**
quickly	went	away
angrily	stalked	out
reluctantly	refused	

The adverbs work into all the basic patterns, complicating the cluster. They all occur with the verb in Pattern One:

> **D 1 4 2 4 4**
> The men often went away quickly.

> **D 1 2 4 4 4**
> His uncle stalked out angrily sometimes.

> **D 1 4 2 4 4**
> His uncle sometimes stalked out angrily.

Then and *there* adverbs occur in the cluster of Pattern Two:

> **1 4 2 3**
> She often looked beautiful.

> **1 2 3 4**
> She was happy sometimes.

> **1 2 3 4**
> She felt comfortable there.

All of the adverb types occur in the cluster of Pattern Three:

1   2   4   D   1
He was then my helper.

1   2   D   1   4
He was my helper unwillingly.

1   2   D   1   4
He was my helper downstairs.

All occur in the cluster of Pattern Four:

D   1   4   2   D 1   4   4
The quarterback always kicked the ball away vigorously.

1   4   2   D 1   4   4
He generally took his dog outside reluctantly.

● **EXERCISE 20**

A. Write down this sentence on a piece of paper: "The men often went away angrily." Leave plenty of space between the words. Now substitute as many words as you can for the adverbs. This will give you lists of the three types of adverbs:

EXAMPLE   **The men   often   went   away   angrily.**
                      usually   down   happily.
                      never   out   quickly.

You can expect to run out of words for the first column rather quickly.

B. Write two simple examples of each of the basic sentence patterns.

EXAMPLE   **The birds sing.   (Pattern One)**
          The boys are polite.   (Pattern Two)

C. Now rewrite your sentence patterns, adding as many adverbs as possible. Notice whether the adverbs are *there, thus,* or *then* adverbs.

EXAMPLE   **The birds often sing noisily.**
          The boys are sometimes polite.

21: Verb clusters: P-groups and S-groups

Verbs are also modified by word groups. The most common kinds are the same ones that modify nouns — P-groups and S-groups. The preposition group often comes right after the verb headword:

HEADWORD	MODIFIER	HEADWORD	MODIFIER
2	**P-group**	**2**	**P-group**
went	into the back room	hid	behind a bush
sat	on a tack	rolled	under the couch
died	of palsy	lied	about his age

Since the preposition group contains a noun, we can have a noun cluster developing inside the verb cluster. Still, the P-group as a whole modifies the verb:

VERB CLUSTER

HEADWORD	MODIFIER
2	**P-group**
went	into the room which had been set aside
sat	on a rusty tack with a sharp point
hid	behind a large bush of lovely roses

Sometimes two P-groups in a row modify the same verb headword:

HEADWORD	MODIFIER	MODIFIER
2	**P-group**	**P-group**
rode	into the room	on a bicycle
went	to Toledo	with his uncle
died	of palsy	at the age of eighty

Notice that the last example contains a third preposition group: *of eighty*. But this is part of the noun cluster *the age of eighty*.

S-GROUPS

The S-groups that occur in verb clusters are somewhat different from those that occur in noun clusters. They are introduced by a different set of subordinators — *because, while, if, when,* etc. These subordinators regularly stand outside a sentence pattern, and they make that pattern part of another pattern. For instance, if we say "We went away," we have a sentence. But if we put *because* in front of this pattern, we no longer have a sentence but something that must be part of another construction. The effect of *because* is to make *we went away* a part of another sentence pattern.

Here are some S-groups by themselves. Notice the subordinators before them. Notice that all the basic patterns occur:

	SUBORDINATOR	SENTENCE PATTERN
PATTERN ONE	because	birds sing
PATTERN TWO	although	birds are beautiful
PATTERN THREE	if	he is your friend
PATTERN FOUR	when	he got the money

No matter how long and complicated the sentence pattern is, it will still be part of another pattern if a subordinator stands in front of it:

SUBORDINATOR	SENTENCE PATTERN
because	the little birds that nest in the trees outside our house sing songs that we all like to hear
although	the fellow you told me about last week is one of your best friends

Other common subordinators that work in this way are:

where	after	whether	that
until	since	though	so that
as	where	as if	provided
than	whenever	how	
before	wherever	why	

Some of these words have other uses too.

These subordinators are somewhat different from the subordinators *who*, *which*, and *that* in noun clusters. Subordinators of the *because* type stand outside the pattern they subordinate:

S   1 2   3
He ate because he was hungry.

S   1 2   1
He helped us when he had time.

But subordinators of the *who* type are themselves a part of the pattern they subordinate:

S   2   3
The man who was hungry ate heartily.

Who makes its S-group part of the noun cluster all right. But *who* is itself part of the pattern. When we take out *because* from the word group *because he was hungry*, we are left with a regular sentence pattern: *he was hungry*. But when we take out *who* from the group *who was hungry*, we are left with just a part of a pattern: *was hungry*.

S-groups have several uses. We have seen that they can occur in noun clusters, modifying the noun. They also occur in verb clusters, modifying the verb:

	HEADWORD	MODIFIER
	2	**S-group**
	ate	because he was hungry
	retreated	when the guns opened fire
will	go	if someone pays his way
were	waiting	until she got dressed
	agreed	after we twisted his arm

Several different modifiers may be used to modify the same verb headword. The order isn't quite as rigid as it is in noun clusters, but it isn't altogether free either. If a P-group and an S-group modify the same verb, the P-group ordinarily comes first:

HEADWORD	MODIFIER	MODIFIER
2	**P-group**	**S-group**
walked	into the house	after we twisted his arm
retreated	behind a bush	when the guns opened fire
lied	about his age	because he was told to

We can't very well switch these around. If we do, we get a construction that sounds foreign: *lied because he was told to about his age.* Or we get nonsense: *walked after we twisted his arm into the house.*

If an adverb and a P-group modify the same verb, the adverb may come before the verb, between the verb and the P-group, of after the P-group:

> **slowly** walked into the house
> walked **slowly** into the house
> walked into the house **slowly**

If an adverb and an S-group modify the same verb, the adverb may come before the verb or between the verb and the S-group:

> **slowly** walked after we twisted his arm
> walked **slowly** after we twisted his arm

But it can't ordinarily come after the S-group without producing another meaning, as you can see:

> walked after we twisted his arm **slowly**

SUMMARY

These are the most important features of noun and verb clusters.

Nouns are commonly modified by the following: adjectives, verbs, adverbs, other nouns; determiners; P-groups; S-groups.

Verbs are commonly modified by the following: adverbs; P-groups; S-groups.

Later we shall study a few other kinds of modifiers of both nouns and verbs, but these are enough for now.

● EXERCISE 21

A. Write ten verb clusters in which the verb headword is modified by a preposition group.

EXAMPLE   went to the store
           lay on the sofa

B. Add an adverb to each of the clusters.

EXAMPLE   went off to the store
           lay quietly on the sofa
           sometimes lay on the sofa

C. Write ten verb clusters in which the verb headword is modified by an S-group. Use as many different subordinators as you can.

EXAMPLE   ate an apple because he was hungry
           hurried away before the concert was over

D. Write five verb clusters in which the verb headword is modified by a P-group and also by an S-group.

EXAMPLE   ate peas with his knife because he was hungry
           talked to the soldiers while we were waiting

Part Five

HOW

SENTENCES

ARE BUILT

22 : Pattern parts

We have seen how the words in English speech belong to one or another of a limited number of word classes — nouns, verbs, prepositions, determiners, etc. We have seen how these word classes are arranged to form a limited number of basic patterns. We have seen how patterns may be made parts of other patterns by the use of subordinators. And we have seen how units in the patterns may be enlarged into word clusters by modifiers.

Many of these points we must take up in greater detail later on in our study. But first we must examine another major feature of English sentences: the manner in which the words in an English sentence are arranged in parts or segments.

All of these things are real — in the sense that they are the things a person has to know in order to understand English. When you hear an English sentence or read one, these are the questions you have to know the answers to:

1. What form classes or structure groups do the words belong to? Which are the nouns, which the verbs, which the prepositions and adverbs, and so on?

2. What are the nouns doing? You must not only recognize

the nouns as nouns, you must also recognize them as subjects, objects, or linking-verb complements, or as other structures that we will examine later.

3. What kind of combination is involved? Is something subordinated? If so, how? Is the sentence connected to another sentence? If so, how?

4. What kind of modification is involved? Is a noun modified? If so, by what kind of word? (It makes a difference: a *mess sergeant* is not the same kind of thing as a *messy sergeant*.)

5. What are the major word groups of the pattern, and what are the groups within the major groups? In other words, what are the pattern parts?

These things you absolutely must know in order to understand what a sentence means. Obviously you don't have to know these terms. You can understand English without having heard such terms as *noun, verb, subject, object, pattern*. But you can't understand what a sentence means if you can't tell a noun from a verb; you couldn't tell what was action and what was performer. You can't understand what a sentence means if you can't tell the subject from the object; you wouldn't know whether the man ate the bear or the bear ate the man.

And you can't understand what a sentence means unless you can recognize the pattern parts. You must be able to tell how the words go together in groups.

About 99 percent of the sentences we use are made up of two major pattern parts. (We'll just ignore the other 1 percent.) And each of those two parts is composed of two parts; and each of those is composed of two parts; and so on, until we get down to single words. In other words, English patterns go by twos.

Let's take some examples:

The man at the back was smoking a cigar.

This has two major parts: *the man at the back* is one; *was smoking a cigar* is the other. If we want to write it to show its pattern parts, we write it this way:

The man at the back / was smoking a cigar.

Here are some other examples. We write them first in the ordinary way and then divided into their major pattern parts:

My Uncle Stu married a rich woman.
My Uncle Stu / married a rich woman.
The lad who was holding the lobster fell in.
The lad who was holding the lobster / fell in.

When she got there, the cupboard was bare.
When she got there / the cupboard was bare.

The cupboard was bare when she got there.
The cupboard / was bare when she got there.

Fortunately Charlie was elected treasurer.
Fortunately / Charlie was elected treasurer.

You may be saying to yourself that it doesn't matter how we
cut up such sentences. But it does. We must do it right, or we
come out with the wrong meaning or no meaning at all. Suppose
we did this:

The lad who was holding / the lobster fell in.

Now something is obviously wrong. In the first place we have a
construction that doesn't lead us anywhere: *the lad who was
holding.* On the other side we have a construction that makes
sense but presumably not the sense intended, since we are not
supposed to think that the lobster, rather than the lad, fell in.

In this sentence — and in any good sentence — the signals
in the sentence tell us what the pattern parts are. We know that
lad isn't the subject of *was holding,* because *who* is in the way. If
lad isn't the subject of *was holding,* it must be the subject of *fell.*
If *lad* is the subject of *fell,* *lobster* can't be. So *lobster* must be
the object of *was holding* and therefore part of a modifier of *lad* and
part of the pattern part that *lad* is in. We grasp this in a split
second when we hear the sentence, because we are familiar with
the pattern and the pattern signs.

But in a bad sentence the signs may be lacking. What are the pattern parts of this sentence?

The rulers only did what they pleased.

We can't tell. It might mean that just the rulers, and no one else, did what they pleased; or it might mean that the rulers did nothing else except what they pleased. The pattern parts might be either of these:

The rulers only / did what they pleased.
The rulers / only did what they pleased.

● EXERCISE 22

Let's use a nonsense sentence to review some of the matters we have covered: "The grupple in the scoob was snoping a greefer when a lollyboon perkled in." It isn't hard to identify the various form classes and structure groups:

D   1   P D   1   A   2   D   1   S D   1
The grupple in the scoob was snoping a greefer when a lollyboon
2   4
perkled in.

What else can be said about the sentence? First of all, it's a statement. (A question would begin, "Was the grupple in the scoob snoping a greefer . . .?" and a request would be "Snope that greefer . . .") Secondly, we know what the action is: "snoping" and "perkling." We know who performs which action: a "grupple snopes" and a "lollyboon perkles." We know when the action takes place: in the past. We know the particular structures of the nouns: *grupple* and *lollyboon* are subjects, *scoob* is the noun of a preposition group, and *greefer* is an object. (We assume that if *greefer* were to be a complement, we would have to have the real word *being* or *becoming* in place of *snoping*.) We know what the major pattern parts are: the noun cluster *the grupple in the scoob* is one, and the verb cluster *was snoping a greefer when a lollyboon perkled in* is the other. Basically, the sentence is Pattern Four: 1 2 1 ("The grupple snoped a greefer.") There is another sentence pattern, Pattern One, as part of the verb cluster. It is made part of the cluster by the subordinator *when*.

Here are some more nonsense sentences. First use the symbols to show what form class or structure group each word belongs to. Then give the following information:

a. What is the action?

b. What performs the action?

c. When does the action take place?

d. What are the particular structures of the nouns (subject, object, complement)?

e. What are the major pattern parts of the sentence?

f. What is the basic pattern of the sentence?

g. If there is a subordinated sentence pattern included in the sentence, what is it?

1. A fleem drigged the boiner with a fibbernit. **2.** The leskle in the rantash was very poonish. **3.** Every doag sobbered cobfully while the ramkin spaled. **4.** The old hosker that was dibbling the stoon is my grandax. **5.** Both stuttles should quibber a dracious neg if the goomp bargles in rebeegeously.

1–noun   2–verb   3–adjective   4–adverb
A–auxiliary   D–determiner   V–intensifier   P–preposition   S–subordinator

---

23 : Pattern parts
of whole sentences

We will now examine pattern parts a little more systematically. We will begin with pattern parts of whole sentences. Later on we will proceed to discuss the parts of those parts. Since punctuation is tied closely to the pattern parts, we will notice some points of punctuation as we go along.

If a sentence contains no introductory word or group of words, the pattern is regularly composed of the subject with all its modifiers as one part and the verb with all its modifiers as the other part. In other words, one part is a noun or noun cluster and the other part is a verb or verb cluster.

For instance, in the sentence "The man at the back was smoking his pipe," the parts are these:

D   1   P   D   1   A   2   D   1
The man at the back / was smoking his pipe.

This means that the noun cluster *the man at the back* (as a whole) is subject of the verb cluster *was smoking his pipe* (as a whole). One works as a unit against the other. Notice that no other division makes any sense:

The man / at the back was smoking his pipe.
The man at the back was smoking / his pipe.
The man at the / back was smoking his pipe.

All of these cuts divide elements which belong together.

In the sentence "Every critic of the head of the firm was somewhat timid when the showdown came," the pattern parts are these:

D   1   P   D   1   P   D   1   2L   V   3   S   D
Every critic of the head of the firm / was somewhat timid when the
1   2
showdown came.

We have a noun cluster as one part and a verb cluster as the other. The noun cluster is *every critic of the head of the firm*, with *critic* as the headword. The verb cluster is *was somewhat timid when the showdown came*, with *was* as the headword.

In the sentence "Some of the fellows there should have known better," the parts are these:

1   P   D   1   4   A   A   2   4
Some of the fellows there / should have known better.

Some of the fellows there, the subject with its modifiers, works as a unit against *should have known better*, the verb with its auxiliaries and modifier.

You can't tell anything from the length of the parts. Both may be very short:

Canaries / twitter.

Or the subject part may be long and the verb part short:

Nearly all the pink and yellow Spanish canaries on the mainland that are more than two months old / twitter.

Or the subject part may be very short and the verb part long:

Canaries / sometimes twitter so loudly in the early mornings here that the people staying in the hotel can't get any sleep.

Or they may both be long:

Nearly all the pink and yellow Spanish canaries on the mainland that are more than two months old / sometimes twitter so loudly in the early mornings that the people staying in the hotel can't get any sleep.

Now notice the punctuation in these sentences: there isn't any. We don't usually have any commas in a sentence that consists of just a noun cluster and a verb cluster:

The man at the back was smoking his pipe.
Every critic of the head of the firm was somewhat timid when the showdown came.
Some of the fellows there should have known better.
Nearly all the pink and yellow Spanish canaries on the mainland that are more than two months old sometimes twitter so loudly in the early mornings that the people staying in the hotel can't get any sleep.

If the sentence begins with an introductory word or group of words of any kind, then the two pattern parts are always the introductory words and the rest of the sentence.

S   1   2   4   D   1   2L   3
When she got there / the cupboard was bare.

That is to say, the S-group (as a whole) works as a unit against the rest of the sentence (as a whole). *When she got there* modifies *the cupboard was bare.*

This is the only division that makes any sense. Suppose we ignored the introductory S-group and made the division between the main subject and the main verb. We would get this:

When she got there, the cupboard / was bare.

This won't do. *When she got there, the cupboard* is not a unit. It is not a meaningful part of anything.

S-groups are often used in this way, at the beginning of sentences. In this position, an S-group always works as a unit against the rest of the sentence. Here are some more examples:

If you see Charlie, tell him the boss wants him.
If you see Charlie / tell him the boss wants him.

Since we had plenty of time, we decided to visit Toledo.
Since we had plenty of time / we decided to visit Toledo.

While we were waiting, the roof caved in.
While we were waiting / the roof caved in.

Notice the punctuation. An S-group in this position modifies the rest of the sentence, and it is regularly separated from the rest of the sentence by a comma. Not all introductory modifiers are separated from the sentence in this way, but S-groups regularly are.

Now look at the punctuation of these sentences:

When she got there, the cupboard was bare.
The cupboard was bare when she got there.

We might feel that these mean about the same thing, but the punctuation is different because the pattern parts are different. In "When she got there, the cupboard was bare," the pattern parts are (1) *when she got there* modifying (2) *the cupboard was bare.* But in "The cupboard was bare when she got there," the parts are (1) the noun cluster *the cupboard* and (2) the verb cluster *was bare when she got there.* The S-group *when she got there* is here a part of the verb cluster. In the second sentence there is no punctuation.

Sometimes we have an S-group which comes at the end but modifies the whole sentence. An example is "We decided to visit Toledo, since we had plenty of time." Here the pattern parts are *We decided to visit Toledo* as one and *since we had plenty of time* as the other, and there is a comma between them. We'll go into this sort of thing in more detail later on (pp. 253–54). But usually an S-group in this position is part of the verb cluster and there is no punctuation.

● **EXERCISE 23**

A. Copy these sentences and draw a line between their main pattern parts. In all of these the pattern parts are a noun cluster as one part and a verb cluster as the other.

EXAMPLE   **The house on the corner burned to the ground.**
The house on the corner / burned to the ground.

1. The man on the bench was reading a book. **2.** An old toothbrush peddler wandered into the yard. **3.** Some of the fellows on our side had spikes in their shoes. **4.** A rather old-fashioned picture hung on the wall opposite the fireplace. **5.** The chief of police left before the argument began. **6.** One of the teachers came by while they were fighting. **7.** Charlie got sick sometimes. **8.** Charlie sometimes got sick. **9.** Charlie sometimes got sick when he ate too much ice cream with pickles on the side. **10.** Some of the businessmen who have stores on First Street may object violently if one-way traffic is introduced. **11.** The young circus clown in the center of the arena who was petting the lion laughed heartily. **12.** We didn't think much about it.

B. Write five more sentences in which the main pattern parts are one noun cluster and one verb cluster.

C. In the following sentences the pattern parts are an introductory S-group as one part and a main sentence pattern as the other part. The commas have been left out to make it hard for you. Copy each sentence, cut it into its pattern parts, and put in the comma.

EXAMPLE   **When she got there the cupboard was bare.**
          When she got there, / the cupboard was bare.

1. If you have a minute help me move this piano. **2.** While we're waiting we might as well wash the dishes. **3.** Since he's your brother you should be the one to ask him. **4.** After the police arrived the crowd calmed down a little. **5.** Because he was interested in my welfare he gave me fifty thousand dollars. **6.** As I was going to St. Ives I met a man with seven wives.

D. Write five more sentences in which the pattern parts are an introductory S-group as one part and a main sentence pattern as the other part. Don't forget the comma.

24: Pattern parts of noun clusters

We have seen that any ordinary sentence consists of two main pattern parts. But this isn't the end of it. Each of those two parts also consists of two parts. And each of those parts consists of two parts. And each of those parts consists of two parts — until we work down to individual words. Normal English structure always goes by twos.

Let's turn now to the make-up of noun clusters — groups of words in which the headword is a noun. We'll begin with a whole sentence and cut off a noun cluster for examination:

The genial milk inspector on my right who was smoking a pipe / coughed slightly.

Since this sentence has no introductory elements, the pattern consists of the subject and its modifiers as one part and the verb and its modifiers as the other part. Let's look at the subject:

D   3   1   1   P D   1   S A   2   D   1
The genial milk inspector on my right who was smoking a pipe

Here the headword is the noun *inspector*. This is modified by three modifiers on one side: a determiner (*the*), an adjective (*genial*), and another noun (*milk*). On the other side we find two modifiers: a P-group (*on my right*) and an S-group (*who was smoking a pipe*).

Now the modifiers of a noun in English fit together in such a regular and well-ordered way that one can state a perfectly mechanical rule for cutting a noun cluster into its pattern parts.

Begin with the modifiers *after* the headword. Cut off the one farthest from the headword, then the one next farthest until you are back to the headword. (Ordinarily there are not more than two modifiers after the headword.) Then go to the modifiers in front of the headword. Cut off the one farthest from the headword, then the next, then the next, until you reach the headword.

Let's see how it works:

The genial milk inspector on my right who was smoking a pipe

We have two modifiers after the headword: *on my right* and *who was smoking a pipe*. We cut off the one farthest from the headword:

The genial milk inspector on my right / who was smoking a pipe

This says that *who was smoking a pipe* modifies not just *inspector* and not just *the genial milk inspector*. It modifies the whole cluster: *the genial milk inspector on my right*.

Notice that any other cut would be wrong because it would give us something that is not a unit. For instance:

The genial milk inspector / on my right who was smoking a pipe

This would indicate that it was "my right" that was smoking the pipe. So the cut must be between *right* and *who:*

The genial milk inspector on my right / who was smoking a pipe

Now we are left with one modifier after the headword. We cut that off next:

The genial milk inspector / on my right

This says that the P-group *on my right* modifies not just *inspector* but everything that goes before: *the genial milk inspector*. But it doesn't modify *who was smoking a pipe*.

Now we're back to the headword, so we begin again at the other side, cutting off first the modifier farthest from the headword in front:

The / genial milk inspector

The modifies not just *inspector* but *genial milk inspector*. Now we work in:

genial / milk inspector

Genial modifies not just *inspector* but *milk inspector*. Now we're down to single words:

milk / inspector

Let's cut the whole thing again. First cut the sentence until you're down to a noun cluster. Then cut the modifiers after the headword, beginning with the one farthest out and working in. Then cut the modifiers in front of the headword, beginning with the one farthest out and working in.

The genial milk inspector on my right who was smoking a pipe / coughed slightly.
The genial milk inspector on my right / who was smoking a pipe
The genial milk inspector / on my right
The / genial milk inspector
genial / milk inspector
milk / inspector

Here's another one:

He described some old houses in Toledo that were for sale.

Here a noun cluster is the object of the verb *described*. The noun cluster is *some old houses in Toledo that were for sale*. The headword is *houses.* There are two modifiers after the headword: *in Toledo* and *that were for sale.* There are two modifiers in front of the headword: *some* and *old.* Here are the pattern parts:

some old houses in Toledo / that were for sale

The S-group *that were for sale* modifies *some old houses in Toledo.*

some old houses / in Toledo

The P-group *in Toledo* modifies *some old houses.*

some / old houses

The determiner *some* modifies *old houses.*

old / houses

The adjective *old* modifies *houses.*

Remember one other thing. When a noun cluster is the subject of a verb, it is the headword that is tied to the verb. If the headword is singular, the verb has the form ending in *s* (*walks, helps, goes, has, is, was*) or a past form (*walked, helped, went*). If the headword is plural, the verb has the form without *s* (*walk, help, go, are, were*) or a past form (*walked, helped, went*). Just the headword counts. The other words in the noun cluster have no effect on the following verb:

> The young **fellows** in the car **were** arrested.
> The young **fellow** in the car **was** arrested.
>
> The **houses** in the middle of the block **need** paint.
> The **house** in the middle of the block **needs** paint.
>
> A **man** who understands horses sometimes **helps** me.
> Some **men** who understand horses sometimes **help** me.

● **EXERCISE 24**

A. Here are some noun clusters. Cut them into their pattern parts as we have cut the sentence about the milk inspector on page 117. All of these have two modifiers after the headword and two or three before the headword.

1. the young burglar inside the house who was stealing the silver
2. an indignant farmer from upstate who had been listening **3.** every eligible basketball player in the sophomore class who is interested
4. the new steel bars in the backyard that were recently installed
5. a handsome teacher of mathematics who had just been hired

B. Use each of the noun clusters above in one of the basic sentence patterns, as subject, object, or linking-verb complement.

C. Write five more noun clusters like those above and cut them into their pattern parts.

D. Use each of your noun clusters in one of the basic sentence patterns, as subject, object, or linking-verb complement.

25 : Noun clusters: Complications

Our milk-inspector sentence in the last chapter was a pretty straightforward one. Each word or group of words was an obvious modifier of the noun headword, and they peeled off in order, according to the rule. But the waters can get a lot rougher.

Take another look at the milk-inspector sentence:

The genial milk inspector on my right who was smoking a pipe coughed slightly.

Now look at this one:

The genial milk inspector in the car that had no motor coughed slightly.

The two sentences look very much alike, and they *are* alike *on the first level*. In both sentences the first cut is between the main noun cluster and the main verb cluster:

The genial milk inspector on my right who was smoking a pipe / coughed slightly.

The genial milk inspector in the car that had no motor / coughed slightly.

But the two noun clusters, though they look alike, aren't.

Suppose we make the next cut in the second sentence where we made it in the first:

The genial milk inspector on my right / who was smoking a pipe
The genial milk inspector in the car / that had no motor

What's wrong? Well, the cut says that we have to do here with a motorless inspector. But common sense tells us that the S-group *that had no motor* must apply to *car*. In other words, *that had no motor* isn't a modifier of *inspector* at all. It is a modifier of *car*, the noun in the P-group. So *inspector* has only one modifier following it, and we cut that off first according to rule:

The genial milk inspector / in the car that had no motor

How do we know, in this sentence, that the S-group *that had no motor* applies to the car rather than to the inspector in the car? Presumably, we know because of the general uses of the words. We are accustomed to thinking of cars as having motors (or not having them). But we don't think of motors in connection with inspectors.

Suppose now we come on a sentence with no such clue.

The man with the boy who was making a fuss / left early.

What are the pattern parts of the noun cluster? Does *man* have two modifiers after it or only one? Either is possible:

The man with the boy / who was making a fuss
The man / with the boy who was making a fuss

For here the meanings of the words give no clue. Men can make fusses, and boys can make fusses. We have no way of knowing who is making this fuss.

This is a bad sentence. It is bad because it doesn't contain the signals that will tell the hearer what the pattern parts are. The hearer must grasp the pattern parts in order to understand the sentence. Here he can't.

Here's another bad sentence:

The man with the dog that was making a fuss / left early.

Again we can't tell who is making the fuss, because dogs can make them and men can make them. There are no signals to clue us to the pattern parts.

What signals could there be? Well, in our original sentence we found a signal in the general uses of the words: we think of motors in connection with cars but not in connection with inspectors. But the signals might be more formal and precise than just the general uses of the words. All of the following noun clusters contain the necessary signals:

the man with the boys who were making a fuss   (boys↔were)
the man with the boys who was making a fuss   (man↔was)
the men with the boy who were making a fuss   (men↔were)
the men with the boy who was making a fuss   (boy↔was)
the man with the dog which was making a fuss   (dog↔which)
the man with the dog who was making a fuss   (man↔who)

All of these can be cut into their pattern parts. More important, in each cluster the hearer can grasp the pattern parts accurately. In no cluster is he in doubt about the identity of the fuss maker. The necessary signals are there.

Let's examine these signals more closely. In the first four clusters, the signal is a number signal. There is a subject-verb tie (1↔A 2) which would result if we replaced the *who* with one of the preceding nouns. That noun must be the headword of the S-group. Notice that in each of these clusters the nouns are of different number, one singular and one plural — *man* and *boys* or *men* and *boy*. In the S-group the auxiliary happens to be one which distinguishes between singular and plural — *was* or *were*. If it is *was*, it links the S-group to the singular noun: *man* or *boy.* If it is *were*, it links the S-group to the plural noun — *men* or *boys*.

In the last two clusters we have a signal of quite a different type. Here the signal is in the subordinator itself. We have noticed that in S-groups of this kind — those which modify nouns — the subordinator is generally *who, which,* or *that.* These differ in the kinds of nouns they pattern with. *Who* generally patterns with nouns relating to people: *the boy who, the girl who, my aunt who, the electrician who, the Germans who. Which,* on the other hand, does not ordinarily pattern with such nouns. Instead, it patterns with nouns relating to animals or to things: *the dog which, the light bulb which, the house which, the calf which, the group which, Germany which.*

This contrast provides a clue in sentences like those we are discussing. If there are two nouns ahead of the S-group and one is a person noun and the other isn't, then a *who* will link the S-group to the person noun, whereas a *which* will link it to the non-person noun.

Consequently, all these structures have a signal of some sort, and we can cut them into their pattern parts:

> the man / with the boys who were making a fuss
> the man with the boys / who was making a fuss
> the men with the boy / who were making a fuss
> the man / with the dog which was making a fuss
> the man with the dog / who was making a fuss

But the following clusters cannot be cut into their pattern parts:

> the man with the boy who was making a fuss
> the men with the boy who made a fuss
> the man with the dog that was making a fuss

For here there are no signals which indicate the pattern parts, and consequently the meaning is not made clear. Signals of some sort there must be. Otherwise you write a sentence that can't be understood, and any sentence that can't be understood is a bad sentence.

If your meaning is such that you can use none of these signals to keep the pattern parts clear, then you must express the meaning in some other pattern, perhaps in two sentences:

> The man who was making a fuss left early with his boy.
> The man left early with the boy who was making a fuss.
> The man with the boy left early. The boy was making a fuss.

● **EXERCISE 25**

A. Copy the following clusters and make a slant line to show the two main parts.

1. a traffic patrolman on a motorcycle who was stopping all cars **2.** a noisy discussion group in the back room that meets here every Friday **3.** thirty people in a room that contained ten chairs **4.** a dirty little boy with a big dog which followed him everywhere **5.** the young principal of the high school who answered his letter **6.** some paragraphs in the letter which were afterwards omitted **7.** the nasty remarks in the letter which was sent to the mayor **8.** a lanky cowboy with an old-fashioned revolver who was standing in front of the saloon **9.** the house of a friend of mine which was up for sale **10.** the house of a friend of mine who is anxious to sell

B. Use each of the noun clusters above in a sentence pattern.

C. Write five noun clusters on this pattern: **D 3 1 P-group S-group.** Make sure that each cluster contains a signal to show that the S-group modifies the main headword in the cluster and not the noun in the P-group.

D. Write five noun clusters on this pattern: **D 3 1 P D 1 S-group.** Make sure that each cluster contains a signal to show that the S-group modifies the noun in the P-group and not the main headword of the cluster.

26 : Noun clusters:
Further complications

Sometimes we find complications in the modifiers that precede the headword in a noun cluster. In all the examples we have had so far, each word before the headword was a modifier of the headword, and they peeled off in order:

the / old light bulbs

old / light bulbs

light / bulbs

But suppose we find this construction:

very old light bulbs

It would be wrong to cut off the first word here:

very / old light bulbs

For this would be as much as to say that *very* modifies *old light bulbs*, or that the cluster means that the old light bulbs are very. This is of course nonsense, and we must say that *very* modifies *old* only. We therefore make the first cut after *old:*

very old / light bulbs

If a determiner is involved, the cuts go like this:

some very old light bulbs

some / very old light bulbs

very old / light bulbs

light / bulbs

The rule given on page 116 still holds: begin at the outside and work in, cutting off the modifiers one by one. But notice that while there are four words in front of *bulbs*, there are only three modifiers of *bulbs: some* is the first, *very old* is the second, and *light* is the third.

Here's an example of a similar complication:

a used car salesman

A modifies *used car salesman,* and *car* modifies *salesman,* but surely *used* doesn't modify *car salesman.* It's not the car salesman that is used but the cars he sells. Therefore the cuts go like this:

a / used car salesman
used car / salesman

This construction gives us no trouble, because we're accustomed to thinking of cars, and not salesmen, as used. But how about this one?

a sad fiction writer

Here either meaning is possible. Maybe he's a writer of sad fiction, and maybe he's a fiction writer who is sad. To avoid the ambiguity, we customarily use a hyphen in writing when the adjective is supposed to modify the first noun:

sad-fiction writer

That means that the pattern parts are these:

sad fiction / writer

When we mean the adjective to modify the whole cluster, we do not use a hyphen:

sad fiction writer

That means that the pattern parts are these:

sad / fiction writer

In speech we would not have this problem. Later on (pp. 228–29), we shall see how we pronounce words with different degrees of loudness to resolve ambiguous meanings.

Here are some similar examples:

small-house / painter (paints small houses)
small / house painter (paints houses and is small)

old-book / company (deals in old books)
old / book company (deals in books and is old)

blue-sky / pilot (high-flying aviator)
blue / sky pilot (sad chaplain)

Here is a classic example of how complications can pile up:

pretty little girls' school

There are five possible meanings in this construction, depending on what the pattern parts are. Here are the five:

1. pretty / little girls' school
    little / girls' school
  (a girls' school that is pretty and little)

2. pretty little / girls' school
  (a girls' school that is rather small)

3. pretty / little girls' school
    little girls' / school
  (a pretty school for little girls)

4. pretty little girls' / school
    pretty / little girls'
  (a school for girls who are pretty and little)

5. pretty little girls' / school
    pretty little / girls'
  (a school for girls who are rather small)

So you really have to know what the pattern parts are.

One of the best clues to the pattern parts of a cluster is the word classes the modifiers belong to. *Pretty little girls* is an ambiguous (two-meaning) cluster because we don't know what class *pretty* belongs to. If it is an adjective (like *beautiful*), then it must modify *little girls*. But if it is an intensifier (like *very*), it must modify *little*, since intensifiers don't modify nouns. Notice that neither of these is ambiguous:

> beautiful little girls   very little girls
> beautiful / little girls   very little / girls

In the same way, the pattern parts of *simple singing seamen* are readily grasped:

> simple / singing seamen

And we recognize quite different pattern parts in *psalm singing seamen:*

> psalm singing / seamen

We recognize *psalm* as a noun and perceive that in this position it must pattern with *singing*, not with *singing seamen*.

But this is ambiguous:

> English speaking parrot

We don't know whether this is an English parrot that speaks or a parrot that speaks English.

But despite all of these complications, the basic principle remains the same. When you cut a noun cluster into its pattern parts, you begin with the modifier farthest after the headword and work back to the headword. Then you begin with the modifier farthest in front and work toward the headword.

Here are some final illustrations. Just to make clear what the modifiers are, each group modifier is linked by hyphens.

> the old tree surgeon in-the-yard who-had-been-waiting
> the old tree surgeon in-the-yard / who-had-been-waiting
> the old tree surgeon / in-the-yard
> the / old tree surgeon
>   old / tree surgeon
>   tree / surgeon
>
> an old tree surgeon in-a-yard-which-was-cluttered
> an old tree surgeon / in-a-yard-which-was-cluttered
> an / old tree surgeon
>   old / tree surgeon
>   tree / surgeon

a pine-tree surgeon   a very-happy tree surgeon
a / pine-tree surgeon   a / very-happy tree surgeon
   pine-tree / surgeon   very-happy / tree surgeon
                                            tree / surgeon

● **EXERCISE 26**

A. Copy the following clusters and show their pattern parts by making the first two cuts.

EXAMPLE   a very old man   a / very old man
                              very old / man

1. his rather young wife **2.** a rickety cow barn **3.** some beautiful department stores **4.** a very interesting story **5.** a house moving organization **6.** several quite difficult problems **7.** a broken down lawn mower **8.** every swiftly flowing stream **9.** a disagreeable school principal **10.** her cigar smoking father

B. Where would hyphens be used in the clusters above?

C. Write clusters based on the following formulas. Hyphens are used in the formulas to show which modifiers pattern together as groups. Be sure that the pattern parts are signaled.

EXAMPLE   D 1 P–D–1 S–2L–3
          a man in the yard who was hungry

          D 1 P–D–1–S–2L–3
          a man in the yard which was dirty

1. D 1 P–D–1 S–2L–3   **6.** D 3 1 1
2. D 1 P–D–1–S–2L–3   **7.** D 3–1 1
3. D 3 1 P–D–1   **8.** D 3 1 1 P–D–1 S–A–2
4. D 3 1 S–A–2–D–1   **9.** D 2-ing 1 P–D–1
5. D V–3 1   **10.** D 1–2-ing 1 S–A–2–4

D. Cut each of your clusters into their pattern parts.

E. Use each cluster as part of a basic sentence pattern.

1—noun 2—verb 2L—linking verb 2-ing—verb ending in *ing* 3—adjective 4—adverb
A—auxiliary D—determiner P—preposition S—subordinator V—intensifier

27: Pattern parts of verb clusters

Cutting a verb cluster into its pattern parts is similar to cutting a noun cluster into its pattern parts. But there is one basic difference. We saw that with noun clusters you begin *after* the headword and work back to the headword. In verb clusters you begin with the modifier *before* the headword (usually there's only one) and work in toward the headword. Then you go to the modifier farthest from the headword on the other side and work back to the headword. Let's start with this sentence:

The inspector usually bustled in cheerfully.

Since there are no introductory sentence modifiers, the pattern parts are the noun cluster on one side and the verb cluster on the other:

D   1   4   2   4   4
The inspector / usually bustled in cheerfully.

The verb cluster consists of a verb, *bustled*, with one modifier in front of it and two after it. The pattern consists of the modifier in front as one part and the rest of the cluster as the other:

usually / bustled in cheerfully

That is to say that *usually* doesn't modify *bustled* alone. It modifies the whole thing — *bustled in cheerfully*. That's what the inspector usually did: he bustled in cheerfully. He didn't usually just bustle.

Since there was only one modifier in front of the headword, we go next to the modifiers after it, and we cut off the one farthest from the headword:

bustled in / cheerfully

This means that *cheerfully* doesn't modify *bustled* alone. It modifies *bustled in.* The inspector didn't bustle cheerfully. He bustled *in* cheerfully. But *cheerfully* doesn't modify *usually;* it is part of the structure that *usually* modifies.

That's the basic principle of cutting up a verb cluster. You begin in front, working from the outside in. Then you go to the other side, again working from the outside in.

The complications come only in finding out what is a modifier of the verb and what isn't.

Instead of simple adverbs we might have word groups modifying the verb:

The inspector / usually went to-the-water-cooler when-he-was-thirsty

In this cluster we also have three units modifying the verb headword. One is an adverb, *usually.* Another is a P-group, *to the water cooler.* The third is an S-group, *when he was thirsty.* The cluster works just as *usually bustled in cheerfully* does:

usually / went to the water cooler when he was thirsty
went to the water cooler / when he was thirsty
went / to the water cooler

Usually modifies all the rest of the structure. *When he was thirsty* modifies *went to the water cooler.* *To the water cooler* modifies just *went;* it doesn't modify *when he was thirsty* or *usually.*

Now look at this one:

The inspector / usually went to the water cooler in the hall.

This is slightly different. Here *went* has only two modifiers: *usually* and *to the water cooler in the hall.* For it would be clearly wrong to say that *in the hall* modifies *went to the water cooler.* It modifies *water cooler,* being part of the noun cluster *the water cooler in the hall.* So the verb cluster is cut like this:

usually / went to the water cooler in the hall
went / to the water cooler in the hall

Or suppose we have this:

The inspector / usually went to the water cooler in the hall when he was thirsty.

Again there are three verb modifiers in the cluster:

usually / went to the water cooler in the hall when he was thirsty
went to the water cooler in the hall / when he was thirsty
went / to the water cooler in the hall

Now look at these two sentences:

The inspector / stayed in the room when he was tired.
The inspector / stayed in the room that he had rented.

The first cluster has two groups modifying *stayed: in the room* and *when he was tired.* So it is cut like this:

stayed in the room / when he was tired
stayed / in the room

But the second sentence has just one group modifying *stayed.* *That he had rented* doesn't modify *stayed in the room.* It modifies *room,* being part of the noun cluster *the room that he had rented.* It shows which room he stayed in. It is cut like this:

stayed / in the room that he had rented

Let's take some more examples, some with two modifiers after the verb, some with one:

never ran off with the money
never / ran off with the money
    ran off / with the money
    ran / off

seldom spoke politely to his father
seldom / spoke politely to his father
    spoke politely / to his father
    spoke / politely

arrived in a car with his girl friend
arrived in a car / with his girl friend
arrived / in a car

arrived in a car with no steering wheel
arrived / in a car with no steering wheel

Sometimes we have three modifiers after the verb. The direction is the same — from the outside in:

> bustled in cheerfully sometimes
> bustled in cheerfully / sometimes
> bustled in / cheerfully
> bustled / in

> rode up in a car with his girl friend
> rode up in a car / with his girl friend
> rode up / in a car
> rode / up

> rode up in a car with his girl friend sometimes
> rode up in a car with his girl friend / sometimes
> rode up in a car / with his girl friend
> rode up / in a car
> rode / up

> lived in a hotel when he had enough money
> lived in a hotel / when he had enough money
> lived / in a hotel

> lived in a hotel that had no elevator
> lived / in a hotel that had no elevator

You may remember that adverbs occur in three distinct groups, patterning like *there*, *thus*, and *then*.

	THERE	THUS	THEN
He stopped	by	curiously	sometimes.
He went	away	angrily	later.

Notice that the *then* adverb is usually at the outside of the cluster — fore or aft. In either position it modifies the rest of the cluster:

> stopped by curiously / sometimes
> sometimes / stopped by curiously

The *there* adverb is usually right next to the verb, after it. It modifies just the verb.

stopped / by
went / away

As we've seen, the order of adverbs is quite flexible in English, and sometimes we get a *thus* adverb between the verb and the *there* adverb:

sometimes went quickly away

But the principle of cutting the cluster remains the same — first the words before the verb, then the words after it, from the outside in:

sometimes / went quickly away
went quickly / away
went / quickly

● **EXERCISE 27**

A. Cut these clusters into their pattern parts, following the models in this chapter. The verbs have one, two, or three modifiers after them. Some have one modifier in front of them.

1. often walked in the rain **2.** walked in the rain often **3.** seldom came quickly when he was called **4.** usually looked on quietly **5.** sometimes spoke sharply to the class **6.** always retreated hurriedly in the face of enemy fire **7.** comes over to help us if we ask him **8.** often ate in a restaurant with his mother **9.** often ate in a restaurant with a counter **10.** fell in love with the girl before he knew it **11.** fell in love with the girl who lived next door **12.** generally walked to the store on the corner if he needed exercise

B. Make all of the clusters above parts of sentences by giving them subjects.

C. Write verb clusters based on the following formulas. Hyphens between symbols show word groups.

EXAMPLE

2 P–D–1 P–D–1
went to the store for some eggs

2 P–D–1–P–D–1
went to the store on the corner

1. 4 2 4 4
2. 4 2 P–D–1
3. 2 P–D–1 4
4. 2 P–D–1 S–1–2–4

5. 2 P–D–1–S–2–4
6. 2 4 S–1–2L–3
7. 4 2 4 P–D–1 S–1–2–D–1
8. 4 2 4 P–D–1–S–2–D–1

D. Cut your verb clusters into their pattern parts.

E. Make your verb clusters parts of sentences.

1–noun   2–verb   2L–linking verb   3–adjective   4–adverb
D–determiner   P–preposition   S–subordinator

---

28 : Verb clusters in the basic sentence patterns

We must now go back to the basic sentence patterns and examine the pattern parts of their verb clusters. We have so far talked about four basic sentence patterns:

PATTERN ONE	1↔2	Canaries sing.
PATTERN TWO	1↔2 3	Canaries are beautiful.
PATTERN THREE	1↔2L 1	Canaries are birds.
PATTERN FOUR	1↔2 1	Canaries eat worms.

If we cut these into their pattern parts, they consist of a noun on one side and a verb or verb cluster on the other:

Canaries / sing.	Canaries / are birds.
Canaries / are beautiful.	Canaries / eat worms.

We see that what makes these different is differences in the verb clusters. The noun is the same in all, but the verb clusters are different. In Pattern One it is just a verb; in Two it is a linking verb patterning with an adjective; in Three it is a linking verb patterning with a complement; in Four it is a non-linking verb patterning with an object.

We saw in Chapter 20 that all of these clusters can have modifiers added:

ONE   **Canaries** often **sing** out loudly.

TWO   **Canaries are beautiful** in the spring sometimes.

THREE   **Canaries** usually **are** pretty **birds** when they're well fed.

FOUR   **Canaries** never **eat worms** when they aren't hungry.

Now, so far as pattern parts go, the adjective, complement, and object in the clusters are cut off in the same order as the modifiers. When we cut these clusters into their pattern parts, we treat the adjective or noun just like modifiers — take each one in its turn and cut it off as we work back to the verb head-word.

In Pattern One we have no particular problem:

> Canaries / often sing out loudly.
> often / sing out loudly
> sing out / loudly
> sing / out

In Pattern Two the adjective is just another unit in the verb cluster:

> Canaries / are beautiful in the spring sometimes.
> are beautiful in the spring / sometimes
> are beautiful / in the spring
> are / beautiful

Sometimes modifies all the rest of the verb cluster. *In the spring* modifies *are beautiful*. *Beautiful* works against the headword *are*, because it is part of the basic pattern. Each part works against some other part.

In Pattern Three the complement is just another unit:

> Canaries / usually are pretty birds when they're well fed.
> usually / are pretty birds when they're well fed
> are pretty birds / when they're well fed
> are / pretty birds

Usually modifies the rest of the verb cluster. *When they're well fed* modifies *are pretty birds*. *Pretty birds* works against the headword *are*. (We could even say that *pretty birds* modifies *are*, if we wanted to.)

In Pattern Four the object is just another unit:

> Canaries / never eat worms when they aren't hungry.
> never / eat worms when they aren't hungry
> eat worms / when they aren't hungry
> eat / worms

Never modifies the rest of the verb cluster. *When they aren't hungry* modifies *eat worms*. *Worms* works against *eat*. (Or, if it makes it easier, we could say that *worms* modifies *eat*.)

Remember, however, that any noun can expand into a noun cluster. The basic patterns of the following sentences are alike, but the patterns of the verb clusters are different:

> He / bought a car with the money.
> He / bought a car with no wheels.

In the first cluster there are two units working against the verb — *a car*, which is an object, and *with the money*, which modifies *bought a car*. The pattern parts are these:

> bought a car / with the money
> bought / a car

But in "He bought a car with no wheels," there is just one unit working against *bought* — the noun cluster *a car with no wheels:*

> bought / a car with no wheels

Here are some more examples:

bought a hat / while she was waiting
bought / a hat which she couldn't afford

met a shy bank clerk with a tender smile / when she went to France
met / a shy bank clerk with a tender smile who was very nice to her

Notice what we have left when we cut this last cluster into its pattern parts. We begin with a verb cluster, but when we cut it into its pattern parts we find that it consists of a verb, *met*, as one part and a noun cluster as the other. Let's go on and cut the noun cluster. Remember that when we cut noun clusters, we begin *after* the headword and work back:

```
met / a shy bank clerk with a tender smile who was very nice to her
      a shy bank clerk with a tender smile / who was very nice to her
      a shy bank clerk / with a tender smile
      a / shy bank clerk
          shy / bank clerk
                bank / clerk
```

A noun cluster is always a noun cluster and always cut the same way, no matter whether the noun is a subject, an object, a complement, part of a preposition group, or whatever. And a verb cluster is always cut the same way, no matter what its subject is or how deeply it is buried in the sentence. This is what makes it possible for us to understand long and complicated sentences. They always boil down to familiar units: noun clusters, verb clusters, and a few other structures which we will take up next.

● **EXERCISE 28**

A. Here are some sentence patterns to analyze. First write the sentence and then place the appropriate symbol over each word. Then cut the verb cluster into its pattern parts. Then tell what pattern it is: One, Two, Three, or Four.

EXAMPLE   His father often mows the lawn in the back yard when he has time.

First we put in the symbols:

D   1   4   2   D   1 P D   1   1   S   1   2   1
His father often mows the lawn in the back yard when he has time.

The pattern parts of the sentence are these:

His father ./ often mows the lawn in the back yard when he has time.

The pattern parts of the verb cluster are these:

> often / mows the lawn in the back yard when he has time
>   mows the lawn in the back yard / when he has time
>   mows / the lawn in the back yard

This is Pattern Four, since its base is "His father mows the lawn."

1. The children played noisily in the yard. **2.** We had fish for dinner.
3. She was a foolish little girl sometimes. **4.** His sister was rather foolish
generally. **5.** They never bother innocent people if they can help it.
6. Harry found a book about Indians that he had never read. **7.** Ed
saw a movie about the Marines when he was in Chicago. **8.** The lake
usually was very calm before the wind came up.

B. Write two simple examples of each of the four basic sentence
patterns.

EXAMPLE   **Water boils. Sam was a friend.**

C. Rewrite your eight sentences, adding several modifiers in the
verb clusters.

EXAMPLE   **Water boils at a low temperature in the high mountains.
Sam never was a friend of mine actually.**

D. Cut your sentences into their pattern parts.

EXAMPLE   **Water / boils at a low temperature in the high mountains.
             boils at a low temperature / in the high mountains
             boils / at a low temperature**

           **Sam / never was a friend of mine actually.
            never / was a friend of mine actually
               was a friend of mine / actually
               was / a friend of mine**

In these examples, the verb cluster is cut into all its pattern parts.
Of course one could proceed to cut some of the units that remain.

EXAMPLE   **a friend / of mine
       a / friend**

But you might as well concentrate on the verb clusters here.

29 : Pattern parts
of P-groups and S-groups

The pattern parts of preposition groups and subordinate groups are much simpler than those of noun clusters and verb clusters. The pattern parts of a P-group are always the preposition as one part and everything else as the other part.

P-GROUPS

We'll begin with a sentence and cut it until we reach a P-group:

> A man in a derby hat walked in.
> A man in a derby hat / walked in.
> A man / in a derby hat

The noun cluster *a man in a derby hat* consists of *a man* as one part and the P-group *in a derby hat* as the other part. This P-group, in turn, consists of the preposition *in* as one part and all the rest as the other:

> in / a derby hat

Here are some more examples:

with a shy smile	on the other side	inside the church
with / a shy smile	on / the other side	inside / the church

The P-group might be much longer, but it always consists of the preposition working against all the rest:

> She met a man with a shy smile which she couldn't resist.
> She / met a man with a shy smile which she couldn't resist.
> met / a man with a shy smile which she couldn't resist.

Now we have, on the right, a noun cluster consisting of the words *a man* working against a rather long P-group:

> a man / with a shy smile which she couldn't resist

The P-group consists of the preposition *with* working against all the rest:

> with / a shy smile which she couldn't resist

Now we've cut out another noun cluster. It cuts like any other noun cluster:

> a shy smile / which she couldn't resist
> a / shy smile
> shy / smile

Sometimes we have two P-groups coming in a row. The second may be part of the first, or each may be a separate P-group. Look at these:

> She met a man with a book in his hand.
> She met a man with a book on her way home.

In the first sentence the P-group *in his hand* modifies *book*, so it belongs with the other P-group that begins with *with*. The pattern parts are these:

> She / met a man with a book in his hand.
> met / a man with a book in his hand
> a man / with a book in his hand
> with / a book in his hand
> a book / in his hand
> in / his hand

But the other sentence is different. *On her way home* doesn't modify *book*. It modifies *met a man with a book*. These are the principal pattern parts:

> She / met a man with a book on her way home.
> met a man with a book / on her way home

Now when we write or read or speak or hear sentences like

these, there must always be something to tell us which is which. Otherwise we can't grasp the pattern parts, and the sentence can't be understood. Here's one that can't:

She met a man with a good job in the post office.

Does *in the post office* tell us where she met the man, or does it tell us where his job is?

S–GROUPS

At this point we need to note only one more feature of pattern parts — the pattern parts of S-groups. This is really quite simple.

The pattern parts of an S-group are the subordinator as one part and all the rest of the group as the other. Let's cut off an S-group for inspection:

Because Uncle Henry generally came in early, I grew a little worried.
Because Uncle Henry generally came in early / I grew a little worried.

Here the S-group consists of *because* as one part and *Uncle Henry generally came in early* as the other:

Because / Uncle Henry generally came in early

Now notice what is left on the right side. It is just an ordinary sentence, and it is cut like any other sentence. The first cut separates the noun subject from the verb cluster:

Uncle Henry / generally came in early

The verb cluster is cut just like any other verb cluster: first the modifier on the left, then those on the right, beginning with the ones farthest out:

generally / came in early
came in / early
came / in

An S-group in a noun cluster is just as simple. We'll cut out the units in the next sentence until we find one:

The men on the farm who generally worked late got more money.
The men on the farm who generally worked late / got more money.
The men on the farm / who generally worked late

Now we have an S-group, *who generally worked late*, on the right. This is composed of the subordinator, *who*, working against the verb cluster, *generally worked late*. We cut off the subordinator:

who / generally worked late

Now we have a simple verb cluster:

generally / worked late
worked / late

● **EXERCISE 29**

A. Copy the following P-groups and S-groups and cut them into their pattern parts. Tell what you have left on the right after you make the first cut. It will be either a noun cluster, a verb cluster, or a sentence pattern.

1. in the dog hospital **2.** behind some very old rosebushes **3.** after the visitors went in **4.** that we had never seen him before **5.** until the examination **6.** until the examination began **7.** with the boy in the red shirt **8.** where they buried the bodies **9.** who knew my father **10.** of the men who were here **11.** who were here **12.** since Bert was a good friend of mine **13.** under the table where we put the glasses when the fight began

B. Each of the following sentences contains one or two P-groups or S-groups. Write the sentences, cutting them until you cut out a P-group or an S-group. Then cut the P-group or S-group into its pattern parts. Continue cutting until you have found all the groups in each sentence.

1. The children in the back room howled constantly. **2.** When we got there, the trouble began. **3.** He held the monkey on his lap.

4. After the men with the accordions went away, we ate our oranges. **5.** The fellows who are now here should have the first chance. **6.** All the hens in this coop that have stopped laying eggs will get just one more chance. **7.** Until the music stopped, we all thought that Charlie was in the room. **8.** The girl in the Girl Scout uniform hid behind the sofa. **9.** We went away before the lion in the other cage had been fed. **10.** The coach of the basketball team had got into some trouble because the floor was slippery.

C. Write five P-groups and use them as part of noun clusters or of verb clusters, and tell how you have used them.

EXAMPLE

The men **in the house** gave up.   (part of a noun cluster)
They were standing **behind the door.**   (part of a verb cluster)

D. Write five S-groups and use them as part of noun clusters or of verb clusters or as sentence modifiers, and tell how you have used them.

EXAMPLE

The men **who had been hiding** gave up.   (part of a noun cluster)
They hid **until the excitement died down.**   (part of a verb cluster)
While they were hiding, they ate peanuts.   (sentence modifier)

30: Review of pattern parts

We have now examined the pattern parts of the most common kinds of sentences and sentence units. Once again notice that pattern parts do not just provide a way of analyzing a sentence. They add up to a statement of the way the user of the language understands a sentence. To understand an English sentence, you must know what words go together. If you don't know this, then you can't get the meaning. *Pretty little girls' school* is not clear. Neither is *the man with the boy who was making a fuss.* Neither is *met a man with a good job in the post office.* They are all unclear because they contain no signals telling us what the pattern parts are.

We haven't said all there is to say about pattern parts. There are many sentences in English which you probably wouldn't be able to analyze (though as a user of the language you can certainly grasp their pattern parts.) However, we have gone far enough to be able to analyze most constructions. Let's take a fairly complicated sentence and work it through. Just to be orderly, we'll always follow the left-hand side down to single words before taking up the right-hand side.

Since the young used car salesman who had been accused of income tax evasion refused to hire a lawyer with experience in such cases, most of his friends gloomily gave up hope that he would be acquitted.

On the first level this consists of the introductory S-group as one part and the main sentence as the other:

Since the young used car salesman who had been accused of income tax evasion refused to hire a lawyer with experience in such cases / most of his friends gloomily gave up hope that he would be acquitted.

We'll begin with the first part. This S-group, like all S-groups, consists of the subordinator as one part and the rest of the group as the other:

Since / the young used car salesman who had been accused of income tax evasion refused to hire a lawyer with experience in such cases

That gets us down to a single word on the left. On the right we have what is now just an ordinary sentence. We separate the subject from the verb cluster:

the young used car salesman who had been accused of income tax evasion / refused to hire a lawyer with experience in such cases

On the left we now have a noun cluster. We cut off the last modifier after the headword. There is only one:

the young used car salesman / **who had been accused of income tax evasion**

We keep working down on the left. We cut off the rest of the modifiers of *salesman*, beginning with the one farthest out:

the / **young used car salesman**
young / **used car salesman**

But note the next cut. *Used* doesn't modify *car salesman*.

used car / **salesman**

Now we go back to the last part of the noun cluster we left on the right: *who had been accused of income tax evasion*. This is just an S-group. Cut off the subordinator:

who / **had been accused of income tax evasion**

Now we have a verb cluster in which the headword is *accused*. Begin on the left:

had / **been accused of income tax evasion** *
been / **accused of income tax evasion**

Now we go to the right. There is just one unit to the right of the verb:

accused / **of income tax evasion**

That gives us a P-group. Cut off the preposition:

of / **income tax evasion**

But now be careful. *Income* doesn't modify *tax evasion*.

income tax / **evasion**
income / **tax**

---

* Auxiliaries are cut just like any other units in the verb cluster: begin at the left and work in to the verb. We'll have more examples later (p. 304).

Now we go back to the last unit we left lying on the right. This is *refused to hire a lawyer with experience in such cases.* This is a verb cluster with no units before it and only one unit after it:

refused / to hire a lawyer with experience in such cases

On the right we have another verb cluster with one unit before it:

to / hire a lawyer with experience in such cases *

And one unit after it:

hire / a lawyer with experience in such cases

Now we have another noun cluster. Cut off the modifiers after it, then the modifiers before it:

a lawyer / with experience in such cases
a / lawyer

That gives us another P-group. Cut off the preposition:

with / experience in such cases

Here is another noun cluster:

experience / in such cases

And another P-group:

in / such cases
such / cases

Now we must go back and pick up the right side of the first cut: *most of his friends gloomily gave up hope that he would be acquitted.* This is just an ordinary sentence, so we separate subject from verb cluster:

most of his friends / gloomily gave up hope that he would be acquitted

---

* This construction is one we haven't studied yet, but it is no problem so far as pattern parts go. It is just one more unit.

The left consists of a noun cluster:

most / of his friends

The resulting P-group is simple:

of / his friends
his / friends

Going back, we find another verb cluster: *gloomily gave up hope that he would be acquitted*. Cut off the first unit on the left:

gloomily / gave up hope that he would be acquitted

Then the last one on the right:

gave up / hope that he would be acquitted
gave / up

We have left a noun cluster:

hope / that he would be acquitted

Now an S-group. Cut off the subordinator:

that / he would be acquitted

Now a simple sentence pattern:

he / would be acquitted

And finally a verb cluster:

would / be acquitted
be / acquitted

Here are the steps that we followed. We cut:

1. A sentence into an S-group and a sentence pattern.

2. The S-group into a subordinator and a sentence pattern.

3. The sentence pattern in the S-group into a noun cluster and a verb cluster.

4. The modifiers at the right of the headword in the noun cluster.

5. The modifiers at the left of the headword.

6. The modifiers at the left of the headword in the verb cluster.

7. The modifiers and pattern parts at the right of the headword. (The modifiers are cut off one by one from the left or right of the headword. Each modifier works against what is left at each stage of cutting.)

8. The sentence pattern in the original sentence by following steps 3 through 7. (S-groups within a cluster are cut by following steps 2 through 7. P-groups within a cluster are cut so that we have P on the left and a noun cluster on the right.)

This is a lot of work for one sentence, and you may be saying to yourself that it isn't worth it. Maybe not. But it isn't just a meaningless exercise. It teaches us something about how our language works. It shows how a sentence builds up (or down) from level to level, regularly, in patterns of two. It shows also that what looks like a very complicated sentence is really a series of very simple patterns: simple sentence patterns, S-groups, P-groups, noun clusters, verb clusters.

This shows us how we can understand as much language as we do. It explains how everybody can talk differently and still everybody can understand everybody else. When we meet a new sentence, it isn't a new pattern. It may have new words in it and even new arrangements. But it's never a new pattern. No matter how long or complicated, it always boils down, two by two, to a series of old patterns, familiar patterns that we have heard and used ever since we began to speak English.

● **EXERCISE 30**

A. Cut the following sentences into their pattern parts. Follow the method used on the long sentence in this chapter. Work down on the left side until you get to single words; then go back to the last unit you had on the right side. Write out each unit to be cut, and then draw a line to show the cut.

EXAMPLE

    While we were waiting, the dogs in the kennel barked loudly.
    While we were waiting / the dogs in the kennel barked loudly.

While / we were waiting
     we / were waiting
       were / waiting

          the dogs in the kennel / barked loudly
          the dogs / in the kennel
          the / dogs
             in / the kennel
              the / kennel
                barked / loudly

1. After the guests left, we washed some of the dishes. **2.** The man on the hill was riding toward the barn. **3.** We might row across the lake if the wind dies down. (Notice that the S-group here is part of the main verb cluster; the main verb is *row*.) **4.** The fellow that got arrested was his uncle. **5.** When we heard the news, we locked the doors in a hurry. **6.** They usually keep their horses in our garage when they're in town. (Notice that one cut here comes between *they* and *'re*.) **7.** The boy in the back row had a smile on his face. **8.** When the man on the top floor who was getting in everyone's hair began playing his saxophone at two o'clock in the morning, the people who lived in the flat beneath him called the police on the telephone before the first notes died away.

B. Pick any four of the sentences above and write formulas for them by giving the proper symbols to the words and showing where the ties occur. Then write new sentences from the formulas. Try to keep the pattern parts the same. Here is an example.

OLD SENTENCE

    S   1↔A   2   D 1 P D 1   2   4
    While we were waiting, the dogs in the kennel barked loudly.

NEW SENTENCE

    S   1↔A   2   D   1 P D 1   2   4
    After Bob had gone, some friends of his sister dropped in.

31 : Review of form classes and structure groups

Before going on to the more complicated patterns of English, we had better gather together some of the things we have learned so far. Remember that English sentences are composed of different arrangements of words and that there are two general kinds of words. One kind we have called **form classes.** There are four of them: nouns, verbs, adjectives, and adverbs. The other kind we have called **structure groups.** There are a dozen or so structure groups. So far we have observed five of them: determiners (**D**), patterning like *the;* auxiliaries (**A**), patterning like *can* in *can go, is* in *is going,* or *has* in *has gone;* intensifiers (**V**), patterning like *very;* prepositions (**P**), patterning like *with;* and subordinators (**S**), patterning like *because* or *who.*

We could list the pronouns as a structure group too, since they are rather special. But in the structure of English sentences they work just about as proper nouns do, and in our formulas it is simpler just to give them the symbol 1, along with nouns.

Remember that the structure groups are different in *kind* from the form classes. One difference is that the form classes are very large classes, and the structure groups are very small. Nobody can say how many nouns the English language has, but certainly it has hundreds of thousands. And there are many thousands of verbs, adjectives, and adverbs. On the other hand, there are only about seventy prepositions, about thirty determiners, about twenty auxiliaries. Most of the other structure groups are smaller still. Some contain only two or three words. Some contain only one word.

Another difference is that the individual structure words occur much more commonly than any members of the form classes do. A large part of the language we use is made up of just a handful of structure words repeated over and over — words like *of, the, he, her, it, and, I, will, is* (as an auxiliary). The two most common words in written English are *of* and *the*.

A third difference is that the form classes are **open classes** and the structure groups are **closed classes.** This means that the membership of the form classes is constantly shifting. New nouns and verbs are constantly being created, and old ones are constantly dropping out of use. This is why we can't say how many nouns there are in English. Even if we could find a way of counting them, so many new ones would be born while we were counting that our count would always be inaccurate. It's easy to think of quite common nouns that didn't exist at all a few years ago — like *television, H-bomb, penicillin, flak, veep, jeep.* Whenever someone, for whatever reason, makes a new noise in one of the noun positions, that new noise becomes a noun. *Disappear* is usually a verb. But if someone says "I think I'll do a disappear," for that moment at least *disappear* has become a noun. *Desk* is usually a noun. But if somebody says "He's been desking all day," *desk* has for the nonce become a verb.

But this change and interchange isn't possible with the structure words. The membership of the structure groups changes, to be sure, but very slowly. Whereas new nouns and verbs are constantly being born, a new preposition comes along only every thirty years or so.

This leads us to the fourth major difference between form classes and structure groups: the form classes can be recognized usually by formal signs and signals; the structure groups can't be. Proof of this is that we can have nonsense words in form-class positions in a sentence and still get the general drift of the sentence. Consider this:

When the sloopy wamtupper had eviptally loofed the strambix, the rallopash scomed up his flibbles and skorked.

Obviously, we don't know the meaning of nine of the words in this sentence. But we do know a good deal about the sentence, and we can recognize all the form classes:

1. We know that the sentence is a statement and not a question or a request.

2. We know what the action is. It is loofing, scoming, and skorking.

3. We know who does the action: a wamtupper does the loofing, and a rallopash does the scoming and skorking.

4. We know when the action took place. It all took place in past time, but the scoming and skorking took place after the loofing.

5. We know something about *sloopy*. It's an adjective, and it modifies *wamtupper*.

6. We know something about *wamtupper*. It's a noun. It's something that can loof and be sloopy.

7. We know something about *loofed*. It's a verb. It's something that can be done by a wamtupper. It's something that can be done to a strambix.

8. We know something about *strambix*. It's a noun. It's the sort of thing that can be loofed by a wamtupper.

9. We know something about *rallopash*. It's a noun. It is something that can scome up flibbles and can skork — though it may not do either of these things until some wamtupper has previously loofed a strambix.

10. We know something about *flibbles*. It's a noun. There can be more than one of them. They are things that rallopashes sometimes scome up.

We know, in other words, a good deal about the sentence, without actually knowing the "meaning" of half its words.

But it is only the form classes that are marked and signaled in this way. Notice what happens if we put in real words for the form classes and nonsense syllables for the structure words.

Gork dol beautiful lady splage finally found bine purse, goop minister wrote flio ting words queel smiled.

Now the sentence has no meaning at all. It isn't a sentence at all. It's just nonsense.

● EXERCISE 31

A. Here is a little drama about a speek and a grannyflax. First read the passage aloud. Then copy it out, writing the form-class and structure-group symbols above the words. Use the symbol **C** for the words *and* and *but*. (The first sentence is done to start you out.) Then write down all you have learned about speeks and grannyflaxes — their nature and personal habits.

    D   1 D 1   2   P D   1

One day a speek orgled into a floom. In the center of the floom was a very grutious grannyflax. As everyone knows, speeks geeble granny-flaxes, though grannyflaxes never foober speeks. This grannyflax was niffy and rather kloobful. It had an ignormous spale on its timtam. The speek was quite crebulous. It spanged the spale of the grannyflax and flebbed it stilefully. But the grannyflax still had a boosh. While the speek was flebbing its spale, it baffed the speek on the boobin and rabbled away.

B. Rewrite the paragraph, keeping all the real words as they are, but putting in new nonsense words.

C. Make up a new story, about a queel and a dillymump, to read to the class.

1—noun   2—verb   2L—linking verb   3—adjective   4—adverb
A—auxiliary   D—determiner   P—preposition   S—subordinator
V—intensifier

Part Six

FUNCTION UNITS IN SENTENCE PATTERNS

32 : A new term: Function unit

So far we have studied form classes and structure groups. We have seen what they are and how they are put together to form sentences. We have studied some basic sentence patterns and have seen how these may be complicated by modifiers.

Also we have talked about subjects, objects, linking-verb complements, noun modifiers, verb modifiers, and sentence modifiers. We now need to examine these groups more closely, and we need a general term for them. We shall use the term **function unit**. Thus, a subject is one kind of function unit, an object is another, and a sentence modifier is another. English has a few other function units besides those listed, but we will limit ourselves to these for the moment.

The first thing to notice about function units is their relationship to the word classes. We have no function unit in which just one kind of word occurs; various kinds of words occur in each of the function units.

This is very obvious in the function unit we have called **noun modifiers**. All sorts of words occur as noun modifiers. Here are some examples:

DETERMINERS	**the** man	**a** man	**this** man	**every** man
ADJECTIVES	**happy** man	**foolish** man	**tall** man	
NOUNS	**mountain** man	**New York** man	**college** man	
VERBS	**sleeping** man	**fighting** man	**wounded** man	
ADVERBS	man **upstairs**	man **inside**	man **below**	

they will all adjectives ?

So a noun modifier is obviously not a kind of word. It is simply a relationship between a noun and all sorts of other words.

The same thing is true of subjects and objects and linking-verb complements. So far we have studied just nouns in these positions, because nouns are simple and easy to study. But in the language we use we have all sorts of words occurring as subjects and objects.

Let's look at some of the different kinds of subjects that may occur. First of all, we can have nouns:

That **man** is dangerous.   This **year** is the time to do it.
A leaky **pen** is a nuisance.

Then of course pronouns can occur as subjects. So far as the sentence structure goes, they behave pretty much like nouns:

He is dangerous.   **It** took time.
Nobody knew what time it was.

Adjectives occur as subjects sometimes. When they do, they are usually followed by the form of the verb that is used with plural nouns:

The **poor** were unhappy.   The **hungry** need to be fed.
The **meek** shall inherit the earth.

One reason we know that these subjects belong to the adjective form class is that we can use an intensifier with them, and we cannot with nouns. "The very poor were unhappy."

Verbs occur as subjects. Such verbs usually have either the *ing* form or the simple form with the structure word *to* in front:

Writing is a nuisance.   **To write** takes time.

Writing letters is a nuisance.   **To write** letters takes time.

We even find a stray adverb or so as the subject sometimes:

Now is the time to get those letters written.

We find these different kinds of words as objects also:

NOUN   He hates **spinach**.   ADJECTIVE   He hates the **rich**.

PRONOUN   He hates **me**.   VERB   He hates **writing**.

We find them all patterning with prepositions:

NOUN   Tell it to the **birds**.

PRONOUN   Tell it to **him**.

ADJECTIVE   Give it to the **needy**.

VERB   He needs it for **writing**.

ADVERB   They should have been there by **then**.

In the sentences that we hear and see we must be able to keep these word classes sorted out in the function units in which they occur. That is, we have to know not only whether a word is a subject or object or a noun modifier but also whether it is a noun, an adjective, a verb, or an adverb. It makes a good deal of difference. Look at these sentences:

The youngster had a hard time.

The young had a hard time.

The first one means that some child was in trouble. The second sentence means that a lot of people were in trouble. We understand this because we recognize the subject of the first sentence as a noun and the subject of the second sentence as an adjective.

Or look at this:

> Clean up the mess.
> Clean up the messy.

The meaning is different because the object in the first sentence is a noun and the object in the second is an adjective.

Or this:

> He's a happy man.
> He's a mountain man.

Happy and *mountain* are both noun modifiers, but *happy* is an adjective and *mountain* is a noun, and the sentences are different accordingly.

There are many more details that we might go into — S-groups in the various function units, subordinators in the various function units, different kinds of nouns, pronouns, and verbs in the function units. We could specify the various signals that keep these different forms sorted out. We could list a few more function units in addition to those already named. Some of these matters we shall take up briefly in a later part of the book.

But most of the detail we shall simply pass over. If you speak English, you already command this detail. You know the forms that occur. You know them in the sense that you can use them and can keep them apart. You can respond accurately when other people use them. The thing to do now is to observe — to sharpen your awareness of the language you're living in.

You want also to get a conscious grip of the over-all patterning in English sentences. Remember that there are three large categories: form classes, structure groups, and function units. The form classes and structure groups are kinds of words. The function units are not kinds of words but different relationships that all sorts of words have to one another.

The meanings that we express in our English sentences can be explained by showing the various function units that occur and the various form classes that occur in them.

● **EXERCISE 32**

A. Show the variety of noun modifiers by writing three examples of each of the following. (One example of each is given in parentheses.)

1. D 1   (the man)
2. 3 1   (happy man)
3. 1 1   (mountain man)
4. 2-ing 1   (sleeping man)
5. 1 4   (man upstairs).

B. Show the variety of subjects by writing three examples of each of the following. (One example of each is given.)

1. D 1 verb cluster   (The house burned down.)
2. D 3 verb cluster   (The rich lived well.)
3. 2-ing verb cluster   (Thinking is hard work.)

C. Show the variety of preposition groups by writing three examples of each of the following. (One example of each is given.)

1. P D 1   (in the soup)
2. P D 3   (for the needy)
3. P 2-ing   (by thinking)
4. P 2-ing 4   (after going out)
5. P 2-ing D 1   (after eating the soup)
6. P 2-ing D 3   (by helping the needy)

---

33 : Meanings of subjects

So far we have identified the function units **subject, object, linking-verb complement, noun modifier, verb modifier,** and **sentence modifier.** We have also noticed the unit that follows a preposition to form part of a preposition group. We may now ask what general meaning words have when they appear in these different function units. But we should be aware that we do not use the meanings to recognize the units. It's the other way around. When we see or hear an English sentence, we identify the different units by recognizing the different arrangements of words in the patterns. It is only after we have recognized the arrangement that we get a clue to the meaning.

The subject is the function unit that can have the widest variety of meanings. A subject in English sentences may have one of five distinct meanings. We'll look at four of them now and the other one later on.

DOER OF THE ACTION

Probably the most common meaning of the subject is **doer of the action.** The subject has this general meaning whenever the verb is not a linking verb and whenever it is not followed by the auxiliary *be* and the past-tense form of the verb. Here are some sentences in which the subject means doer of the action.

	1	A	2		
The	canaries		twittered.		
My	father		spoke	up angrily.	
Old	soldiers		die	with their boots on.	
	Charlie	was	sobbing	quietly.	
	He		quit.		

	1	A	2		1	
	Charlie	was	peeling	a	grape.	
The	woodsmen		destroyed	the	forest.	
	Everybody		liked	the	spinach.	
My	father		beat		me	frequently.
	They	were	skinning	some	lions.	

Any word occurring as subject in one of these patterns has the general meaning of doer of the action. The canaries do the twittering, my father does the speaking, Charlie does the sobbing and the peeling, and so on.

Sometimes the meaning is rather vague. Sometimes the verb doesn't suggest any very obvious kind of action and consequently the subject isn't a very obvious doer. Look at the one following:

1   2
The house needs a coat of paint.

Needing doesn't really suggest much action in the way *speaking* or *destroying* does, and consequently *house* isn't so obviously a doer here. Nevertheless, we grasp the meaning of the sentence in the same general way as we do those above. The sentence makes the same impression on our minds: the canaries do something — they twitter; the house does something — it needs a coat of paint.

Or look at these:

	1	**2**	
The	man	stayed	there.
The	man	lay	there.
The	man	was	there.

Here we have no action at all, unless *staying*, *lying*, and *being* are actions. Nevertheless, we grasp these as the same pattern as "The man walked there," "The man smoked there," "The man died there." In each sentence *man* has the general meaning of doer of the action, though the action is obvious in some sentences and vague in others.

Here's one in which the meaning is quite turned around:

1   2
This   car   rides   easily.

Now we may feel that cars don't actually ride. People ride cars, or ride in cars. But that's just the situation in the world outside the language. The meaning in the sentence is that the car rides. The sentence *says* that the car rides. And the meaning of the subject is doer of the action. Quite often the meanings in the language seem all out of step with the factual world. That's one of the things that makes the language so interesting.

Here are some other sentences like "This car rides easily." In all of them the subject has the meaning of doer of the ac- tion:

That material won't wash.   His play reads well.
These neckties will sell like hot cakes.   His play won't act.

THAT WHICH IS DESCRIBED

The second kind of meaning that a subject may have is **that
which is described.** The subject has this meaning when it occurs
in the pattern 1 2 3:

The man was foolish.

Here there's no action at all, vague or otherwise. Consequently
there is no doer of the action. The subject is simply the person
(or thing) described by the verb cluster that follows. *The man*
is described by *was foolish.*

We have had many examples of this 1–2–3 pattern before.
Here are a few more:

His sister is beautiful.   The stew tasted awful.
Charlie felt sick.   Her house seemed clean.
The doctor appeared uncertain.

THAT WHICH IS IDENTIFIED

The third kind of meaning for a subject is **that which is identified.** The subject has this meaning in the pattern 1 2L 1. Here
the linking verb is usually either *be* or *become:*

That man is my father.

Here the subject, *man*, isn't a doer, and the verb cluster, *is my
father*, doesn't exactly describe the subject. It simply links up
the subject with another noun and in this way identifies the
subject. Here are some more examples:

She was the boss.   These may be the ones.
Charlie is my friend.   His doctor is a phony.
He became my uncle when he married my aunt.

UNDERGOER OF THE ACTION

The fourth meaning for subjects is **undergoer of the action.** Here is an example:

Charlie was knocked down by Henry.

Here *Charlie* is the subject, and there is an action — "knocking down." But Charlie isn't the doer of the action. Henry is. Charlie is the one who undergoes the action.

The subject has the meaning of undergoer of the action whenever it occurs in this pattern:

1 A 2-ed
(be)

The word *be* under the symbol for *auxiliary* means that the auxiliary is to be some form of the word *be: am, is, are, was, were, will be, must have been,* and so on. The symbol **2-ed** means that the verb is to be a past form. Whenever we get this auxiliary with a past form of the verb, the subject has the meaning of undergoer of the action:

1		A (be)	2-ed	
The	culprit	was	caught	by the police.
Her	brother	was	seen	in Idaho.
	Charlie	was	knocked down	by Henry.
The	camels	were	fed.	
	You	're	whipped.	
	These	should be	cleaned.	
	He	was	stung.	
The	pie	might be	finished.	

● **EXERCISE 33**

A. Write five sentences with the basic pattern 1 2 — like "My uncle went away," "The girl on the sofa sobbed loudly," "Charlie took off for Mexico on his motorcycle." What general meaning do all your subjects have?

B. Write five sentences with the basic pattern 1 2 1 — like "He hates sandwiches," "Somebody found the gasoline," "The man on my left blew his nose." What is the meaning of the subjects?

C. Write five sentences with the basic pattern 1 2 3 — like "She was pretty," "My doctor got sick," "His story sounded rather fishy." What is the meaning of the subjects?

D. Write five sentences with the pattern 1 2L 1 — like "He was a good friend," "That's my sister," "His older brother is a teammate of mine," "They became our neighbors." What is the meaning of the subjects?

E. Write ten sentences with the pattern 1 A 2-ed. The auxiliary
                                        (be)
must be some form of *be*, and the verb must be a past form. Examples are "He was arrested," "The sandwiches were found," "His donkey must have been pushed off a cliff." What is the meaning of the subjects?

34: Meanings of other function units

OBJECTS

The units **object** and **linking-verb complement** have rather simple meanings compared to subjects. An object has the general meaning **undergoer of the action.** That's the meaning of *Sam*, for instance, in this sentence:

Charlie shot Sam.

Here the action is shooting; Charlie, the subject, performs the action of shooting; and Sam, the object, undergoes the action of shooting.

Here are some more objects with the meaning of undergoer of the action:

They found the **alligators**.	The house needed a **coat** of paint.
He studied the **lesson**.	I raced **him** to the house.
We climbed a **mountain**.	I raced the **motor**.

We noted in studying the meanings of subjects that the action sometimes is rather vague, so that the doing of the action is vague too. In the same way the undergoing of the action may be vague, as in "The house needed a coat of paint," or "He had a dollar." But since *coat* and *dollar* in these sentences are in the same pattern as *Sam* in "Charlie shot Sam," we grasp them in the same way. They all mean, in some sense or other, undergoer of the action.

Don't forget that subjects can mean undergoer of the action, too. This is the meaning of subjects in the pattern **1 A 2-ed**:

	1	**A** (be)	**2-ed**
	Sam	was	shot (by Charlie).
The	alligators	were	found.
The	lesson	was	studied.
A	coat of paint	was	needed.

LINKING-VERB COMPLEMENTS

Linking-verb complement is the name we gave to the second noun in the basic pattern **1 2L 1**:

He is my **friend**.	He became my **friend**.

The subject in this pattern has the meaning of that which is identified. Obviously the linking-verb complement has the meaning of that which identifies the subject. The boldface words in the following sentences are all linking-verb complements with this meaning. Notice that the identification is more obvious in some than in others:

That man is the **boss.**   All the world's a **stage.**
This bird is a **robin.**   He became a **mortician.**
He's an **athlete.**   Now is the **time** to start.
My time is your **time.**

UNITS FOLLOWING PREPOSITIONS

Another function unit is the word or word group that follows
a preposition to form a preposition group: *in the house, around the
corner, after the dance, according to the latest reports.* It's impossible
to indicate a meaning for this function unit. There are as many
meanings as there are prepositions — more, in fact, because
some prepositions have more than one meaning. But we can
note some general meanings that frequently occur: place or
position, *in the house, under the bed;* time, *after the dance;* manner,
with a shrug of his shoulders. It is also interesting to note that the
meaning of doer of the action can be expressed by a preposition
group:

Sam was shot by Charlie.

Here *Charlie,* patterning with the preposition *by,* has the meaning
of doer of the action of shooting.

MODIFIERS

The other function units so far named are modifiers — noun
modifiers, verb modifiers, and sentence modifiers. The meanings of these are closely tied up with the form classes that occur
as modifiers, but they are rather complicated. We will notice
just some of the obvious ones.

Adjectives modifying nouns most generally indicate some
quality that the noun has:

handsome lad   greedy pig   nervous mother

Thus, *handsome* modifying *lad* indicates that the lad has the quality of handsomeness; the pig has the quality of greediness, and so on.

Nouns modifying other nouns have a great variety of meanings. Perhaps the best word to cover all of them is **identification,** though this is very vague. Here are examples:

> grocery lad   (the lad who works in the grocery)
> kitchen sink   (the sink in the kitchen)
> Chicago lawyer   (the lawyer who works in Chicago)
> nerve specialist   (the doctor who specializes in nerves)

One thing that these modifiers do *not* do is state the quality of the nouns they modify.

Verbs modifying nouns are particularly interesting; 2-ing verbs name the action that the noun does:

> weeping mother   drooping flowers   screaming girls

In the first one, for example, *weeping* names the action which the mother performs. Thus the relationship between *weeping* and *mother* is exactly the same as that between *weeps* and *mother* in "The mother weeps." The patterns are different of course. In "The mother weeps," *mother* is the subject of the verb *weeps*. In "weeping mother," *weeping* is a modifier of the noun *mother*, which may be in any of a number of function units:

> The **weeping mother** was carried off.   (subject)
> I silenced the **weeping mother.**   (object)
> This is my **weeping mother.**   (linking-verb complement)

But the relationship of *weeping* to *mother* remains the same; *weeping* names the action, and *mother* is the doer of it.

A 2-ed verb modifying a noun generally names the action that the noun undergoes:

> invited guests   potted plants   insulted mother

In "invited guests," *invited* names the action that *guests* undergoes: somebody invited the guests. We don't say, of course, that *guests* is the object of *invited*. An object is a particular unit in a particular pattern: the second noun in the basic pattern 1 2 1. But the meaning relationship between *invited* and *guests* is the same in "The invited guests came in" and "He invited the guests."

So we see that the same meaning can often be expressed in quite different function units. In all of the following, *guests* has the meaning of undergoer of the action:

He invited the guests. (object)　　The guests were invited. (subject)

invited guests (headword of a noun cluster, which might occur in any function unit)

ADVERBS

Adverbs modifying nouns usually have the meaning **time** or **place**:

the men **there** (place)　　the letter **inside** (place)
the people **below** (place)　　the fight **afterward** (time)

Verb modifiers usually have the meaning **time, place,** or **manner**. These meanings can be expressed by various kinds of modifiers:

TIME　　went **later** (adverb)
　　　　went **after dinner** (P-group)
　　　　went **when he wanted to** (S-group)

PLACE　　went **down** (adverb)
　　　　went **that way** (noun)
　　　　went **to the store** (P-group)

MANNER　　went **quickly** (adverb)
　　　　went **on his bicycle** (P-group)
　　　　went **as he was** (S-group)

In addition, P-groups and S-groups express various more special meanings when they modify verbs. These meanings depend upon the particular prepositions and subordinators used.

We will take up sentence modifiers and their meanings a little later on.

● **EXERCISE 34**

A. Here you are given some verbs naming actions and some nouns naming doers of the action. For each set, write three sentences, each expressing the meaning of doer of the action in a different way. For instance, if the action were *weeping* and the doer *mother*, you might write these sentences:

My mother wept bitterly.   **Bitter tears were wept by my mother.**
I comforted my weeping mother.

In each of these the action is weeping and the mother does it.
Now, write three sentences for each of the following pairs.

ACTION	DOER	ACTION	DOER
1. awakening	lion	4. investigating	committee
2. burning	fire	5. attacking	troops
3. singing	girls	6. moving	finger

B. Here the nouns name possible undergoers of the actions. Write three sentences for each set, expressing the meaning of undergoer of the action in three different ways. If the action were *writing* and the undergoer *message*, you might have these sentences:

Jim wrote a message.
The message had been written long before.
We got a written message telling us what to do.

In each of these the action is writing and the message undergoes it.
Now, write three sentences for each of these pairs.

ACTION	UNDERGOER	ACTION	UNDERGOER
1. inviting	guests	4. frightening	child
2. breaking	arm	5. speaking	word
3. stealing	money	6. burning	hand

35 : Some other basic statement patterns

We have so far studied just four basic statement patterns, and it is time now to notice a few more. But first let us look again at the original four.

Pattern One is basically just a subject and a verb, though of course both subject and verb may have modifiers:

    1   **2**
Canaries twitter.

      1   **2**
The little canaries in the trees twitter when they're feeling good.

Pattern Two is basically a subject, a linking verb, and an adjective:

    1   **2**   **3**
Canaries are yellow.

      1   **2**   **3**
The little canary in this cage is especially yellow in the spring.

Pattern Three is basically a subject, a linking verb, and a linking-verb complement:

    1   **2L**   **1**
Canaries are birds.

    1   **2L**   **1**
Canaries that behave themselves are the finest birds in the world.

Pattern Four is a subject, a verb, and an object:

     1   **2**   **1**
Canaries eat worms.

      1   **2**   **1**
The canary we own wouldn't eat worms if it were starving.

Now before going on to other basic statement patterns, we must add something to our formulas. We need a way of showing whether two nouns refer to the same person or thing or to different persons or things. Examine the difference between the third and fourth patterns:

1   2L   1   **1   2   1**
Canaries are birds.   Canaries eat worms.

One way to explain the difference is to say that the first sentence contains a linking verb and the second does not; that, in fact, is what the formula does. But another way to explain it is to say that in the first sentence *canaries* and *birds* refer to the same things and that in the second *canaries* and *worms* refer to different things. So in these:

He is Charlie.   He saw Charlie.

In the first sentence, *he* and *Charlie* are the same person. In the second they are different people.

In our formulas we can indicate whether two nouns refer to the same person or thing or to different persons or things by putting small letters after the noun symbol. For instance, 1^a, 1^b would mean "two nouns referring to different persons or things"; and 1^a, 1^a would mean "two nouns referring to the same person or thing."

1^a 2 1^a   **1^a 2 1^b**
He is Charlie.   He saw Charlie.

Notice that there are two ways of writing a formula for the sentence "He is Charlie." One is 1 2L 1. (If the verb is a linking verb, the nouns will necessarily refer to the same person or the same thing.) The other is 1^a 2 1^a. (If the two nouns refer to the same person or the same thing, the verb will necessarily be a linking verb.) Indeed, if we had no patterns except those so far studied, we wouldn't have to use the small letters; we could just distinguish between **2** and **2L**. But this won't work in all patterns.

Another thing to notice is that the small letter itself doesn't tell whether the noun is subject, object, or some other function unit. We give the letter *a* to the first noun (or pronoun) in the sentence. If the second noun refers to the same thing, we use *a* for it, too; if it refers to something else, we use *b*. If the third noun refers to a third thing, we use *c*, and so on. For example:

$$\textbf{D } 1^a \textbf{ P D } 1^b \textbf{ P D } 1^c \textbf{ 2 } 1^a$$
The man at the back of the room is Charlie.

Charlie is 1^a because it refers to the same person that *man* does.

This brings us to the next basic statement pattern:

$$1^a \textbf{ 2 } 1^b \textbf{ } 1^c$$

There are three nouns, all referring to different people or different things, one before the verb and two after it. In this pattern, the first noun is the subject and is tied to the verb; the third noun is an object; and the second noun is what is called an **indirect object**. Here are some examples:

SUBJECT				INDIRECT OBJECT		OBJECT	
D	1^a	**2**	**D**	1^b	**D**	1^c	
The	teacher	taught	the	students	their	arithmetic.	
The	man	gave	his	son	some	money.	
Some	friends	sent	those	children	an	accordion.	
My	brother	lent		me	his	skates.	
	Charlie	mailed		Bert	a	package.	
His	aunt	sang		us	a	song.	
	She	gave		him	the	gate.	

But we must always know whether the second two nouns refer to different persons or things or to the same person or thing. If they refer to the same person or thing, we get an entirely different pattern:

$$1^a \textbf{ 2 } 1^b \textbf{ } 1^b$$

Here the first noun is still the subject and is tied to the verb. But the second noun is the object, and the third noun is what is called an **object complement.** Here are some sentences:

SUBJECT			OBJECT			OBJECT COMPLEMENT
D	**1**ᵃ	**2**	**D**	**1**ᵇ	**D**	**1**ᵇ
The	girls	considered	the	boy	a	fool.
The	class	elected		Charlie		president.
The	team	made		Sam	their	spokesman.
The	boy	thought	the	girl	an	idiot.
	We	found		him	a	help.

Here *boy* and *fool* refer to the same person; so do *Charlie* and *president*, *Sam* and *spokesman*, and so on.

Slightly different is the pattern in which we have an adjective in place of the object complement:

	SUBJECT			OBJECT	ADJECTIVE
D	**1**ᵃ	**2**	**D**	**1**ᵇ	**3**
The	boys	considered	the	girls	idiotic.
The	girls	thought	the	fellows	foolish.
	That	made		me	sore.
	I	believed		him	honest.

So we have three new basic patterns:

$$1^a \; 2 \; 1^b \; 1^c \qquad 1^a \; 2 \; 1^b \; 1^b \qquad 1^a \; 2 \; 1^b \; 3$$

We also have two new function units. The second noun in the first pattern is an indirect object. The third noun in the second pattern is an object complement.

Naturally these patterns can be modified and expanded in all the usual ways:

D	**V**	**3**	**1**ᵃ	**P**	**D**	**1**ᵇ	**2**	**D**	**3**	**1**ᶜ	**P**
Some	rather	foolish	friends	of	the	family	sent	those	awful	children	in

D	**1**ᵈ	**1**ᵉ	**D**	**1**ᶠ
the	Smith	house	an	accordion.

This is basically 1^a 2 1^b 1^c; *friends* is the subject, *children* is an indirect object, and *accordion* is an object.

These patterns may also appear in an S-group:

S 1^a 2   D 1^b 3 1^a 2 1^b D 1^c
Since I believed the man honest, I lent him some money.

1^a 2   4   S   D 1^b 2 1^c 1^c
Everything went well after the class elected Charlie president.

● **EXERCISE 35**

A. Write five sentences with the basic pattern 1^a 2 1^b 1^c — like "Some friends of mine gave me a party on my birthday." Try to use a different verb each time.

B. Write five sentences with the basic pattern 1^a 2 1^b 1^b — like "I found Ralph a big help in an emergency." Try to use different verbs.

C. Write five sentences with the basic pattern 1^a 2 1^b 3 — like "We all thought Ralph rather helpful." Try to use different verbs.

D. Write sentences based on the following formulas. These start easy and get harder so that they become rather like puzzles. Solve as many as you can. Follow the formulas exactly.

1. 1^a 2 D 1^b
2. D 1^a P D 1^b 2 D 1^c
3. D 1^a 2 D 1^a
4. D 1^a 2 4
5. D 1^a P D 1^b 2 1^a
6. 1^a 2 1^b D 1^c
7. D 1^a A 2-ing D 1^b
8. D 1^a 2 V 3

9. D 1^a 2 1^b D 1^c
10. 1^a A 2 3
11. S D 1^a 2 4, D 1^b 2 D 1^c
12. 1^a A 2 P D 1^b
13. D 1^a 2 1^b D 1^b
14. D 3 1^a 2 D 1^b 3
15. D 1^a 2 4 S D 1^b 2 D 1^c
16. D 1^a S 2 4 2 1^a

17. D V 3 1^a P D 1^b 2 D 3 1^c P D 1^d 1^e D 1^f
18. 1^a 2 1^b D 3 1^c S 1^b 2 1^a D 1^a
19. S 1^a 2 D 1^b 3, 1^a 2 1^b D 3 1^c
20. D 1^a S 2 1^b D 1^c 2 4 S D 1^d P D 3 1^e 2 4

1—noun   2—verb   3—adjective   4—adverb
A—auxiliary   D—determiner   P—preposition   S—subordinator   V—intensifier

36: Gender

One of the things we learn when we learn English is that there is a striking difference in the use of the words *he, she, it*. We learned to use the pronouns *he–him* to replace words like *boy, Charlie, father,* the pronouns *she–her* to replace words like *girl, Susie, mother,* and the pronoun *it* to replace words like *tree, house, car:*

Charlie is bleeding badly; **he** needs a doctor.
Susie isn't dressed yet; **she'll** be late.
My **car** won't run; **it** has no motor.

We might be tempted to say that we learned to use *he–him* to refer to male beings, *she–her* for female beings, and *it* for things that could not be classified as male or female. But this gets the story backwards. We did not first receive instruction in biology and then proceed to use the pronouns accordingly. Instead we began to use the pronouns as we heard other people use them, and this use of the pronouns helped us to sort the world into "males," "females," and "things in neither grouping."

This use of these pronouns in English goes by the name of **gender.** We say that a noun is of the **masculine gender** if *he* or *him* substitutes for it:

The boy climbed the tree.   The tree towered over the boy.
He climbed the tree.   The tree towered over **him.**

We say that a noun is of the **feminine gender** if *she* or *her* substitutes for it:

My mother parked the car.   The car baffled my mother.
She parked the car.   The car baffled **her.**

We say that a noun is of the **neuter gender** if *it* substitutes for it:

My mother parked the car.   The car baffled my mother.
My mother parked **it.**   **It** baffled my mother.

We need to notice right away that sex and gender are not the same things. Sex is a matter of biology; gender is a matter of language. Sometimes things which have no sex take the substitutes *he* or *she* and so are of the masculine or feminine gender. An obvious example is *ship*. Ships have no sex, but the word *ship* usually takes *she* as the substitute:

> **The ship sailed away.**
> **She** sailed away.

On the other hand, mosquitoes do have sex, but when we have to do with mosquitoes, we do not usually inquire into their sex. We simply make the word neuter gender:

> **The mosquito buzzed around my ears.**
> **It** buzzed around my ears.

We bring up the matter of gender here because it has a bearing on sentence structure. It happens that the distinction between masculine and feminine doesn't matter much. The distinction may be of absorbing interest in life, but in English sentence structure masculine nouns and feminine nouns operate in pretty much the same way. However, neuter nouns sometimes work differently.

We can begin, then, by separating two groups of nouns: (1) those for which the substitute pronouns are *he, she, him*, or *her;* (2) those for which the substitute pronoun is *it*. For simplicity we will call the first the **he group** and the second the **it group:**

HE NOUNS		IT NOUNS	
boy	Charlie	tree	Kansas City
girl	lawyer	razor	medicine
father	assistant	automobile	assistance
mother	ship	garbage	mosquito

We can show these nouns to belong to these groups by showing the words that substitute for them.

The girl sat under the tree.
She sat under **it.**

The boy bought a razor.
He bought **it.**

Your assistant would be grateful for some assistance.
He would be grateful for **it.**

The ship was covered with garbage.
She was covered with **it.**

If we were to go on trying nouns in sentences to see what their substitutes are, we would find that most nouns in English would go into one list or the other, and the lists could be made very long.

Not all English nouns would go into one list or the other, however. Some nouns would not go into either, and some would go into both. Suppose we try a sentence containing the word *dog:*

The dog was eating a piece of meat.

We find that either *he–she* or *it* might substitute:

He was eating a piece of meat.
It was eating a piece of meat.

The same thing is true of *baby:*

The baby was playing with a rattle.
She was playing with a rattle.
It was playing with a rattle.

So we have a third group: one for which the substitute may be either *he–she* or *it*. We will label it the **he–it group:**

HE NOUNS	HE–IT NOUNS	IT NOUNS
boy	baby	rattle
girl	child	tree
mother	dog	house
uncle	horse	mistake

In most of the sentences that we deal with in this book it doesn't matter what the gender of the nouns is. But sometimes it does matter, and when it does we have to be able to show the gender in the formulas. We do this by writing *he*, *he–it*, or *it* under the symbol for the noun. Like this:

D 1ᵃ 2 D 1ᵇ D 1ᶜ
(he)   (he–it)   (it)

This means that the first noun must be of the masculine–feminine gender (have the substitute *he* or *she*); the second noun must be of the masculine–feminine or neuter gender (have the substitute *him–her* or *it*); the third noun must be of the neuter gender (have the substitute *it*). All of the following sentences would satisfy the formula:

> The boy gave the baby a rattle.
> My father fed the dog some cheese.
> The cowboy taught his horse a lesson.
> His mother gives her cats their baths.

We wouldn't in actual practice substitute pronouns in both parts of these sentences. We might say "The boy gave it a rattle," but we would hardly say "The boy gave it it." Nevertheless *rattle* is an *it* word, as we see by comparing "The rattle broke and "It broke," with *it* substituting for *rattle*.

● EXERCISE 36

A. Take a piece of paper and write three column headings: *he* nouns, *he–it* nouns, and *it* nouns. Then go through the following sentences and put each of the nouns in one of the three columns. If the substitute would be *he*, *she*, *him*, or *her* put it under *he* nouns. If it would be *it*, put it under *it* nouns. If it might be either, put it under *he–it* nouns. If the noun is plural, just think what the substitute would be if it were singular.

1. The boy gave the baby a rattle. **2.** His mother painted the house. **3.** The dog was gnawing on a bone. **4.** The doctor gave his patient a pill. **5.** Our cat caught a mouse. **6.** A good soldier keeps his gun clean.

7. Alexander was leading a small child by the hand. **8.** Alarmed by the hunter, the deer bounded away. **9.** Mrs. Jenkins found a beetle in the salad. **10.** The mule wasn't used to saddles. **11.** This company makes mash for pigs. **12.** The hen laid an egg and cackled proudly at Edna.

B. Write sentences from the following formulas. Make sure that you use nouns from the gender groups indicated.

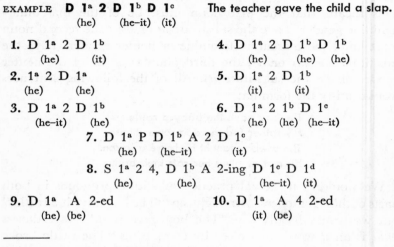

EXAMPLE   **D 1ᵃ 2 D 1ᵇ D 1ᶜ**   **The teacher gave the child a slap.**
             (he)   (he–it)   (it)

1. D 1ᵃ 2 D 1ᵇ   **4.** D 1ᵃ 2 D 1ᵇ D 1ᵇ
     (he)   (it)   (he)   (he)   (he)

2. 1ᵃ 2 D 1ᵃ   **5.** D 1ᵃ 2 D 1ᵇ
    (he)   (he)   (it)   (it)

3. D 1ᵃ 2 D 1ᵇ   **6.** D 1ᵃ 2 1ᵇ D 1ᶜ
    (he–it)   (he)   (he)   (he)   (he–it)

         7. D 1ᵃ P D 1ᵇ A 2 D 1ᶜ
              (he)   (he–it)   (it)

         8. S 1ᵃ 2 4, D 1ᵇ A 2-ing D 1ᶜ D 1ᵈ
               (he)   (he)   (he–it)   (it)

9. D 1ᵃ A 2-ed   **10.** D 1ᵃ A 4 2-ed
   (he) (be)   (it) (be)

1–noun   2–verb   4–adverb
A–auxiliary   D–determiner   P–preposition   S–subordinator

---

37 : *Th* nouns

In the last chapter we divided nouns into three groups according to the pronouns that substitute for them. Some nouns, however, cannot be replaced by pronouns at all. For example, consider the sentence "The milkman brought the milk last Wednesday." We can substitute *he* for *milkman* and *it* for *milk*:

The milkman brought the milk last Wednesday.
He brought it last Wednesday.

But we cannot substitute *it* or any other pronoun for *last Wednesday*. We cannot turn the sentence into "He brought it it" or "He brought the milk it."

There is, however, something we can substitute for *last Wednesday*. We can substitute the adverb *then:*

The milkman brought the milk last Wednesday.   He brought it then.

Or consider "My father prunes the tree this way." We can substitute the pronoun *he* for *my father* and the pronoun *it* for *the tree*. We can't substitute any pronoun for *this way*. But we can substitute the adverb *thus:*

My father prunes the tree this way.   He prunes it thus.

In some sentences, *way* may have the substitute *there:*

My brother went that way.   He went there.

So now we have four groups of nouns, arranged according to the words that substitute for them:

1. A *he* group — nouns for which the substitute is *he, she, him,* or *her* (in the plural *they* or *them*):

boy	salesman	opponent
girl	farmer	helper
mother	uncle	friend
father	aunt	rival
doctor	actress	student

2. An *it* group — nouns for which the substitute is *it* (in the plural *they* or *them*):

tree	garbage	sleep
lawn	doorknob	silence
apple	mouse	leaf
advice	mosquito	water
lesson	beauty	dream

3. A *he–it* group — nouns for which the substitute may be either *he*, *she*, *him*, *her*, or *it* (in the plural *they* or *them*):

dog	child
horse	baby
pig	tot
deer	cat

4. A group for which the substitute is *thus*, *then*, or *there*. We will call this the **th group**, after the first letters of *thus*, *then*, and *there*. A noun in this group is a **th noun**:

this way	next October
last Wednesday	this Monday
some day	every night
yesterday afternoon	each week end

Th nouns generally occur with determiners as shown.

When we want, in our formulas, to show that a noun belongs to the *th* group, we will write (*th*) under the 1, just as we write (*he*), (*it*), and (*he–it*) for the other groups:

D	1ᵃ	2	D	1ᵇ	D	1ᶜ
	(he)			(it)		(th)
The	milkman	brought	the	milk	last	Wednesday.
My	father	prunes	the	tree	this	way.

Just as we found some words, like *change*, which are sometimes nouns and sometimes verbs, so we find some nouns that belong now to one substitute group and now to another. For instance, for one of its meanings *pupil* is *he*, but for another *pupil* is *it*:

D	1ᵃ	A	2	D	1ᵇ
	(he)				(it)
The	pupil	was	learning	his	lesson.

D	1ᵃ	P D	1ᵇ	A	2
	(it)		(it)		
The	pupil	of his	eye	was	dilated.

A word like *Wednesday* might be in the *th* or in the *it* group.

D 1^a   2   D   1^b   D   1^c
 (he)   (it)   (th)

The man brought the money last Wednesday.

D   1^a   2   D   1^a   P   D   1^b
    (it)   (it)   (it)

Last Wednesday was the day of the meeting.

If we actually can't tell which group a noun belongs to, then the sentence will have two possible meanings:

The club will choose next Wednesday.

This may mean "The club will select next Wednesday as the day to do something" — with *Wednesday* as an *it* noun. Or it may mean "The club will do its choosing next Wednesday" — with *Wednesday* as a *th* noun. We couldn't write the formula for this sentence, because we wouldn't know whether to write (*it*) or (*th*) under *Wednesday*. If we can't write a formula for a sentence, the sentence is an ambiguous one that has either no meaning or no clear meaning.

Here's an interesting one. As you may know, the old Roman roads are sometimes called "ways." So the following sentence would have two meanings, at least in writing:

The Romans built this way.

It might mean that they built this road or that they built in this manner, or in this direction. The following sentence, however, would have only one meaning:

D   1^a   2   D   1^b   D   1^c   D   1^d
    (he)   (it)   (th)   (th)

The Romans built this way this way this way.

It means "The Romans built this road in this direction in this manner."

Now that we have identified *th* nouns, we can make a little correction of a statement made earlier. We identified the indirect object as the noun after the verb in the pattern 1^a 2 1^b 1^c. We said that the second noun in this pattern is an indirect object and the third noun an object:

D	**1**[a]	**2**	**D**	**1**[b]	**D**	**3**	**1**[c]
(he)			(he)				(it)

The boy gave his sister a bad time.

But of course we were assuming that the last noun in the pattern was not a *th* noun. If the last noun is a *th* noun, then the noun after the verb is an ordinary object, not an indirect object.

D	**1**[a]	**2**	**D**	**1**[b]	**D**	**1**[c]
(he)			(it)			(th)

The principal opened the school this morning.

The *th* nouns occur as additions to all of the patterns we have studied. They may occur at the end of the patterns:

D	**1**[a]	**2**	**4**	**D**	**1**[b]
	(he)				(th)
That	man	came	early	last	week.
My	mother	sleeps	late	every	Sunday.

D	**1**[a]	**2**	**D**	**1**[b]	**D**	**1**[c]
	(he)			(it)		(th)
My	brother	saw	the	movie	this	afternoon.
Indians	clean	their		fish	this	way.

D	**1**[a]	**2**	**D**	**1**[b]	**D**	**1**[c]	**D**	**1**[d]
	(he)			(he)		(it)		(th)
His	father	gave	the	salesman	a	check	last	night.
We	found		him		a	tire	this	way.

D	**1**[a]	**2**	**D**	**1**[a]	**D**	**1**[b]
	(he)			(he)		(th)
My	friends	were	the	winners	that	time.
Charlie	is		the	flunkey	this	week.

D	**1**[a]	**2**	**D**	**1**[b]	**D**	**1**[b]	**D**	**1**[c]
	(he)			(he)		(he)		(th)
The	chief	called	the	man	a	coward	this	morning.
We		elected		him		chief	last	Tuesday.

Or the *th* nouns may come at the beginning of the pattern:

> Last week that man came early.
> Every Sunday my mother sleeps late.
> This afternoon my brother saw the movie.
> Last night his father gave the salesman a check.
> That time my friends were the winners.
> This morning the chief called the man a coward.
> Last Tuesday we elected him chief.

The *th* nouns do not very often come in the middle of the pattern. We may sometimes hear people say "My father this afternoon gave the salesman a check" or "My friends that time were the winners." But the position at the beginning or end is much more common.

Notice also that *th* nouns meaning "thus" or "this way" normally occur only at the end. "This way the Indians clean their fish" would sound somewhat unnatural.

So far as pattern parts go, *th* nouns work like adverbs or S-groups. If they come at the beginning of the pattern, they modify all the rest of the pattern:

> Last night his father gave the salesman a check.
> Last night / his father gave the salesman a check.
>
> That time my friends were the winners.
> That time / my friends were the winners.

But if they come at the end of the pattern, they are part of the verb cluster. They are cut off in order with the other members of the verb cluster:

> My friends were the winners that time.
> My friends / were the winners that time.
>   were the winners / that time
>
> My mother usually sleeps late every Sunday.
> My mother / usually sleeps late every Sunday.
>   usually / sleeps late every Sunday
>   sleeps late / every Sunday

● **EXERCISE 37**

A. Write four column headings on a piece of paper: *he* nouns, *he–it* nouns, *it* nouns, and *th* nouns. Then go through the following sentences and put each of the nouns into one of the four columns. If the substitute would be *he, she, him,* or *her,* put the noun under *he* nouns. If it would be *it,* put it under *it* nouns. If it might be either, put it under *he–it* nouns. If the substitute would be *then, thus,* or *there,* put the noun under *th* nouns. If the noun is plural, just think what the substitute would be if it were singular.

1. The man ate a sandwich. **2.** His mother bought a car last Monday. **3.** Mr. Weaver taught his son a lesson. **4.** My sister waved her hair this morning. **5.** The pig refused to eat the mash that time. **6.** Every day Elsie milked thirty cows. **7.** A small child was eating dirt happily. **8.** The cowboys tie a bowline this way. **9.** All the pictures fell off the wall last night. **10.** My aunt is having an operation next week.

B. Write sentences from the following formulas. Be sure you use nouns from the gender groups indicated.

EXAMPLE   **D 1ᵃ 2 D 1ᵇ D 1ᶜ D 1ᵈ**
            (he)   (he–it) (it)   (th)

The teacher gave the child a slap this morning.

1. D 1ᵃ 2 D 1ᵇ D 1ᶜ
      (he)   (it)   (th)

2. D 1ᵃ 2 4 D 1ᵇ
      (he)   (th)

3. D 1ᵃ 2 D 1ᵃ D 1ᵇ
      (he)   (he)   (th)

4. D 1ᵃ D 1ᵇ 2 D 1ᶜ
      (th)   (he)   (it)

5. D 3 1ᵃ P D 1ᵇ A 2-ing D 1ᶜ D 1ᵈ
        (he–it)   (it)   (it) (th)

6. D 1ᵃ 1ᵇ 2 D 1ᶜ 3
      (th) (he)   (he)

7. D 1ᵃ 2 D 1ᵇ S D 1ᶜ 2 D 1ᵈ
      (he)   (it)   (it)   (th)

8. D 1ᵃ S 2 4 D 1ᵇ 2 D 1ᵃ
      (he)   (th)   (he)

1–noun   2–verb   3–adjective   4–adverb
A–auxiliary   D–determiner   P–preposition   S–subordinator

38: More meanings of function units

We may now return to the function units identified in the last few chapters and say a little more about their meanings. We'll begin with indirect objects. You remember that an indirect object is the noun after the verb in the pattern 1^a 2 1^b 1^c. (This is so unless 1^c is a *th* noun. We will assume that 1^c is not a *th* noun unless so specified.)

	SUBJECT			INDIRECT OBJECT		OBJECT		
D	1^a	**2**	**D**	1^b	**D**	1^c		
My	father	gave	the	man	some	money.		
I		sent	my	brother	a	letter.		
	Alice	played		us	a	record.		
His	uncle	gave	the	house	a	coat	of	paint.

The meaning of the indirect object might be said to be **receiver of the action,** or the person for whom something is done. In the first sentence the man receives the money. In the second the brother gets the letter. In the third the record is played for us. Usually the indirect object indicates a person, but sometimes it does not. In the fifth sentence a house receives a coat of paint.

Any meaning that we can indicate for a function unit is bound to be general and sometimes vague. The indirect objects in the following sentences indicate receiver of the action, but not so obviously as those in the first examples:

> I ran **Charlie** a race. We dropped **him** a hint.
> He asked **me** the way. Forgive **us** our sins.

Nevertheless, they occur in the same structure, and we grasp them in the same way. They all have a common general meaning: receiver of the action — the person (or thing) for whom the action is done.

Remember always that it isn't the meaning that tells us the structure; it's the structure that tells us the meaning. We don't know that these words are indirect objects by perceiving that they have the meaning of receiver of the action. We know that they have the meaning of receiver of the action by perceiving that they are indirect objects. It's the arrangement of the words in the pattern that tells us that they are indirect objects.

We can see this to be true by noting that the meaning of receiver of the action can be expressed by other structures besides indirect objects. For instance, it can be expressed by preposition groups:

I sent a letter **to my brother.**   Alice played a record **for us.**
My father gave some money **to the man.**

This meaning can also be expressed by the subject in certain patterns. In the following sentences, the subject has the meaning of receiver of the action:

The man was given some money.   We were played a record.
My brother was sent a letter.   The house was given a coat of paint.

So we must add receiver of the action to the list of meanings that subjects can have. That makes five general meanings in all:

DOER OF THE ACTION   The man gave the house a coat of paint.
THAT WHICH IS IDENTIFIED   The man is a painter.
THAT WHICH IS DESCRIBED   The man is skillful.
UNDERGOER OF THE ACTION   A coat of paint was applied.
RECEIVER OF THE ACTION   The house was given a coat of paint.

A FINE POINT

Here's an oddity. If you find the going too sticky, skip it. But it's a nice illustration of the signaling system of our language. Starting with the following formula, we can get two different structures:

$$1^a \ A \ 2\text{-ed} \ 1^b$$
(be)

In one the subject has the meaning of undergoer of the action and in the other it has the meaning of receiver of the action.

D	1ᵃ		A	2-ed	D	1ᵇ	
			(be)				
The	house		was	given	a	coat	of paint.
A	coat	of paint	was	given	the	house.	
The	boy		was	given	a	girl	(as a partner.)
A	girl		was	given	the	boy	(as a partner.)

These pairs are not particularly important in English structure. The second one in each pair doesn't actually occur very often. But they are interesting because they show how the structure of the sentence tells us the meaning. If we say "The boy was given a girl," we know that the boy is the receiver of the action, and the girl is the undergoer; the girl is brought over and introduced to the boy. But if we say "A boy was given the girl," we know that the boy is the undergoer and the girl the receiver; the boy is brought over and introduced to the girl. How do we know?

Well, since the sentences are identical except for the determiners, it must be the contrast between the determiners that tells us. In a structure of this type, if the subject is preceded by a specific determiner (*the, this, that, my, his*, etc.) and the other noun is preceded by a general determiner (*a, some, an, one, several*), the subject will have the meaning of receiver of the action and the other noun will have the meaning of undergoer of the action. We can put this in the formula by marking *s* for "specific" and *g* for "general" under the *D*'s:

D	1ᵃ	A	2-ed	D	1ᵇ
(s)		(be)		(g)	
The	boy	was	given	a	girl.
That	girl	was	given	some	boy.
My	uncle	was	sent	an	assistant.

But if the determiner for the subject is general and the other determiner is specific, the subject will have the meaning of undergoer of the action.

D	1ª	A	2-ed	D	1ᵇ
(g)		(be)		(s)	
A	boy	was	given	the	girl.
Some	girl	was	given	the	boy.
An	assistant	was	sent	my	uncle.

If there is no such contrast between specific and general determiners, the sentence will have two possible meanings. In the following sentences, you can't tell who gets whom:

> The boy was given the girl.
> An assistant was sent an uncle.

Another signal that can operate in this structure is a contrast in the gender groups that the nouns belong to. You will remember that there are *he* nouns (*boy, girl, uncle, lawyer*), *he–it* nouns (*dog, baby, horse, monkey*), and *it* nouns (*bone, paper, house, ticket*). If a *he* noun contrasts with a *he–it* noun or an *it* noun, the *he* noun will mean receiver and the *it* or *he–it* noun will mean undergoer:

D	1ª	A	2-ed	D	1ᵇ
	(he)				(it)
The	boy	was	given	the	bicycle.
My	uncle	was	sent	the	paper.

In these the *he* subjects, *boy* and *uncle*, mean receiver.

D	1ª	A	2-ed	D	1ᵇ
	(it)				(he)
The	bicycle	was	given	the	boy.
The	paper	was	sent	my	uncle.

The *it* subjects, *bicycle* and *paper*, mean undergoer.

D	1ª	A	2-ed	D	1ᵇ
	(he)	(be)			(he–it)
The	boy	was	given	the	dog.
My	uncle	was	given	the	baby.

The *he* subjects, *boy* and *uncle*, mean receiver.

D	**1**ᵃ	**A**	**2-ed**	**D**	**1**ᵇ
	(he–it)	(be)			(he)
The	dog	was	given	the	boy.
The	baby	was	given	my	uncle.

The *he–it* subjects, *dog* and *baby*, mean undergoer.

If the contrast is between a *he–it* noun and an *it* noun, the *he–it* noun means receiver and the *it* noun means undergoer.

D	**1**ᵃ	**A**	**2-ed**	**D**	**1**ᵇ
	(he–it)	(be)			(it)
The	baby	was	handed	the	rattle.
The	dog	was	fed	the	meat.

The *he–it* subjects, *baby* and *dog*, mean receiver.

D	**1**ᵃ	**A**	**2-ed**	**D**	**1**ᵇ
	(it)	(be)			(he–it)
The	rattle	was	handed	the	baby.
The	meat	was	fed	the	dog.

The *it* subjects, *rattle* and *meat*, mean undergoer.

As was said at the beginning, these contrasts aren't a very important part of English structure. Actually, it's more usual to avoid the contrast by saying "The dog was fed the meat" for one meaning and "The meat was fed to the dog" for the other.

But the point they illustrate *is* important. That is, that all the meanings we get from our English sentences we get from form and pattern and contrasts of form and pattern. This is why in studying English structure we must always begin with the form and pattern and let these lead us to the meaning, instead of beginning with the meaning and not paying any attention to the form.

If two meanings — like receiver and undergoer — are to be separated, there must be signals to separate them. We have seen that these meanings can be expressed in several different structures, all kept apart by form signals, of which one is gender — regularly sorted for us by our pronouns. We can actually indicate these structures by formulas, sets of symbols. Each formula will lead directly to just one structure and not to two different and contrasting structures.

In some places the signals that separate structures have become weak. We have seen that the contrast between receiver and undergoer is sometimes signaled by just the contrast between gender groups or between different sets of determiners. When this happens, the possibility of ambiguity — two possible meanings — is increased. Then the language always tends to change, to find stronger signals for separating the meaning.

This is precisely why it is more common nowadays to say "The meat was fed to the dog" instead of "The meat was fed the dog," or "A boy was given to the girl" instead of "A boy was given the girl." "A boy was given the girl" has come too close to "The boy was given a girl." The signals have grown weak.

● **EXERCISE 38**

A. Write sentences from these formulas. Then decide whether the nouns in your sentences mean performer, receiver, or undergoer of the action.

1. D 1ᵃ 2 D 1ᵇ D 1ᶜ
2. D 1ᵃ 2 1ᵇ D 1ᶜ
3. 1ᵃ 2 1ᵇ D 1ᶜ
4. S 1ᵃ 2 1ᵇ D 1ᶜ, D 1ᵈ 2 D 1ᵃ
5. D 1ᵃ S 2 1ᵇ D 1ᶜ 2 D 1ᵈ
6. D 1ᵃ   A 2-ed D 1ᵇ
   (he) (be)   (it)
7. D 1ᵃ   A 2-ed D 1ᵇ
   (he) (be)   (he–it)

8. D 1ᵃ   A 2-ed D 1ᵇ
   (it) (be)   (he)
9. D 1ᵃ   A 2-ed D 1ᵇ
   (he–it) (be)   (he)
10. D 1ᵃ   A 2-ed D 1ᵇ
   (he–it) (be)   (it)
11. D 1ᵃ A 2-ed D 1ᵇ
   (s)   (g)

B. Write sentences from these formulas. Here all of the basic pat-

---

1–noun   2–verb   3–adjective   4–adverb
A–auxiliary   D–determiner   P–preposition   S–subordinator   V–intensifier

terns we have studied are included. Note the occurrence of objects, linking-verb complements, indirect objects, and object complements.

1. D 1^a 2 4
2. D 1^a 2 D 1^b
3. D 1^a 2 3
4. D 1^a 2 1^b D 1^c
5. D 1^a P D 1^b 2 D 1^a

6. D 1^a 2 D 1^b D 1^b
7. D 1^a P D 1^b 2 P D 1^c
8. D 1^a 2 D 1^b 3
9. D 1^a S 2 4 2 D 1^a
10. S 1^a 2 4, D 1^b 2 D 1^c D 1^d
11. S D 1^a 2 D 1^b D 1^c, 1^d 2 4
12. 1^a 2 1^b D 1^b S 1^b 2 V 3
13. S D 1^a 2 4, D 1^b S 2 1^c D 1^d 2 D 1^e
14. 1^a A 2-ing D 1^b S D 1^c 2 4 D 1^d

39: Statements with subject after the verb

In all the statement patterns we have studied so far, the subject comes before the verb. In the basic patterns — with no modifiers — the subject is the noun directly in front of the verb:

	SUBJECT	VERB	
The	people	went	away.
	Charlie	looked	silly.
	We	rented	some bicycles.
My	father	gave	the waiter a smile.
The	waiter	thought	my father stingy.

If the subject has modifiers after it, another noun or so may come between the subject and the verb. Most common is the noun in the preposition group:

The man in the **car** needed a shave.
The paintings on the **wall** were horrible.
The kid with the yellow **shoes** is Charlie.

Or we might have an S-group, possibly with nouns in it, coming between the subject and the verb:

> The man **who was sitting in the car** needed a shave.
> The pictures **that Al hung on the wall** were horrible.
> The girl **his parents wanted him to marry** was a wrestler.

But subjects don't always come before the verb in statements. We have one common pattern and several uncommon patterns in which the verb comes first. The common pattern is one using the structure word *there*. This word is in a class by itself; no other English word patterns quite like it. In our formulas we shall indicate it by simply writing it in. When we need to refer to it, we shall simply call it **structure word there**. As we'll see, there is also an adverb *there*, different from the structure word *there*.

The basic pattern is **there 2 D 1 4**. The 2 and the 1 are tied, that is, the noun is the subject of the verb.

there	2	D	1	4
There	was	a	man	here.
There	were	some	men	here.
There	were	some	men	there.
There	is	a	piano	upstairs.
There	are	two	pianos	·upstairs.
There	's	a	hammer	somewhere.
There	were	six	horses	there.

We might have other constructions in place of the adverb at the end. It's very common, for example, to have a P-group here:

there	2	D	1	P	D	1
There	is	a	dog	in	the	kennel.
There	are	two	dogs	in	the	kennel.
There	was	a	meadow	across	the	river.
There	were	some	meadows	across	the	river.
There	's	a	clown	in	this	class.
There	are	six	clowns	in	this	class.

In this pattern the verb is nearly always *be* (*is, are, was, were*). The most obvious exception is the verb *come* in the expression "there comes a time":

there   2 ← D → 1

| There | comes | a | time | when we have to give in. |
| There | comes | a | time | when such things don't matter. |

Notice that this structure word *there* is quite different from the adverb *there*. The adverb means "in that place." But the structure word doesn't have any place meaning; it doesn't have much meaning of any kind, in fact. It's just a way of getting the sentence started. Also the two words are usually pronounced differently. Structure word *there* is pronounced with light stress, and adverb *there* with heavy stress. From some speakers this has produced a difference in vowel sound, so that structure word *there* is sometimes pronounced with the vowel of *were*.

Notice also that whereas various other adverbs will substitute for adverb *there*, nothing will substitute for structure word *there* without changing the basic pattern of the sentence.

there	**2**	**D**	**1**	**4**
There	is	a	man	there.
There	is	a	man	here.
There	is	a	man	upstairs.
There	is	a	man	inside.
There	is	a	man	below.
There	is	a	talk	afterwards.

Another pattern in which the verb comes before the subject in statements is the pattern 4 2↔1. Usually there is something else at the end of the pattern — an adverb, an adjective, or some other structure:

4	**2** ←	**D**	→ **1**	
Seldom	were	the	men	there.
Seldom	was	the	train	on time.
Rarely	was	the	dinner	edible.

4	**2**	**D**	**1**	
Not once	were	the	boys	ready.
Not often	was		anyone	around.
Never	were	the	tools	where we left them.

The adverbs starting these sentences are the ones that most often occur in this pattern — time adverbs with some kind of negative meaning. Other verbs than *be* may occur, but with other verbs we use an auxiliary and make the pattern 4 A↔1 2 instead of 4 2↔1. Notice that the tie is between the auxiliary and the subject, not between the verb and the subject:

4	**A**	**D**	**1**	**2**	
Seldom	does		he	get	here on time.
Seldom	do	the	men	get	here on time.
Rarely	can		we	depend	on them.
Not once	did		he	admit	his stupidity.

This pattern used to occur much more frequently in English than it does now.

In addition to the examples given, we sometimes use a 4–2–1 pattern with the adverbs *here* and *there* and the verbs *go* and *come:*

There goes Charlie.   **Here comes Louie.**   **Here goes nothing.**

Where *there* occurs in this pattern, it is the adverb *there*, not the structure word *there*.

In written English we make some use of the statement pattern P D 1 2↔1:

P	**D**	**1**	**2**	**1**	
Into	the	room	came	Charlie.	
Down	the	stairs	walked	my father.	
In	the	sky	blazed	a new star.	

But these have a definite literary ring to them and would not be heard often in conversation.

By and large nowadays we like to put the subject before the verb in statements. The really important exception is the pattern with structure word *there:* "There is a man under the table." The other statement patterns with verb before the subject appear to be slowly dying out.

● EXERCISE 39

A. Write ten statement patterns using structure word *there:* "There was a man here," "There were some men here," "There's a basketball under the couch," etc. Let five of them have singular subjects and five plural subjects.

B. Read through a piece of written English and copy out the first five statements that contain structure word *there.* If you encounter any other statements with the verb before the subject, copy them out too. (Be sure they're statements, not questions.)

C. Write sentences from the following formulas.

1. there 2 D 1 4   **4.** 4 2 D 1 P D 1
2. there 2 D 1 P D 1   **5.** 4 A D 1 2
3. 4 2 D 1 4   **6.** 4 A D 1 2 P D 1

1—noun   2—verb   4—adverb
A—auxiliary   D—determiner   P—preposition

40: Review of function units

We have so far studied the following function units: subject, object, linking-verb complement, indirect object, object complement, noun modifier, and verb modifier. Remember that these are not word classes. Various classes of words occur in each of the function units. This is most obvious with noun and verb modifiers. Practically any kind of word can modify a noun, including other nouns. Practically any kind of word can modify a verb, including (though we haven't had examples yet) other verbs.

This variety isn't quite so obvious in function units other than noun and verb modifiers. The words most likely to occur as subjects and objects are nouns and pronouns. Indeed, practically all of our illustrations of these units have used nouns or pronouns. But we have seen that other word classes move into these units, too, occasionally:

ADJECTIVE AS SUBJECT	**The reckless** sometimes get hurt.
VERB CLUSTER AS SUBJECT	**Eating greedily** is bad manners.
ADVERB AS SUBJECT	**Now** would be a good time.
P-GROUP AS SUBJECT	**Over the fence** is out.

The subject is in a sense the most important of the function units. It occurs in all of the basic statement patterns; together with the verb it forms the heart of statement patterns. The central characteristic of the subject is that it is tied to the verb; that is, the number of the subject — singular or plural — affects the form of the verb.

None of the other function units occur in all of the basic statement patterns. In fact, the occurrence or non-occurrence of the other function units is what makes the difference between most of the basic patterns.

If a sentence consists of just a subject tied to a verb and no other function units, we have one sort of pattern (1 **2** or 1 **2 4**):

Children play.
Children play noisily.
Children play around.

If an object occurs, this function unit gives us a different pattern (1[a] **2** 1[b]):

Children play games.
Mothers beat children.

If a linking-verb complement occurs as a function unit, the pattern is different still. This pattern has a linking verb, of course, and it is the verb that gives the signal (1^a **2** 1^a):

> Children are little devils.
> Charlie became a good hitter.

The indirect object construction is a function unit giving still another basic pattern (1^a **2** 1^b 1^c):

> He tossed me the ball.
> She gave him the gate.

And then there is the pattern with the object complement as a function unit (1^a **2** 1^b 1^b):

> He called me a liar.
> We made him chairman.

In addition to these patterns, we have singled out three others of importance in English statements. The one with an adjective after a linking verb (1 **2L** 3):

> The idea sounded good.

The one with an adjective in place of a noun as object complement (1^a **2** 1^b 3):

> We thought him silly.

And the one with structure word *there* (**there** **2** 1):

> There are seventeen boys in the class.

All of these function units have meanings which can be described more or less accurately. The object names whatever undergoes the action; the indirect object names whatever receives the action, the person for whom the action is done; the linking-verb complement identifies the subject.

The subject has a complicated set of meanings. It often means doer of the action:

> Alfred strangled the tiger.
> The dentist smiled happily.

Or the subject may mean "that which is described":

> She was very pretty.
> The dentist seemed happy.

In another construction, the subject means that which is identified:

> Alice is my best friend.
> The speaker was a Hungarian.

Followed by the auxiliary *be* plus a past form of the verb, the subject usually means undergoer of the action:

> The tiger was strangled by Alfred.
> He was hit by a pitched ball.
> The dog was hit.

If this pattern has a noun after the verb, the subject usually means receiver of the action:

> The dog was given a bone.

But in this construction, too, it occasionally means undergoer of the action:

> A bone was given the dog.

The signals separating the last two are the determiners and the gender groups the nouns belong to, as was explained in Chapter 38.

Don't forget that we can recognize these meanings of the function units only *after* we have recognized the structure — with very few exceptions. Then the recognition of the various function units and their meanings is automatic. This is obvious when we use nonsense words in place of real nouns. We can still recognize subjects, objects, linking-verb complements, and so on, if we have enough other signals, and we can tell whether they mean doer of the action, undergoer of the action, receiver of the action, or whatever.

For instance, in the sentence "My gribble spooved a yellow

plong," all the function units and their meanings are clear. *Gribble* is the subject, and *plong* is an object. The gribble does the spooving, and the plong gets spooved.

In "Some ammit gave the drigglenitch a scrope," *ammit* is the subject, *drigglenitch* is the indirect object, and *scrope* is the object. In "The ramlip considered me a blengnether," *ramlip* is the subject, and *blengnether* is an object complement.

Naturally, we must have plenty of signals in the pattern in order for these nonsense words to be identified in one structure or another. These signals may be structure words, word endings, word order, gender, or various other things. Sometimes the signals will be in other nouns or verbs. For instance, if we wish to produce the linking-verb complement construction, we must use the real verbs *be* or *become*, because the signal lies in these:

The boggle was becoming a flib.

If we were to say "The boggle was droging a flib," the reader would probably take this as the more common 1ᵃ 2 1ᵇ pattern and would understand *flib* as an object.

Similarly, we would probably understand "The glug was gragging the burk a drimble" as the indirect-object construction. The less common objective-complement pattern needs to be signaled by one of a dozen or so real verbs — *consider, think, believe,* etc.

In our usual discourse we naturally use real words, or try to, and these are, of course, an important part of the signaling system. But the central fact remains that we don't derive the pattern from the meaning. We derive the meaning from the pattern, always.

● **EXERCISE 40**

A. Name the function unit of each of the nouns in the following sentences. If the noun is a subject, tell whether it means doer of the action, undergoer of the action, receiver of the action, that which is described, or that which is identified.

1. The stuboltz yawned and walked away. **2.** That lipe is obviously a scallaham. **3.** The fringle was drobing a helpless little squinch. **4.** A drope handed the nage a dipwit. **5.** At first I thought the sclub a callowdash. **6.** The roke had been badly scottled. **7.** The roke had been given a skimby. **8.** A skimby had been given the roke. **9.** When the dragert frappled in, the listwich burged the plex and doggered away. **10.** The stromp was rather crageful, so the nompers were carefully endarpled.

B. Write sentences from the following formulas. Notice the various function units that you get from the formulas and notice the different basic patterns.

1. D 1 2 3

2. D 1 2 4

3. D 1ᵃ 2 D 1ᵃ

4. there 2 D 1 4

5. there 2 D 1 P D 1

6. D 1ᵃ 2 D 1ᵇ

7. D 1ᵃ P D 1ᵇ 2 D 1ᶜ

8. D 1ᵃ 2 D 1ᵇ D 1ᶜ
       (he)   (he)   (it)

9. D 1ᵃ 2 1ᵇ D 1ᵇ
      (he) (he) (he)

10. D 1ᵃ 2 D 1ᵇ D 1ᶜ
       (he)   (it)   (th)

11. D 1ᵃ D 1ᵇ 2 D 1ᶜ D 1ᵈ
       (th)   (he)   (he)   (it)

12. D 1 A 2-ed
         (be)

13. D 3 1 P D 1 A 4 2-ed
              (be)

14. D 1ᵃ   A 2-ed D 1ᵇ
       (he) (be)   (it)

15. D 1ᵃ   A 2-ed D 1ᵇ
       (it) (be)   (he)

16. D 1ᵃ   A 2-ed D 1ᵇ
       (he–it) (be)   (it)

17. D 1ᵃ   A 2-ed D 1ᵇ
       (he) (be)   (he–it)

18. S D 3 1ᵃ 2 4, D 1ᵇ A 2-ing D 1ᶜ

19. D 1ᵃ S 2 D 3 1ᵇ 2 D 1ᶜ D 1ᵈ

20. D 1ᵃ P D 3 1ᵇ 2 4 S D 1ᶜ 2 D 1ᵈ D 1ᵈ

1–noun   2–verb   3–adjective   4–adverb
A–auxiliary   D–determiner   P–preposition   S–subordinator

Part Seven

JOINING

SENTENCE

PATTERNS

41 : Conjunctions

We now come to another kind of expansion that happens in English sentences. This kind of expansion happens when various sentence parts occur in pairs connected by structure words called **conjunctions**. As we shall see, conjunctions sometimes join whole sentence patterns. But first we shall examine them as they occur between parts of patterns.

Conjuctions are words that pattern like _and_. In our formulas we shall give conjunctions the symbol **C**. Conjunctions can crop up in almost any place in the patterns we have studied. Take a look at these examples.

In place of a simple 1 2 pattern, we can have 1 **C** 1 2, in which the conjunction joins two noun subjects:

1	2		1	C	1	2
Canaries	twitter.		Canaries	and	storks	twitter.
Charlie	wept.		Charlie	and	Alfred	wept.
Kindness	failed.		Kindness	and	charity	failed.
Sue	works.		Sue	and	Cynthia	work.

Notice something about the last example. Two subjects joined by *and* have the same effect on a verb that a plural subject has: "He *works*," but "He and his brother *work*."

In place of 1 2 3, we might have 1 C 1 2 3:

1	2	3
Canaries	are	stupid.
Henry	looks	sick.
Charlie	seems	groggy.

1	C	1	2	3
Canaries	and	storks	are	stupid.
He	and	Henry	look	sick.
Charlie	and	Glooba	seem	groggy.

Naturally the nouns that the conjunction connects don't have to be simple nouns. They can be noun clusters:

This canary **and** that stork are stupid.
The yellow canary on your right **and** the nearby stork are stupid.

The nouns joined by the conjunction might be objects:

D   1ᵃ   2   D   3   1ᵇ   C   D   3   1ᶜ
My father bought a yellow canary and a large stork.

Or they might be indirect objects:

D   1ᵃ   2   D   1ᵇ   C   D   1ᶜ   D   1ᵈ
My father gave the canary and the stork some seeds.

Or we might expand the pattern 1ᵃ 2 1ᵇ 1ᶜ so that each of the function units occurs as a pair, with a conjunction between:

D   1ᵃ   C   1ᵇ   2   D   1ᶜ   C   D   1ᵈ   D   1ᵉ   C   1ᶠ
My father and mother gave the canary and the stork some seeds and water.

Conjunctions may also join two verbs. In place of 1 2, we might have 1 2 C 2:

1	2	1	2	C	2
Canaries	twitter.	Canaries	twitter	and	sputter.
Charlie	wept.	Charlie	wept	and	struggled.
Nobody	left.	Nobody	rose	and	left.

In place of **1 2 3**, we might have **1 2 C 2 3**:

D	1	2	C	2	V	3
The	canary	seemed	and	was	rather	stupid.
The	dinner	smelled	and	tasted		awful.

Or a conjunction may join two adjectives:

D	1	2	3	C	3
The	canary	was	stupid	and	dirty.
The	dinner	tasted	foul	and	poisonous.

Or even — though it isn't so likely to happen in actual conversation or writing — we might have every part of a **1–2–3** pattern expanded:

1	C	1	2	C	2	3	C	3
Canaries	and	storks	seem	and	are	stupid	and	ugly.
Charlie	and	Allan	looked	and	smelled	fresh	and	clean.

We might go on, putting conjunctions between almost any pattern parts. Sometimes they join P-groups:

P-group	C	P-group	
The lamp	by the window	and	near the door	is broken.

Sometimes they join S-groups:

S-group	C	S-group
He'll come	if he feels like it	and	if he has time.

Conjunctions can expand practically any part of a sentence.

So far the only conjunction we have used is *and*. In most of the positions in which we have used *and*, *or* will substitute. So *or* is a conjunction too:

1	C	1	2	3	C	3
Canaries	and	storks	are	stupid	and	ugly.
Canaries	or	storks	are	stupid	or	ugly.

D	1	C	D	1	2	1	C	1
My	father	and	my	mother	kept	canaries	and	storks.
My	father	or	my	mother	kept	canaries	or	storks.

But is also a conjunction, though it won't occur in all the positions in which *and* and *or* occur. It commonly occurs between adjectives or adverbs:

1	2	3	C	3
Canaries	are	beautiful	and	stupid.
Canaries	are	beautiful	or	stupid.
Canaries	are	beautiful	but	stupid.

1	2	4	C	4
He	searched	quickly	and	carefully.
He	searched	quickly	but	carefully.

Now, look back over the examples given in this chapter and notice the punctuation. There isn't any punctuation inside the sentences; that is, there are no commas. We shall see in a moment that punctuation is used sometimes with conjunctions. But when the conjunction just stands between two parts of a sentence pattern, there is ordinarily no punctuation.

Sometimes instead of just a pair of sentence parts we have three or four with a conjunction between the last two. When that happens, commas are ordinarily used in this fashion:

1,	1,	1,	C	1	2	4

Charlie, Alfred, Eggstone, and Sam went away.

D	1,	D	1,	C	D	1	2	4

The man, the boy, and the donkey laughed heartily.

1	2	4,	2	D	1,	C	2	P	D	1

He turned around, saw his aunt, and fell to the floor.

D	1	2	3,	3,	C	V	3

The car was new, beautiful, and very expensive.

Combinations like these are called **series**. When we have a series of sentence parts, we have commas separating the several parts. In magazine and book writing there's usually a comma between the last two parts, in front of the conjunction, as in the examples above. In newspaper writing this last comma is often omitted. But when we have just a pair of sentence parts with a conjunction between them, we usually have no comma.

● EXERCISE 41

A. You'll remember that the constantly recurring larger parts of sentences are noun clusters, verb clusters, P-groups, and S-groups. Write five sentences in each of which two noun clusters are joined by a conjunction. Let the clusters be subjects, objects, indirect objects, or whatever occurs to you. An example would be "He bought a suit with two pairs of pants and a necktie which had a picture of Lincoln on it." Here the *and* connects the cluster *a suit with two pairs of pants* and the cluster *a necktie which had a picture of Lincoln on it.* The two clusters are objects.

B. Write five sentences in each of which two verb clusters are joined by a conjunction. An example would be "He bought a suit with two pairs of pants and gave it to his grandfather." The verb clusters are: *bought a suit with two pairs of pants* and *gave it to his grandfather.*

C. Write three sentences in each of which two P-groups are joined by a conjunction, like "The ball rolled across the floor and under the sofa."

D. Write three sentences in each of which two S-groups are joined by a conjunction, like "He was a fellow that I'd seen before but whose name I couldn't remember" or "I didn't know whether I could do it or whether I really wanted to."

E. Write sentences from the following formulas.

1. 1 C 1 2 3
2. D 1 C D 1 2 3
3. D 1 2 C 2

4. D 1 2 3 C 3
5. 1 C 1 2 3 C 3
6. D 1ᵃ 2 D 1ᵇ C D 1ᶜ D 1ᵈ

7. D 1ᵃ 2 D 1ᵇ C D 1ᶜ D 1ᵈ C D 1ᵉ
8. D 1ᵃ 2 D 1ᵇ C 2 D 1ᶜ
9. D 1 S 2 3 C 3 2 4
10. D 1ᵃ S 2 3 C 3 2 4 C 2 D 1ᵇ
11. D 1 2 P D 1 C P D 1
12. 1ᵃ 2 S 1ᵇ 2 D 1ᶜ C S D 1ᵈ 2 4

1—noun   2—verb   3—adjectives   4—adverb
C—conjunction   D—determiner   P—preposition   S—subordinator

42 : Conjunctions between statement patterns

In the examples given in the last chapter, all the conjunctions joined *parts* of sentence patterns. Conjunctions are also used to join whole sentence patterns, one to another.

Compare the four combinations below. In the first three, *and* joins parts of patterns. In the last one, the *and* joins two whole patterns. Notice the punctuation.

1   C   1   2
Canaries and storks twitter.

1   2   C   2
Canaries twitter and sputter.

1   C   1   2   C   2
Canaries and storks twitter and sputter.

1   2,   C   1   2
Canaries twitter, and storks sputter.

In the first sentence the conjunction joins two subjects. In the second it joins two verbs. In the third, one conjunction joins two subjects, and the second joins two verbs. But in the fourth sentence, the conjunction joins two statement patterns. It makes one sentence out of what would otherwise be two sentences.

Commonly when a conjunction joins two sentence patterns, we put a comma in front of the conjunction. When a conjunction joins parts of a pattern, we generally don't use a comma (unless we have a series).

Any of the statement patterns we have studied might be joined to another statement pattern by a conjunction:

1   2   3,   C   1   2   3
Charlie is handsome, and Eggstone is repulsive.

D   1   2   4,   C   D   1   2   4
The canaries chirped noisily, and the storks went away.

D   1ᵃ   2   1ᵇ,   C   D   1ᵃ*   2   1ᵇ
My father collected butterflies, and my uncle shot quail.

D   1ᵃ   2   D   1ᵇ   D   1ᶜ,   C   D   1ᵃ   2   D
The contractor gave the mayor a check, and the mayor phoned his

1ᵇ   D   1ᶜ
secretary her instructions.

In all of these examples the patterns joined are of the same type. But the patterns don't have to be of the same type. A conjunction can connect any kind of pattern to any other kind of pattern:

1ᵃ   2,   C   1ᵃ   2   3
Charlie slept, and Eggstone grew impatient.

D   1ᵃ   2   3,   C there 2 D   1ᵃ   P D   1ᵇ
The door was open, and there was no guard in the corridor.

1ᵃ 2   1ᵇ   D 3   1ᶜ,   C   1ᵃ   2   4
I gave Agnes a cold look, and she went away.

We have so far used *and* to illustrate the use of the conjunction. Half a dozen other conjunctions may replace *and* between two sentence patterns:

The door was open, **and** there was no guard in the corridor.
The door was open, **but** there was a guard in the corridor.
The door was open, **so** there was a guard in the corridor.
The door was open, **for** there was a guard in the corridor.
The door was open, **yet** there was no guard in the corridor.
The door was open, **or** there was a guard in the corridor.

---

* When we write formulas for sentences with two or more main patterns, like this one, it is simplest to begin a new series of noun letters (1ᵃ, 1ᵇ, 1ᶜ) with each new pattern.

Sometimes the word *nor* appears in this position as a conjunction. But when *nor* is used, the second pattern undergoes a reversal, as if it were a question, and there is commonly a negative word, like *not*, in the first pattern.

The door was not locked, nor was there a guard in the corridor.

Here is another example of the different conjunctions:

> **Eggstone grew impatient, and Charlie slept.**
> **Eggstone grew impatient, but Charlie slept.**
> **Eggstone grew impatient, so Charlie slept.**
> **Eggstone grew impatient, for Charlie slept.**
> **Eggstone grew impatient, yet Charlie slept.**
> **Eggstone grew impatient, or Charlie slept.**
> **Eggstone didn't grow impatient, nor did Charlie sleep.**

There's one other wrinkle in punctuating structures of this type. The comma after the first pattern is what might be called minimum punctuation. That is, you generally have at least that much. But you could have more: a semicolon or a period. All of the following would be conventional in American writing or printing:

> **Eggstone grew impatient, yet Charlie slept.**
> **Eggstone grew impatient; yet Charlie slept.**
> **Eggstone grew impatient. Yet Charlie slept.**

Nobody can put down rules on how to choose among punctuation variations of this type. A writer develops a feeling by becoming familiar with the structures and then watching what other writers do with them.

In general, the period is a sharp break, the semicolon somewhat less sharp, and the comma a minor pause. You'll do well to think of the semicolon as more like the period than like the comma. You can generally interchange periods and semicolons without offending anybody. But in some structures you can get into trouble if you interchange semicolons and commas.

As we have seen, you can interchange them all in the structure we are now concerned with: two sentence patterns with a conjunction between them. The comma tends to combine the patterns into one sentence; the semicolon or period breaks them into two. Good writers do it both ways, though the comma is more likely to appear when the two patterns are short, the semicolon or period when they are long.

One effect of using a semicolon or period in this position is to throw more emphasis on the second pattern. Compare these:

> Eggstone grew impatient, yet Charlie slept.
> Eggstone grew impatient. Yet Charlie slept.

The reader is brought to a stop at the end of the first pattern. He takes the second separately and thinks, "Good heavens! Imagine that silly Charlie sleeping while poor old Eggstone grew impatient."

That's about all there is to conjunctions. They may join parts of a pattern, or they may join two patterns. Conjunctions used to join parts of a pattern are principally *and* and *or*, with *but* coming in at certain positions. Conjunctions used to join two whole patterns are *and, or, nor, for, yet, so, but*. The most common punctuation practice is to use no punctuation when the conjunction joins two parts of a pattern but to use a comma (or a semicolon or a period) when it joins whole patterns.

Writers don't always observe even this practice, but it is fairly general.

● EXERCISE 42

A. Write ten sentences in which a conjunction joins two statement patterns. Use each of the seven conjunctions at least once.

B. Write a series of seven sentences like the "Eggstone grew impatient, and Charlie slept" example on page 208. The patterns remain the same, but the conjunction changes. You may find that you have to make slight variations in the patterns, however, according to which conjunction you use.

EXAMPLE   He's my uncle, and I like him.
He's my uncle, but I don't like him.
He's not my uncle, nor do I dislike him.

C. Write a sentence with a conjunction between two sentence patterns. Then write it twice more to illustrate the different types of punctuation described on page 208.

D. Write sentences from the following formulas.

1. 1 2 C 2
2. 1 C 1 2
3. 1 C 1 2 C 2

4. 1 2, C 1 2
5. 1 2 3, C 1 2 3
6. D 1 2 3, C 1 2

7. D 1 C D 1 2 4, C 1 2 4
8. D 1 2 3, C there 2 D 1 4
9. D 1^a 2 D 1^b, C D 1^a 2 D 1^b D 1^c
10. D 1 2 C 2 4, C D 1^a 2 D 1^b
11. D 1 2 P D 1 C P D 1, C D 1 2 4
12. 1, 1, C 1 2 4, C D 1^a 2 D 1^b
13. D 1^a 2 D 1^b, 2 D 1^c, C 2 4
14. D 1 2 3, 3, C 3, C D 1 2 3
15. 1^a 2 1^b D 1^c C D 1^d, C 1^a 2 1^b D 1^b

1—noun   2—verb   3—adjective   4—adverb
C—conjunction   D—determiner   P—preposition   S—subordinator

---

43 : Sentence connectors

Another structure group, different from conjunctions, sometimes stands between two sentence patterns. We will call this group **sentence connectors.** Sentence connectors are somewhat similar to conjunctions, but in some ways they pattern differently. They are punctuated differently too.

Sentence connectors are words that pattern like *therefore.* We will give them the symbol T, after the first letter in *therefore.* Here are their principal positions:

<pre>
  1   2;   T   1   2   3
</pre>
Charlie slept; **therefore** Eggstone grew impatient.
<pre>
  1   2;   1   T   2   3
</pre>
Charlie slept; Eggstone **therefore** grew impatient.
<pre>
  1   2;   1   2   3   T
</pre>
Charlie slept; Eggstone grew impatient **therefore.**

Notice how sentence connectors resemble conjunctions:

1. Both conjunctions and sentence connectors may join two sentence patterns.

2. Both conjunctions and sentence connectors may stand directly between the patterns they join.

Now notice how they are different:

1. Conjunctions may join parts of patterns; sentence connectors just join whole patterns. *Therefore* could replace *and* in the sentence "Canaries twitter, and storks sputter." But *therefore* could not replace *and* in the sentence "Canaries and storks twitter and sputter."

2. When they join whole patterns, conjunctions must stand directly between the patterns. Sentence connectors may stand directly between the patterns or may come at the end of the second pattern or may come in the middle of the second pattern. *And* could replace *therefore* in the sentence "Canaries twitter; therefore storks sputter." But *and* could not replace *therefore* in "Canaries twitter; storks therefore sputter" or in "Canaries twitter; storks sputter therefore."

A dozen or so words occur commonly as sentence connectors. Here are some examples:

Charlie slept; **therefore** Eggstone grew impatient.
Charlie slept; **consequently** Eggstone grew impatient.
Charlie slept; **however,** Eggstone grew impatient.
Charlie slept; **moreover,** Eggstone grew impatient.
Charlie slept; **hence** Eggstone grew impatient.

The door was open; **therefore** there was a guard in the hall.
The door was open; **nevertheless** there was no guard in the hall.

The door was open; **furthermore** the hall was unguarded.
The door was open; **besides,** the hall was unguarded.
The door was open; **indeed** the whole place was open.
The door was open; **thus** we managed to escape.

All of these will move around in the second pattern, just as *therefore* will:

Charlie slept; Eggstone **consequently** grew impatient.
Charlie slept; Eggstone, **however,** remained alert.
The door was open; the hall, **furthermore,** was unguarded.
The door was open; the whole place, **indeed,** was open.
The door was open; the whole place was open, **indeed.**

The punctuation here is worth paying some attention to. When a sentence connector joins two patterns, you have a semicolon or a period at the end of the first pattern:

The boys went away; however, the girls stayed awhile.
The boys went away. However, the girls stayed awhile.

He looked hungry; I therefore offered him some food.
He looked hungry. I therefore offered him some food.
He looked hungry. I offered him some food therefore.

It doesn't make much difference whether you have a semicolon or a period. If you want the reader to tend to bring the patterns together, you use a semicolon; if you want him to tend to keep them apart, you use a period. But you cannot have a comma or no punctuation at all.

Another question is whether you put a comma after the *T* word or not. This is harder to answer. Sometimes you do and sometimes you don't.

Writers of English used to use more punctuation than they do now. It used to be that a sentence connector at the beginning of a pattern practically always had a comma after it. At the end of the pattern, it always had a comma in front of it. In the middle there was a comma on each side.

This isn't always so now. If you'll look back at the examples, you'll see that *however* is set off by commas in all positions.* So are *moreover* and *besides*. *Furthermore* and *indeed* are set off in some sentences. The others are not set off. This represents fairly common practice among modern American writers. Use your judgment on these words. Reading the sentence aloud might help, and watching what other writers do surely will.

Anyway the important thing is to get a semicolon or a period after the first pattern whenever a *T* word occurs in the second.

---

* There's a peculiarity about *however* that sometimes gives a little trouble. It sometimes is used as a subordinator, as in these sentences:

However I do it, I always get it wrong.   **I don't like fish however it is cooked.**

When it patterns like *because* or *whenever*, as here, you don't put a comma after it.

● **EXERCISE 43**

A. Write ten sentences, using a different sentence connector in each.

B. Write each of the ten sentences again, shifting the position of the sentence connector.

C. In which of the twenty sentences could a conjunction be substituted for the sentence connector? What conjunction might occur? In which sentences could no conjunction be substituted?

D. Write sentences from the following formulas.

1. 1 2; T 1 2

2. 1 2; T 1 2 3

3. 1 2; 1 2 3 T

4. D 1 2 4; T D 1ᵃ 2 D 1ᵇ

5. D 1ᵃ 2 D 1ᵇ, C D 1 2 4

6. 1 C 1 2 4; T D 1ᵃ 2 D 1ᵃ

7. there 2 D 1 4; T D 1ᵃ 2 D 1ᵇ

8. D 1ᵃ 2 D 1ᵇ; D 1ᵃ 2 D 1ᵇ T

9. D 1 2 C 2 4, C D 1ᵃ 2 D 1ᵇ C D 1ᶜ

10. D 1ᵃ 2 D 1ᵇ; D 1 T 2 4

11. D 1ᵃ 2 D 1ᵇ D 1ᶜ; T there 2 D 1 P D 1

12. D 1 2 3; D 1ᵃ T 1ᵇ D 1ᵇ

1—noun   2—verb   3—adjective   4—adverb

C—conjunction   D—determiner   P—preposition   T—sentence connector

44: Punctuation
and how it grew

We have been concerned in the last two chapters with punctuating sentence patterns, and we shall have more to say about punctuation in the chapters that follow. Perhaps it would be a good idea to pause here to think a little bit about punctuation in general. Who decides what punctuation is proper? How did punctuation begin?

Punctuation is a part of writing, but it isn't nearly as old as writing is. The punctuation marks that we use today are only a few hundred years old, but men have been writing for at least six thousand years. The oldest kind of writing is picture writing. If you wanted to write "man," you just drew a picture of a man. If you wanted to write "the man is eating," you drew a picture of a man eating. A modern example of picture writing is Chinese. The Chinese characters don't look much like pictures, because they have changed over the centuries, but that's how they began.

Picture writing isn't very satisfactory. You have to draw too many pictures. It's very hard to learn to read and write Chinese because you have to memorize thousands of figures and what they stand for.

The great step forward in writing was taken about three thousand years ago. That was when the notion developed of making marks that stand not for words or ideas but for sounds. This was a great advance because it was much simpler. There's no limit to the number of ideas that a language can express. But there's a strict limit to the number of distinctive sounds that it uses: twenty or thirty or forty. So instead of having five thousand different figures in the writing system, it was possible to write with a couple of dozen.

The ancient Phoenicians and the ancient Greeks had developed this new system of writing. (That's probably one reason why they became so powerful.) But they didn't develop a punctuation system. The Greeks wrote all in large letters, with no separation between words or patterns, like this:

THISISWHATANCIENTGREEKLOOKEDLIKEOFCOURSEITISNTGREEK
ITSENGLISH

The Romans, whose civilization followed the Greek civilization, slowly improved the writing system. They learned to make a distinction between small letters and large letters and to reserve the large letters for special occasions. In the manuscripts of the Middle Ages it was customary to make the first letter in a book or a chapter a large and beautifully decorated letter — a picture, actually — and to make all the others small. This first letter, since it came at the head of the manuscript, was called a "capital," from the Latin word for "head," *caput*.

Capital letters came to be used in other places besides the head of a chapter, and when printing was invented, in the fifteenth century, the printers learned to make two sets of letters, one small and one large. As they worked, they kept the two sets in separate cases on a slanting stand in front of them. The little letters were in the lower case, and the large ones were in the upper. So printers usually speak not of small letters and capital letters but of lower-case and upper-case letters.

Practices in the use of capitals have changed gradually since the invention of printing. It used to be customary to use a capital letter not only at the beginning of each sentence but also for the first letter of each noun. Now we capitalize just proper nouns, words derived from proper nouns, and the pronoun *I*, in addition to the first word in the sentence.

Punctuation, too, was a growth of the Middle Ages and the early days of printing. The first people to use anything like our modern punctuation were priests and preachers, who would mark their manuscripts so they would know where to pause in delivering their sermons. They used squiggles and dots and combinations of squiggles and dots, and the early printers cast type to represent these marks too. From these grew our commas, semicolons, and periods.

The people who had most say in establishing the conventions of capitalization and punctuation (and spelling too, incidentally) were the printers of the sixteenth and seventeenth centuries. In 1500 everything was chaos, and everyone rode off in his own direction. But by 1700 regular habits and ways of punctuating had gradually grown and become established. Punctuation has changed since 1700 but slowly and in a more or less uniform way.

The people who rule on punctuation nowadays and keep it in line are not so much the printers as the editors and publishers — the people who put out books, magazines, and newspapers. When an editor receives a manuscript, he goes over it and makes sure that it conforms to usual practices in punctuation (and in other matters too) before he sends it on to the printer. This ensures that the punctuation in the books we read is pretty much alike, and this is a break for the reader. When he sees a semicolon, he knows it means that a certain kind of structure is in progress and not just that the writer is fond of semicolons. This signal makes for faster and more accurate reading.

Even so, punctuation practice changes as reading skill grows. As a people, we seem to be growing more and more skillful in reading. Fifteen hundred years ago nobody read without moving the lips, actually forming the sounds that the letters represented. Nowadays most people can read with the lips tightly closed. Furthermore, we have learned to pick up larger and larger stretches with single movements of the eye.

One result of this is that modern writers use less punctuation than writers did a hundred years ago. We try not to chop up the line with marks but to leave it open, so that the reader can take a longer sweep. In addition there has been a shifting of the marks that are used. Often the modern writer uses no punctuation where commas were formerly used, uses commas where semicolons were used, and semicolons where earlier writers would have used periods. The comma tends to move into semicolon territory and the semicolon into period territory.

Punctuation is complicated, as language is complicated. You can't expect to find half a dozen rules that will solve all your punctuation problems. Where we can, we will link up punctuation practices with sentence patterns and with certain structure groups — like conjunctions, sentence connectors, and subordinators. But even here it is just general practice that is being described. Since writers and editors are individuals in a free country, they don't always feel bound to keep in the same grooves.

Later on we will talk about certain features of the sound system called **intonation** and show how this is connected to punctuation habits.

Always the best teachers of punctuation are the experts — the professional writers. As you read, notice the different punctuation marks that are used and observe how they relate to the patterns in the sentence. As you write, imitate and experiment.

● **EXERCISE 44**

A. You can learn how to punctuate just by reading, if you keep your eyes open and notice the structures that are punctuated. Get a magazine and a newspaper and see what they do about punctuating the following structures. Notice whether there is any difference in their practices. There may be.

1. How are series of structures punctuated? That is, where would commas be used in expressions like "The man the boy and the donkey went through the gate walked over the hill and lay down in the grass"? Is newspaper practice the same as magazine practice?

2. Do commas always occur before conjunctions that join two sentence patterns? Are they ever omitted? Is any other kind of punctuation ever used?

3. When an S-group occurs before a sentence pattern ("When she got there the cupboard was bare"), do the editors use a comma after the S-group or not?

4. A colon (:) consists of two dots, one above the other. Colons are not used in the same way as semicolons. See if you can find three or four colons in your magazine or newspaper. What structures come before the colons? What structures come after them?

B. If you can get hold of a book printed in the eighteenth century or earlier, study the punctuation of a page or two. Probably it will seem to you overpunctuated by modern standards.

1. If the material were being printed today, what changes do you think would be made?

2. Notice the capitalization too. Do you find any differences between the older practices and ours?

3. Do you find any differences in spelling?

---

45 : Conjunctions, sentence connectors, and subordinators

The punctuation used between statement patterns in present-day English writing is based very largely on the contrast of three structure groups: conjunctions, sentence connectors, and subordinators. Anyone studying punctuation will find it very convenient to have these three groups firmly in mind and be able to tell them apart.

A **conjunction,** you will remember, is a word that patterns like *and*. It has two distinct possibilities. It may stand between parts of patterns.

The donkey **and** the dog strolled down the road.
The donkey strolled down the road **and** observed the scenery.
We knew that it was late **and** that we had to hurry.

Or it may stand between whole patterns:

The donkey strolled down the road, **and** the dog observed the scenery.
We knew that it was late, **but** there was nothing we could do about it.

A **sentence connector** is a word that patterns like *therefore*. It regularly joins two patterns, not parts of patterns. It occurs either at the beginning of the second pattern or inside the second pattern or at the end of the second pattern:

We knew it was late; **therefore** we hurried.
We knew it was late; we **therefore** hurried.
We knew it was late; we didn't hurry, **however**.

Subordinators are of two types. First we have forms like *who, whose, whom, which, that*. These occur in patterns that are parts of noun clusters or verb clusters. Their feature is that they not only subordinate the pattern but also are a part of the pattern. They replace the subject or object or a determiner in the pattern they subordinate.

The fellow **who** helped most was Charlie.
I wonder **which** he meant.
These are the people **whose** car got hit.

Subordinators of this type aren't very easily confused with conjunctions or sentence connectors, and we won't say any more about them here.

The other kind of subordinators are those that pattern like *because*. These subordinators stand at the head of a sentence pattern and make that pattern a part of another pattern. The subordinated pattern can come either before the other pattern or after it:

Because he helped us, we gave him some money.
We gave him some money **because** he helped us.

So we have three groups to keep separate:

CONJUNCTIONS

and	or	nor	so
but	for	yet	

SENTENCE CONNECTORS

therefore	however	hence	indeed	consequently	nevertheless
also	moreover	thus	in fact	accordingly	furthermore

SUBORDINATORS

when	because	if	after	provided	whereas
where	since	as	before	whenever	that
while	whether	lest	until	wherever	

One way to keep the groups separate, obviously, is to memo-rize the lists. But since the members of the different groups shift around a little and sometimes turn up in unexpected places, it is better to understand the patterning. Here is how they are alike and how they are different.

The three groups share one position: they will all stand between two sentence patterns:

Sentence pattern, **and** sentence pattern.
Sentence pattern; **therefore** sentence pattern.
Sentence pattern **because** sentence pattern.

That is, we can say:

The men went away, **and** the boys were noisy.
The men went away; **therefore** the boys were noisy.
The men went away **because** the boys were noisy.

Sentence connectors are different because they move around in the second pattern and conjunctions and subordinators don't:

Sentence pattern; **therefore** sentence pattern.
Sentence pattern; sentence **therefore** pattern.
Sentence pattern; sentence pattern **therefore.**

We can say:

> The men went away; **therefore** the boys were noisy.
> The men went away; the boys, **therefore,** were noisy.
> The men went away; the boys were noisy, **therefore.**

But conjunctions and subordinators do not pattern this way. We do not say "The men went away; the boys, and, were noisy" or "The men went away; the boys were noisy because."

Subordinators are different because the whole subordinated pattern can appear before the other pattern; at least this is true for most subordinators:

> Sentence pattern **because** sentence pattern.
> **Because** sentence pattern, sentence pattern.

We can say:

> The men went away **because** the boys were noisy.
> **Because** the boys were noisy, the men went away.

Conjunctions and sentence connectors do not pattern this way. We do not say "And the boys were noisy, the men went away" or "Therefore the boys were noisy, the men went away."

So that's the difference. Conjunctions, sentence connectors, and subordinators all join patterns. Conjunctions must stand between the patterns they join; sentence connectors may stand between the patterns or may occur in or after the second pattern. Subordinators appear at the head of the pattern, not in or after it, but the whole pattern may occur either at the beginning or at the end of the sentence.

Since the three groups pattern differently, they have come to have different structural meanings, and they are punctuated differently by American writers and editors. Here are the usual ways of punctuating them in the shared position:

CONJUNCTIONS

> The men went away, and the boys were noisy.
> The men went away; and the boys were noisy.
> The men went away. And the boys were noisy.

SENTENCE CONNECTORS

The men went away; therefore the boys were noisy.

The men went away. Therefore the boys were noisy.

SUBORDINATORS

The men went away because the boys were noisy.

Some subordinators sometimes have a comma before them in this position. We'll take that up when we study intonation.

● **EXERCISE 45**

A. Make up sentences using the words below to connect sentence patterns. Use each word in each of its possible positions; that will mean one sentence for each conjunction, two for each subordinator, and three for each sentence connector.

1. however	**3.** since	**5.** nevertheless
2. for	**4.** but	**6.** while

B. Make up sentences using the words below to connect sentence patterns. Use them only in the shared position, between the patterns, but punctuate them in all the ways shown on pages 221–22; that will mean three sentences for each conjunction, two for each sentence connector, and one for each subordinator.

1. yet	**3.** consequently	**5.** furthermore
2. if	**4.** so	**6.** until

C. Write sentences from the following formulas.

1. D 1 2 4, C D 1 2 4   **3.** D 1 2 4; T D 1^a 2 D 1^b

2. D 1^a 2 D 1^b S D 1 2 3   **4.** D 1 2 4; D 1^a 2 D 1^b T

5. D 1 2 4, C there 2 D 1 P D 1

6. D 1 2 4; there 2 D 1 4 T

7. D 1^a 2 D 1^b D 1^c S D 1 2

8. D 1 2 3; T D 1^a 2 D 1^b S D 1 2

9. S D 1 2 4, D 1^a 2 D 1^b, C D 1 2

10. S D 1 2 3, 1^a 2 D 1^b; T 1 2 S D 1 2 4

1—noun   2—verb   3—adjective   4—adverb
C—conjunction   D—determiner   P—preposition   S—subordinator
T—sentence connector

Part Eight.

INTONATION

AND

PUNCTUATION

46 : Phonemes

In punctuating, it sometimes helps to pay attention not only to the word classes that make up the patterns but also to the way the patterns would sound if we spoke them. In order to do this we will take a look at the sound system of English.

English speech is made up, first of all, of thirty-three sound units which we call **phonemes.** A phoneme is not exactly a single sound. It is more a collection of similar sounds which, in spite of their slight differences, sound the same to a native speaker of the language. If the native speaker hears them as the same, they are the same for him, and they make up one phoneme.

For example, say the word *papa* with your hand an inch or so in front of your mouth. You may feel a puff of breath after the first *p* but not after the second. These two sounds are actually quite different. Speakers of some languages, hearing these sounds, would be surprised to learn that we use the same letter to indicate them. The *p* in *spin* is a third sound, and the *p* in *top* a fourth. But to a speaker of English they are all the same, and we say that they are varieties of the phoneme /p/. (We enclose phonemes in diagonal lines.)

Different languages have different numbers of phonemes.

English, as was said, has thirty-three — twenty-four consonants and nine vowels.

The ordinary alphabet won't work for writing English phonemes because, among other things, it has only twenty-six letters. For this reason we have to use a special phonemic alphabet when we want to indicate actual sounds. Here is the alphabet, with key words to show what sounds the letters stand for. Some of the key words may be misleading, because some of the words are pronounced differently in different parts of the country. But this ought to give you a general idea.

VOWELS

/i/	the vowel sound in *sit, bit, hit, pin*
/e/	the vowel sound in *set, bet, men, bed*
/æ/	the vowel sound in *hat, bat, can, mad*
/ɨ/	the vowel sound in *just,* as it is usually pronounced in "He was just here"
/ə/	the vowel sound in *but, done, sun, mud*
/a/	the vowel sound in *hot, not, cot.* (But some speakers have /ɔ/ in these words.)
/u/	the vowel sound in *put, book, foot*
/o/	the first part of the vowel sound in *go, dome, poke*
/ɔ/	the vowel sound in *law, wash, taught*

CONSONANTS

/p/	the first sound in *pat*		— *th* — in ordinary spelling, but a single sound)
/t/	the first sound in *tap*		
/k/	the first sound in *cat*	/s/	the first sound in *sack*
/b/	the first sound in *bat*	/š/	the sound spelled *sh* in *shack*
/d/	the first sound in *dot*	/v/	the first sound in *vine*
/g/	the first sound in *get*	/ð/	the sound spelled *th* in *then* (A different sound from the sound in *thin*)
/c/	the sounds spelled *ch* in *church* (A single sound)		
/j/	the first sound in *jury*	/z/	the first sound in *zeal*
/f/	the first sound in *find*	/ž/	the sound spelled *s* in *measure*
/θ/	the first sound in *thin* (Spelled with two letters	/m/	the first sound in *met*

CONSONANTS

/n/	the first sound in *net*	/r/	the first sound in *rag*
/ŋ/	the sound spelled *ng* in *sing*	/w/	the first sound in *wet*
	(A single sound)	/y/	the first sound in *yet*
/l/	the first sound in *lag*	/h/	the first sound in *hit*

The last three phonemes occur not only as consonants but also as vowels. They combine with some of the simple vowels listed above to make vowel combinations, or diphthongs. Here are some examples:

/iy/	the vowel sound in *beet*	/ow/	the vowel sound in *go*
/ey/	the vowel sound in *mate*	/aw/	the vowel sound in *house*
/ay/	the vowel sound in *mine*	/uw/	the vowel sound in *soon*
/ɔy/	the vowel sound in *boy*	/eh/	the vowel sound in *yeah*

Now here are some whole words written first in ordinary spelling and second in phonemic spelling. Remember that words are sometimes pronounced differently by different people or even by the same person at different times. These pronunciations would occur for many speakers if the words were uttered separately. In connected speech some would be different.

cat	/kæt/	bridge	/brij/	boat	/bowt/
bet	/bet/	length	/leŋkθ/	knight	/nayt/
ship	/šip/	said	/sed/	those	/ðowz/
sing	/siŋ/	thatch	/θæc/	finger	/fiŋgər/
either	/iyðər/	about	/əbawt/	singer	/siŋər/
bought	/bɔt/	dream	/driym/	warmth	/wɔrmpθ/
moon	/muwn̩/	peel	/piyl/	name	/neym/
thug	/θəg/	sack	/sæk/	shame	/šeym/

You will see that phonemic spelling is quite different from ordinary spelling. Ordinary spelling used to be much more phonemic than it is now. What has happened is that the spelling became more or less fixed several centuries ago, while the language went right on changing. So now we still put in letters for sounds that ceased to be pronounced hundreds of years ago, and often we don't put in letters for sounds that are pronounced now.

This is what makes it hard to spell English. We have many letters that represent different sounds. For instance the letter *a* stands for /æ/ in *hat*, for /ey/ in *name*, for /ə/ in *about*, for /a/ in *father*, and for /ɔ/ in *hall*. The combination *ng* stands for /ŋ/ in *sing* and *singer* but for /ŋg/ in *finger* and for /ŋk/ in *length*.

On the other hand, we often have the same sound represented by two or more different letters. The sound /ay/ occurs in *my*, *shine*, and *light*. The sound /e/ occurs in *bet*, *said*, and *bread*.

There is one good thing that can be said about English spelling: it's standard. That is, we all spell words the same way, no matter how we pronounce them. This is what makes it possible for people all over the English-speaking world to read one another's writing. There are tremendous differences in our pronunciations, but we all spell about the same.

● EXERCISE 46

A. It isn't very hard to learn to read phonemic writing. At first one has to keep checking back to the alphabet and the key words, but before long one remembers the letters, and since each letter stands for just one sound, the reading is easy. Try it on these words. Write each one as it would appear in ordinary spelling.

1. /kæt/	13. /buk/	24. /steyj/	35. /pæc/
2. /kæp/	14. /ðis/	25. /jəj/	36. /məðər/
3. /træp/	15. /θik/	26. /yuw/	37. /mežər/
4. /trik/	16. /riŋ/	27. /yuwθ/	38. /pležər/
5. /triyt/	17. /klæŋ/	28. /hwət/	39. /ciyp/
6. /kriym/	18. /klæn/	29. /huw/	40. /brɔl/
7. /teym/	19. /klæm/	30. /deynjər/	41. /kɔt/
8. /teyk/	20. /šeyk/	31. /ərest/	42. /bay/
9. /howl/	21. /rowzəz/	32. /tiycər/	43. /hæpi/
10. /hawl/	22. /ərawnd/	33. /futbɔl/	44. /bətən/
11. /towz/	23. /cip/	34. /growiŋ/	45. /fowniym/
12. /bət/			

B. Now try some phonemic writing. Put the following words into phonemic spelling. If you feel that a word has more than one pronunciation, write the one that you think you would be most likely to use.

1. cat	**13.** sting	**24.** not	**35.** machine
2. bat	**14.** help	**25.** note	**36.** much
3. ban	**15.** neat	**26.** such	**37.** event
4. bang	**16.** bee	**27.** shave	**38.** dreary
5. hang	**17.** buy	**28.** scratch	**39.** broom
6. hung	**18.** bough	**29.** race	**40.** English
7. ham	**19.** brought	**30.** rapid	**41.** brother
8. hail	**20.** blush	**31.** plague	**42.** which
9. pale	**21.** chick	**32.** oven	**43.** photograph
10. mud	**22.** foot	**33.** father	**44.** strength
11. dread	**23.** suit	**34.** thorn	**45.** asked
12. flap			

---

47 : Intonation

Besides the thirty-three vowels and consonants, English has a series of phonemes of an entirely different kind — or rather of three different kinds. These are the features called **stress, pitch,** and **juncture.** Taken together, stress, pitch, and juncture make up what we call **intonation.** Every time we utter a sentence, we use some kind of intonation, and the meaning of our sentences changes according to the intonation we use.

The whole story of English intonation is a very complicated matter, and we won't try to explain all the details here. But it is easy to see some of the contrasts of intonation and to realize that we react accurately to them whenever we hear English.

STRESS

Probably the simplest feature of intonation to understand is stress. **Stress** is simply the loudness or softness with which we utter the different syllables in the speech stream. We make use of stress all the time in forming our sentence patterns. For instance, if we use the word *subject* as a noun, we pronounce the *sub* louder than the *ject:*

What's the súbject?

But if we use it as a verb, we pronounce the *ject* part louder:

We'll subjéct him to an examination.

We have the same contrast in *íncrease* and *incréase*, *prótest* and *protést*, *réfuse* and *refúse*, and many other pairs.

But that's by no means all there is to stress in English. Each speaker of English makes use of four different stresses — four degrees of loudness — when he speaks his sentences. The names and symbols for them are these:

Primary, the loudest degree /´/
Secondary, the next to loudest /^/
Tertiary, the third from loudest /ˋ/
Weak, the softest /˘/

Here's a sentence that has all of them:

The Whíte Hoùse is a whĭte hoûse.

If you'll pronounce the sentence naturally, you'll see that you don't say "White House" quite as you say "white house." The difference is mainly in the stress.

Stress usually distinguishes adjectives modifying nouns from nouns modifying nouns. You may remember our ambiguous sentence "He's a sweet salesman," where you can't tell whether the salesman is sweet or sells candy. But this is ambiguous in writing only. In speech, *sweet* will have secondary stress if it's an adjective but primary stress if it's a noun.

He's a sweet salesman.   (The salesman is sweet.)
He's a sweet salesman.   (He sells candy.)

Stress is so important that if the speaker gets the stresses mixed up the result is likely to be nonsense. You might not be surprised to get a "writing desk" for Christmas. But you would probably be very much surprised if you got a "writing desk."

PITCH

The second feature of intonation is pitch. **Pitch** is caused by the vibration of the sounds as they come from our mouths. If they vibrate fast — say 800 times a second — we get what we call **high pitch.** If they vibrate slowly — say 200 times a second — we get **low pitch.**

We are all familiar with pitch, because we know, for example, that women's voices are generally higher than men's and that adults' voices are lower than children's. What most people don't realize, however, is that each of us — whether his voice is generally high or generally low — makes use of four contrasting pitch points or pitch phonemes. We give these numbers, not names. The highest pitch phoneme is /4/; the next to highest is /3/; the next to lowest is /2/; the lowest is /1/.

We can also indicate them by drawing lines above and below the letters. A line just over the letters means pitch /3/; a line well above the letters means pitch /4/; a line just under the letters means pitch /2/; and a line well below the letters means pitch /1/.

For instance, suppose we want to mark the pitch on the sentence "What are you doing?" This could be said in several ways, but the most common way would be to begin on pitch /2/, to stay on that until the stressed syllable is reached, to rise to /3/ on the stressed syllable, and then to fall to /1/. Like this:

What are you do ing?

We use pitch for many purposes in our sentences. It is closely bound up with the structural patterns of our sentences. But we also use it to express such meanings as surprise, indignation, insistence, panic, boredom, and many others. For example, one could put a note of panic into the question "What are you doing?" by rising to the fourth pitch instead of the third:

What are you ⌐do⌐ing?

Or if one is just sort of exasperated with the other person and what he's doing, he might say:

What ⌐are⌐ you ⌐do⌐ing?

Often we make jokes by deliberately using the wrong pitch. Here's one:

What did you put in the ⌐sa⌐lad? Alice?

In place of:

What did you put in the ⌐sa⌐lad, Alice?

JUNCTURE

The third part of intonation is juncture. **Juncture** is a way of breaking or stopping the speech flow. English intonation seems to go in fours, and there are four junctures just as there are four stresses and four pitches; the first one, however, is quite different from the other three. Junctures are named after the symbols used to indicate them.

The first juncture is called **plus juncture** because it is marked with a plus sign: $/+/$.

The second juncture is called **single bar juncture.** It is marked with one upright line or bar: $/|/$.

The third juncture is called **double bar juncture.** It is marked with two upright lines: $/\|/$.

The last juncture is called **double cross juncture.** It is marked with two crossing lines: $/\#/$.

Plus juncture is a special kind of break between phonemes. It is the difference between *I scream* and *ice cream*. In *I scream* we have plus juncture before the /s/ phoneme: /ay+skriym/. In *ice cream* the plus juncture comes after the /s/ phoneme: /ays+kriym/. The reason that the two sounds are different is that in *I scream* we have the kind of /s/ that comes at the beginning of a word and the kind of /k/ that comes after /s/; but in *ice cream* we have the kind of /s/ that comes at the end of a word and the kind of /k/ that comes at the beginning. This is what plus juncture does; it breaks up the phonemic flow and makes words, although the phonemic words are not always identical with the ones we commonly write.

The other junctures come at the end of groups of words. These junctures are closely tied up with stress and pitch. If a sentence has only one primary (loudest) stress, then we won't have any junctures inside the sentence. But if we have two primary stresses, then we will have a single bar or double bar juncture between them.

For instance, we can say the sentence "The man on your right is her brother" with just one primary stress; then there is no juncture inside the sentence:

The man on your right is her bróther.

Or we can say it with two primary stresses; then there will be a single bar juncture after the first primary stress:

The man on your ríght | is her bróther.

If there are three primary stresses, there will be two single bar junctures:

The mán | on your ríght | is her bróther.

This would be a very slow and emphatic way of saying the sentence.

The difference between single bar, double bar, and double cross juncture is a matter of what happens to the pitch. If the pitch stays the same, we have single bar; if it goes up a little (but not to the next pitch level) we have double bar; if it goes down a little, we have double cross.

The sentence "The man digging in the garden is Mr. Jones" might have one or two single bar junctures, depending on the number of primary stresses; or it might have none at all:

> The mán | digging in the gárden | is Mr. Jónes.
>
> The man digging in the gárden | is Mr. Jónes.
>
> The man digging in the garden is Mr. Jónes.

But the sentence "Mr. Jones, digging in his garden, found a worm" would be pronounced quite differently. There would be three primary stresses with double bar junctures separating them:

> Mr. Jónes ‖ digging in his gárden ‖ found a wórm.

That is, the pitch would rise slightly after *Jones* and after *garden*. The pitch would be something like this:

> Mr. ⌐Jon⌐es, digging in his ⌐gar⌐den, found a ⌐wo⌐rm

Double bar juncture corresponds more or less to a comma in writing.

Double cross juncture is a slight drop in pitch. Notice in the last example that a slight drop is shown at the very end, after *worm*. This is a double cross juncture, in its usual place at the end of a sentence:

> Mr. Jones ‖ digging in his garden ‖ found a worm #

By and large, double cross junctures in speech correspond to semicolons and periods in writing.

Here are a few more examples showing primary stresses and the different junctures. There would be other ways of saying some of these of course:

> Where are you góing #
>
> Where áre | you góing #

Running into the house ‖ Agnes told us the news #

We invited Al ‖ who had a car #

Al ‖ who had a car ‖ offered to take us #

Al had a car # therefore we had to invite him #

Al had a car # he wouldn't ‖ however ‖ let us use it #

People who own cars are pretty lucky #

People who own cars | are pretty lucky #

● EXERCISE 47

A. Intonation is hard to study because it is so difficult to say something and listen to it at the same time. We won't try to identify all the stresses, pitches, and junctures as they occur in our sentences. All we need to do is develop a general awareness of some of the contrasts and notice how they affect sentence meaning. Say the following groups of sentences as naturally as you can. Can you detect a difference in stress? On what words do the primary stresses fall?

1. He's a good salesman.
He's a car salesman.
2. That's a blackbird.
That's a black bird.
3. He looks like his mother   (not his father).
He looks like his mother   (but acts like his father).
He looks like his mother   (but his sister doesn't).

B. Frequently we shift the primary stress to get a different emphasis or to express a different feeling. Pronounce the following sentences observing the different locations of the primary stress. What changes in meaning or feeling are indicated?

1. Where are you going?

2. Where are you going?

3. Where are you going?

4. Where are you going?

5. Where are you going?

C. Pronounce the following pairs of sentences as naturally as possible. Where does the pitch rise and fall? How do the sentences in each pair differ in meaning?

1. Was he mad?
   Was he mad!

2. Are you reading Shakespeare?
   Are you reading, Shakespeare?

3. Why are you washing, Alice?
   Why are you washing Alice?

4. Watch this rock skip.
   Watch this rock, Skip.

5. What are you eating, Charlie?
   What are you eating? Charlie?

D. The phonemes in *yellow drug* and *yellowed rug* are the same: /yelowdrəg/. What is the difference in the pronunciation? Spell each expression in phonemic spelling, this time putting in the plus juncture. Do the same for these pairs.

1. a name — an aim   /əneym/
2. flight wrap — fly trap   /flaytræp/
3. needed rain — need a drain   /niydədreyn/

E. Pronounce each of the following sentences three times — first with one primary stress, then with two, then with three. When you put in two primary stresses, you will have one single bar juncture. Where? With three primary stresses you will have two junctures. Where?

1. The fellow in the office needs a shave. 2. The child petting the skunk is my kid brother. 3. My mother peels potatoes with a soup spoon.

F. The following sentences contain double bar and double cross junctures. Where do they come and which are they? Say the sentences aloud and try to hear the short rises (double bar) and the short falls (double cross).

1. My Aunt Flora, who lives in Albany, owns seven goats. 2. My kid brother, looking guilty, tried to sneak away. 3. We all wanted to help him; however there was nothing we could do. 4. We all wanted to help him. There was nothing, however, that we could do. 5. Sam wanted the car badly, but he didn't have enough money. In fact, he didn't have any money at all.

48: Intonation and punctuation

We've gone into this long discussion of speech sounds largely in the hope that you would find it interesting but also because it might help you with some of your writing problems. Obviously speech isn't a very dependable guide to spelling. You might know that a word is pronounced /breyk/ and not know whether to spell it *break* or *brake*.

Still, speech is a sort of guide, and you want to use it as far as it will take you. If you notice what goes on in speech, you might avoid such spelling as "studing" for the word pronounced /stədiyiŋ/. If you get mixed up on *too* and *to*, you might notice that in "It's too bad he went to town" the *too* is pronounced /tuw/ and the *to* is pronounced /tə/. If you have trouble about doubling final consonants, notice that doubled consonants reflect a difference in vowel sound: *pinned*, /pind/; *pined*, /paynd/; *dinned*, /dind/; *dined*, /daynd/; *ratted*, /rætəd/; *rated*, /reytəd/; *hopped*, /hapt/; *hoped*, /howpt/; and so on.

Naturally we can't spell as we speak; we have to spell in the conventional way. Neither can we speak as we spell; if we did, we'd be talking as people talked five or six hundred years ago. But wherever speech does clue us to the spelling of a word, we should follow the clue.

Much the same thing is true in punctuation. We have punctuation in speech as well as in writing. In speech the punctuation is composed of double bar junctures and double cross junctures, plus complicated patterns of pitch and stress. This speech punctuation doesn't relate exactly to written punctuation any more than phonemic spelling does to ordinary spelling. But it does have a good deal of relation, which is sometimes worthwhile to observe.

Think of single bar juncture as being "no comma" juncture. Where speech has single bar, writing usually has no punctuation. The sentence "The man on your right is my brother" might have one single bar juncture or two or none, depending on the number of primary stresses:

> The man on your right is my bróther.
> The man on your ríght | is my bróther.
> The mán | on your ríght | is my bróther.

When single bar juncture occurs, there will be a pause, perhaps a rather long one. But the pitch will stay the same, going neither up nor down, and there will be no comma in writing:

> The man on your right is my brother.

Think of double bar juncture as "comma juncture." Most of the places in which double bar occurs are places where writers and editors have come to use commas in writing:

> Al ‖ who is on your right ‖ is my brother.
> Al, who is on your right, is my brother.

Or look at it the other way. If you are reading aloud, you will probably react to a comma by putting in a double bar juncture — that is, a slight rise in pitch at the end of the word before the comma.

Think of double cross juncture as "semicolon or period juncture." Double cross juncture — a slight fall in pitch at the end of a word — comes mostly at the end of sentence patterns, and it is the most common kind of juncture to come there. Double cross junctures suggest a period or a semicolon:

> Al went back to the house # he had forgotten his money #
> Al went back to the house. He had forgotten his money.
>
> Al had no money # consequently he couldn't buy the car #
> Al had no money; consequently he couldn't buy the car.

As we read, we generally react to a period or a semicolon by putting in a double cross juncture — that is, a drop in pitch.

You must not suppose that writers always punctuate in writing as they do in speaking. Just as there are differences between sound and spelling, so there are differences between intonation and punctuation. In many places editors have regularized punctuation according to the word classes that occur instead of trying to follow intonation patterns.

For example, the sentence "Al had no money; consequently he couldn't buy the car" could be spoken in two ways — with double cross or with double bar juncture:

Al had no ⌐mon⌐ey, consequently he couldn't buy the ⌐ca⌐r.
Al had no ⌐mon⌐ey consequently he couldn't buy the ⌐ca⌐r.

The first sentence has double bar (rise) after *money;* the second has double cross (fall). But this would commonly be punctuated as if it always had double cross at this point. That is, it would have a semicolon or a period before *consequently*, not a comma, as explained in Chapter 43.

For this reason it is better to let the word structure guide you to the punctuation wherever it will. If a sentence connector (like *therefore*, *consequently*, *moreover*) stands between two sentence patterns, put a semicolon or a period before it, whatever you feel the intonation might be.

But in many situations the word structure is not a good guide, and then we must rely on what we know of the intonation patterns. We shall have several examples of such situations later on.

Furthermore, it is interesting to realize that the only reason we have the punctuation we do is that the intonation was there in speech to begin with. The reason our ancestors started putting commas and periods in sentences was that they wanted to mark these rises and falls in pitch which we now call double bar and double cross junctures.

● **EXERCISE 48**

A. Read the following sentences aloud. If you can manage to read them naturally, you will probably get a double bar juncture (rise) where the commas occur and a double cross (fall) where the periods and semicolons occur. See if you do.

1. His mother kept rabbits in the back yard. **2.** His mother kept rabbits in the back yard, and his father raised large crops of carrots. **3.** His mother kept rabbits in the back yard. And his father raised large crops of carrots. **4.** He lived in Wichita when he was young. **5.** When he was young, he lived in Wichita. **6.** Although he was too proud to ask for it, he needed the money badly. **7.** He needed the money badly, although he was too proud to ask for it. **8.** He needed the money badly; however he was too proud to ask for it. **9.** He needed the money badly. He was, however, much too proud to ask for it. **10.** Bert Brazil, who was very good at math, helped me with my problems. **11.** I got some help from Bert Brazil, who was very good at math. **12.** Having forgotten his key, Stan slept on the front porch. **13.** Stan, having forgotten his key, slept on the front porch. **14.** Stan slept on the front porch, having forgotten his key. **15.** We didn't want to drop in on the Joneses without warning; moreover, we didn't know their address, and it wasn't in the phone book.

B. Copy out the following sentences, omitting the juncture signs and putting in commas, semicolons, or periods where the intonation calls for them.

1. Peeling off his clothes ‖ Charlie dived into the water # **2.** The little man behind the counter | was cracking walnuts # **3.** We usually rode the bus ‖ for we had no car # **4.** We rode the bus | only because we had no car # **5.** The warden felt | that he had stopped the riot # the prisoners ‖ however ‖ were still restless # **6.** Susan ‖ seeing Harry smile ‖ felt a little foolish # **7.** His uncle ‖ a lawyer ‖ gave him some free advice # **8.** He was very tired | and rather hungry # but he wanted to finish the job # **9.** Nobody can prove they did it # there weren't any witnesses # **10.** If you have time ‖ I'd be glad of your help # however if you're busy ‖ I can do it myself.

49 : Sentence modifiers

Let's review pattern parts a little. You'll remember that English structure goes by twos. A sentence is ordinarily made up of two pattern parts. Each of those parts is made up of two parts, each of those of two, and so on until we get down to word units. For instance the first pattern parts of the sentence "The children on this block usually go to school on Saturdays" are the noun cluster and the verb cluster:

The children on this block / usually go to school on Saturdays.

Cutting a noun cluster, you begin on the right:

The children / on this block

A P-group consists of the preposition plus all the rest:

on / this block

Cutting a verb cluster, you begin on the left:

usually / go to school on Saturdays
go to school / on Saturdays
go / to school

But the top pattern parts of a sentence do not always consist of (1) the noun cluster that is the subject and (2) the verb cluster. The main sentence pattern may be modified by something else. If it is, the top pattern parts are the main sentence pattern as one part and whatever modifies it as the other. Here's an example:

Because the schools are so crowded, the children on our block go to school on Saturdays.

Here the S-group *because the schools are so crowded* modifies the whole pattern that follows. The pattern consists of the S-group as one part and the main sentence pattern as the other.

Because the schools are so crowded / the children on our block go to school on Saturdays.

We call a structure that works as a unit against a main sentence pattern a **sentence modifier.** Sentence modifiers are regularly separated from the sentences they modify by double bar juncture. In writing, this is usually, though not always, indicated by a comma.

Various structures can be sentence modifiers. Here are some more:

> Since it was hot / we went swimming.
> Usually / we go swimming every week end.
> Holding the reins in his teeth / Sumner whipped the horses.
> Next week / my cousins from Montana are going to visit us.
> On the way to the store / I ran into Charlie.
> Afraid of what might happen / he called the police.

This is an obvious position for sentence modifiers: in front of the sentence patterns they modify. Here they are marked as sentence modifiers by the position as well as by the double bar juncture. They can't be part of the noun cluster because they stand outside of it. They aren't part of the verb cluster because they aren't connected to it. They are just sentence modifiers.

But sentence modifiers do not always come before the sentences they modify. Sometimes they come after, and sometimes they come in the middle. Here the double bar juncture becomes a stronger signal, because it carries more of the burden of keeping the sentence modifier separate from the other parts of the sentence. Study these:

> Standing on the bridge, the skipper studied the weather.
> The skipper, standing on the bridge, studied the weather.
> The skipper studied the weather, standing on the bridge.

In each sentence the pattern parts are *standing on the bridge* as one and *the skipper studied the weather* as the other. In speech the rise of double bar juncture would separate the two parts wherever they touch.

Standing on the bridge ‖ the skipper studied the weather #
The skipper ‖ standing on the bridge ‖ studied the weather #
The skipper studied the weather ‖ standing on the bridge #

The junctures are especially important in the last two sentences. If these were spoken with no junctures or with single bar, the sentences would have a different meaning. Suppose this occurred:

The skipper standing on the bridge | studied the weather #

This would make *standing on the bridge* not a sentence modifier but a part of the noun cluster *the skipper standing on the bridge.* It would suggest that the ship had several skippers and that the one standing on the bridge studied the weather while the others did other things.

Or suppose this occurred:

The skipper studied the weather standing on the bridge #

This would make *standing on the bridge* a part of the verb cluster *studied the weather standing on the bridge.* We would have the weather standing on the bridge and the skipper studying it.

Thus when the sentence modifier comes inside or at the end of the pattern it modifies, the double bar juncture becomes more important and must be clearly heard. In writing, the commas that indicate double bar become more important too. As we shall see, we sometimes leave out the comma when the sentence modifier comes at the beginning of a sentence, where the position marks it clearly as a sentence modifier. But we don't leave out the commas when the sentence modifier comes inside or at the end of the sentence it modifies.

NOTE ON MEANING

It is easier to understand sentence modification in some constructions than in others. Look at these two:

Since he had nothing to do, the skipper studied the weather.
Standing on the bridge, the skipper studied the weather.

In the first sentence it is pretty clear that the idea of the first pattern applies as a whole against the idea of the second pattern as a whole. It doesn't apply against just some part of the second pattern.

But in the second sentence the verb cluster *standing on the bridge* seems more closely connected to *the skipper* than to anything else in the main pattern. And it is. We'll take this up again in Chapter 51, where we'll see that when a verb cluster occurs in this position, the performer of the action is regularly named by the subject of the main pattern. Here the skipper is the one who stands. If we don't make this connection, we might get a peculiar sentence, like "Standing on the bridge, the weather was studied." Here the weather seems to be standing on the bridge.

Because of this close connection some students of language would prefer not to call verb clusters of this sort sentence modifiers. They would say that in "Standing on the bridge, the skipper studied the weather," the cluster *standing on the bridge* doesn't modify anything really; it just gives an added fact about the skipper. And so in the other positions, between the subject and the verb cluster and at the end of a sentence pattern:

> The skipper, standing on the bridge, studied the weather.
> The skipper studied the weather, standing on the bridge.

These contrast with the construction in which the verb cluster is a noun modifier:

> The sailor standing on the bridge studied the weather.

One can explain the difference by saying that in the sentence about the skipper who is standing on the bridge, the verb cluster is not a modifier; it's just an added statement made about the skipper. In the sentence about the sailor, the cluster is a noun modifier; it indicates which of several possible sailors is meant.

We see the same contrast in the use of S-groups of the *who* type:

The skipper, who was on the bridge, studied the weather.
The sailor who was on the bridge studied the weather, while the other sailors coiled rope.

The main difference — and it bears repeating — between this and other sentence modifiers is that the subject of the main pattern names the performer of the action of the verb cluster. The skipper studies and the skipper stands.

● EXERCISE 49

A. What are the top pattern parts of the following sentences? That is, where would the first cut come?

1. Whistling a tune, my brother walked down the street. **2.** Albert rode to the store on his bike. **3.** Albert usually rode to the store on his bike. **4.** Usually Albert rides to the store on his bike. **5.** On Saturday mornings Albert rides to the store on his bike. **6.** When she got home, she took a bath. **7.** She took a bath when she got home. **8.** Although she was fairly clean, she took a bath. **9.** She took a bath, although she was fairly clean. **10.** Poking around in the ruins, Herbert found a skull. **11.** He was rather tired, having worked all day. **12.** We invited a hundred people, hoping that most of them wouldn't come.

B. Say these sentences aloud, trying to hear the different junctures. Then copy each sentence, putting in suitable punctuation.

1. Since we need help ‖ we might invite Bob # **2.** Running into the house ‖ Sylvia fell on her face # **3.** Sylvia ‖ running into the house ‖ fell on her face # **4.** The young lady skinning the camel | is Louisa # **5.** Whatever you do ‖ don't tell my mother # **6.** The younger children ‖ by the time the day was over ‖ had had all the exercise | they wanted # **7.** I haven't seen him | since he moved to Springfield # **8.** We seldom speak ‖ since we just argue | when we do #

50: Verb clusters again

When we studied verb clusters, we studied them mostly in just one of the many sentence positions in which verbs occur. This is the position in which the verb is tied to a noun, its subject. In this position the verb cluster and its subject produce a sentence pattern.

Presently we shall examine verb clusters in various other positions. But first let's look again at some of the different kinds of verb clusters that occur in this position. The verb can pattern with modifiers, objects, and complements to form various kinds of verb clusters:

2   4
The man / walked away.

2   P D 1
The man / walked to the store.

4   2   P D 1
The man / usually walked to the store.

2   P D 1   D   1
The man / walked to the store every Saturday.

2   D 1
The man / milked the cow.

2   D 1ᵃ   D   1ᵇ
The man / gave my father the money.

2   D 1ᵃ D 3   1ᵃ
The man / called my father a great man.

2   V   3
The man / looked rather foolish.

This is the most important position for verbs — tied to the noun and constituting the heart of the sentence pattern. But verbs and verb clusters occur in various other positions too. They occur as noun modifiers, sentence modifiers, parts of preposition groups, subjects, and objects. Indeed, they can occur in any of the different function units. Compare these:

2   4

The man / walked away.

2   4

The man walking away / looks angry.

In the first sentence *walked away* is a verb cluster tied to the subject *man*. In the second sentence *walking away* is a verb cluster modifying *man*. It is part of the noun cluster of which *man* is the headword:

the man / walking away

The verb cluster that is tied to the subject in the second sentence is *looks angry*.

Here are some more verb clusters as noun modifiers:

2   P   D   1

The man walking to the store / looks angry.

2   D   1

The man milking the cow / wants some help.

2   D   1^a **D   1**^{b}

The man giving my father the money / is the mayor.

2   V   3

The man looking rather foolish / is my Uncle Herbert.

2   D   1^a **D   1**^{a}

Anybody calling my father an idiot / is asking for trouble.

You see that the verb cluster may have several different relationships with other parts of the sentence. It may be tied to a subject or it may modify a noun or function in other ways. But this has no effect on the make-up of the cluster itself. The various pattern parts occur in the verb cluster in all of the different functions of the cluster.

Verb clusters often pattern with prepositions and form part of a P-group.

    2   P D   1   D   1
By walking to the store every day, Harry kept in shape.

    2   D   1
After milking the cow, I went in to breakfast.

    2   D 1ᵃ D 1ᵇ
The mayor was accused of giving my father the money.

    2   D 1ᵃ D 1ᵃ
I knocked him down for calling my father an idiot.

In the sentences above the structure of the clusters is just the same as it would be in these:

2   P D 1   D   1   **2   D 1ᵃ D 1ᵃ**
He walked to the store every day.   He called my father an idiot.

Verb clusters can also occur as subjects and objects:

    2   P D 1   D   1
Walking to the store every day / kept Harry in shape.

    2   D 1ᵃ D 1ᵃ
Calling a man an idiot / can get you into trouble.

    2   1ᵃ D 1ᵇ
I remembered giving him the money.

The *ing* form (*walking, calling, giving,* etc.) is very common for verbs occurring in these function units — subject, object, etc. But other forms occur too. The past tense form is common for verbs occurring as noun modifiers:

    2-ed P 1
The money given to me / was counterfeit.

    2-ed P 1
Themes written in pencil / are hard to read.

    2-ed   1
He came with a fellow called Steve.

A very common form for verbs in the different function units is the simple form with the word *to* in front: *to go, to try, to buy a car,* and so on. This seems to us such a common and basic form of verbs that we often use it when we refer to verbs; that is, we speak of the verb *to be,* the verb *to write,* etc.

The word *to* patterning with verbs in this way is in a group by itself. When we want to refer to it in formulas, we will simply write it in.

Verb clusters with *to* have the same structure as other verb clusters:

$$\textbf{to 2 \quad P \quad D \quad 1}$$
It's about time to quit for the day.

$$\textbf{to \quad 2 \quad D \quad 1}$$
It's too early to milk the goats.

$$\textbf{to \quad 2 \quad P \quad 1}$$
There's a man here to talk to you.

$$\textbf{to \quad 2 \quad 1}^{a}\textbf{ D \quad 1}^{b}$$
My only purpose was to give him the money.

$$\textbf{to \quad 2 \quad 1}^{a}\textbf{ D \quad 1}^{b}$$
To give him the money was my only purpose.

● **EXERCISE 50**

A. Construct four verb clusters, any kind. For instance, you might have something like "walk to the store," "peel the apple with a knife," "strummed happily on his guitar," "found something new to think about every day." Now for each of your clusters write four sentences, using the verb cluster as a different function unit in each one, and tell how you have used it. Use any form for the verb: **2, 2-ing, 2-ed,** or **to 2.**

EXAMPLE

Charlie walked to the store. (main verb in the pattern, tied to the subject)
The people walking to the store looked tired. (modifier in the noun cluster)
He killed some time by walking to the store. (part of the P-group)
Walking to the store was a lot of fun. (subject)

B. Write sentences from these formulas. Each formula is broken into its two main pattern parts to make it a little easier.

1. D 1 / 2 4	**8.** 2-ing P D 1 / 2 D 3 1
2. D 1 2-ing 4 / 2 D 1	**9.** P 2-ing D 1 / 1 2 D 1
3. D 1 2-ing P D 1 / 2 D 1	**10.** D 1 2-ed P D 1 / 2 3
4. D 1 / 2 P D 1	**11.** D 1 / 2 to 2 D 1
5. D 1 / 2 D 1	**12.** to 2 D 1 / 2 D 1
6. D 1 2-ing D 1 / 2 4	**13.** to 2 D 1ᵃ D 1ᵇ / 2 V 3
7. 1 / 2 D 1 2-ing D 1	**14.** D 1 / 2 1 2-ed P D 1

15. D 1 2-ing D 1ᵃ D 1ᵇ / 2 D 1

1—noun   2—verb   3—adjective   4—adverb
D—determiner   P—preposition   V—intensifier

---

51 : Verb clusters
as sentence modifiers

Besides occurring in the different function units noted in Chapter 50, verb clusters often occur as sentence modifiers. (The reason for the use of this term here is discussed at the end of Chapter 49.) Like other sentence modifiers, they are regularly separated from the sentence they modify by a double bar juncture (rise) in speech. In writing they are regularly marked off from the sentence they modify by a comma or commas.

Here's an example of a verb cluster as a sentence modifier:

Walking through the park, Sam saw a buzzard.

In speech the pitch would be something like this:

Walking through the ⌐pa⌐rk‿ Sam saw a ⌐buz⌐zard

Notice the slight rise after *park.* That's double bar juncture marking off the verb cluster from the sentence pattern it works against.

Here are some more examples of verb clusters as sentence modifiers. The commas show where double bar juncture would come in speech.

> Reaching for another banana, I began my story.
> Sailing through the air, the dish of pudding hit the wall.
> Bending over, the officer tied his shoe.

Here's another thing to notice. Although the verb cluster modifies the whole sentence, it has a special connection with the subject of the main pattern. It names an action that the subject of the main pattern performs. In the examples above, the officer is the one who bends over, the dish of pudding is what flies through the air, "I" am the one who reaches for another banana.

If you don't watch this, you're likely to get sentences like these:

> Reaching for an other banana, a funny thing happened.
> Sailing through the air, the wall was struck.
> Bending over, the shoe was quickly tied.

Now a thing seems to be reaching, a wall sailing, a shoe bending.

Verb clusters other than 2-ing clusters also occur as sentence modifiers, for example, 2-ed verbs and *to* verbs:

> Caught in the act, Sam looked guilty.
> Shocked by his rudeness, I socked him in the nose.
> To get to the center of town, you have to take a bus.

Verb clusters as sentence modifiers don't have to come before the patterns they modify. They can come at the end or in the middle. Here is an example, first with the pitch shown and then with ordinary punctuation:

> The ⌐di⌐sh, sailing through the ⌐ai⌐r, hit the ⌐wa⌐ll
> The dish, sailing through the air, hit the wall.

Here the junctures (and in writing the commas) are a very important signal because they are often the only signal that the cluster is a sentence modifier and not a noun modifier. In the other position — in front of the sentence — the position itself is a signal. But if the cluster is inside the sentence, the entire meaning may depend on the junctures. Our example might be pronounced with different intonation and have a different meaning:

The dish sailing through the ai r | hit the wa ll

This would suggest that there are several dishes involved; perhaps one is sliding off the table, one is rolling toward the fireplace, and one is sailing through the air. The cluster *sailing through the air* tells which dish hit the wall. It is here a noun modifier, part of the noun cluster *the dish sailing through the air*. It would be written without commas:

The dish sailing through the air hit the wall.

But with double bar juncture the verb cluster becomes a sentence modifier. It just adds another idea to the main sentence, as if one were to say "The dish sailed through the air, and the dish hit the wall."

Or look at this:

The of ficer, bending o ver, tied his sh oe

This means that there was an officer who bent over and tied his shoe. It would be punctuated with commas marking off the sentence modifier:

The officer, bending over, tied his shoe.

But this one is different:

The officer bending o ver tied his sh oe

Here there are at least two officers. The one bending over tied his shoe while the one standing up looked at the scenery. It would be written without commas.

Sometimes, to be sure, there are other signals besides the junctures. For instance, if the subject in the main pattern is a proper noun, the verb cluster will always be a sentence modifier, not a noun modifier. It will always have double bar junctures and be written with commas:

Sam, strolling through the park, saw a buzzard.
Greenland, being very cold, is a rather uncomfortable place to live.

Other types of verb clusters appear in this position too:

Alice, shocked by Sam's rudeness, stuck out her tongue at him.
The paper, having been written in pencil, was difficult to read.

The other position for verb clusters as sentence modifiers is at the end of the sentence pattern they modify. Here also they are signaled by the double bar juncture:

The farmer showed us his ⌐rab⌐bits, beaming with ⌐pri⌐de

Take out the double bar juncture here and you get nonsense. The verb cluster would then be a noun modifier, not a sentence modifier, and the rabbits would be beaming with pride.

This position for verb clusters as sentence modifiers isn't so common as the others, but we use it every now and then. Here are a few more examples:

Belinda wept bitterly, shocked at Sam's behavior.
The officer picked up a pin, peering at it closely.
I ran back to the house, having forgotten my portable cement mixer.

Notice that wherever it occurs the verb cluster modifying the sentence has a close meaning relationship with the subject of the main pattern. In the examples above, Belinda is the one who is shocked, the officer is the one who peers, and "I" am the one who has forgotten.

● EXERCISE 51

A. Pronounce these sentences aloud, trying to notice the junctures. Your voice should rise for double bar, fall for double cross, and remain level for single bar. Then copy the sentences, putting in the punctuation.

1. Feeling a little sick ‖ I went to bed # **2.** Anyone finding a yellow purse | should take it to the office # **3.** Martha ‖ digging into her purse ‖ paid the waiter # **4.** The people sitting in the back row | couldn't hear much # **5.** My father ‖ sitting in the front row ‖ heard everything # **6.** Having looked into my mouth ‖ the dentist shuddered # **7.** The dentist shuddered ‖ having looked into my mouth # **8.** A policeman pushed forward ‖ disturbed by what was going on. **9.** A fireman ‖ climbing to the third floor ‖ collapsed | and fell to the ground # **10.** The fireman climbing to the third floor | collapsed and fell to the ground #

B. Write three sentences, each with a 2-ing verb cluster as a sentence modifier. Put the verb cluster at the beginning of the sentence. Then see whether it could occur also within the sentence or at the end. Some can and some can't.

C. Write a sentence with a 2-ed verb cluster as a sentence modifier.

D. Write a sentence with a *to* verb cluster as a sentence modifier.

E. Write sentences from the following formulas.

1. 2-ing D 1 ‖ 1 2 4
2. 1 ‖ 2-ing D 1 ‖ 2 4
3. 1 2 4 ‖ 2-ing D 1
4. D 1 2-ing D 1 | 2 4
5. 2-ed P D 1 ‖ 1 2 D 1
6. D 1 ‖ 2-ing 4 ‖ 2 D 1
7. D 1 ‖ 2-ed P D 1 ‖ 2 P D 1
8. 1 ‖ 2-ing D 1 ‖ 2 D 1 2-ing D 1

1—noun   2—verb   4—adverb
D—determiner   P—preposition

52 : S-groups
as sentence modifiers

S-groups very commonly occur as sentence modifiers. Remember that there are two kinds of S-groups: those for which the subordinator is the *because* type and those for which the subordinator is the *who* type. When the subordinator is like *because*, the S-group is generally a sentence modifier or a verb modifier. When it is like *who*, the S-group is a sentence modifier or a noun modifier.

Like other sentence modifiers, the S-group is separated from the sentence pattern it modifies by double bar juncture. This is regularly indicated in writing by a comma.

Let's take the *because* type first. Here's an example, first with the pitch pattern of speech and then with the punctuation of writing:

> Because he was ⌐hun⌐gry Sam ate a ⌐sand⌐wich
>
> **Because he was hungry, Sam ate a sandwich.**

Punctuating S-groups in this position — at the beginning of a sentence — is no problem. Here they're always sentence modifiers, they always have double bar juncture, and they're always followed by a comma:

Since he didn't know any better, the lad ate the stew with his fingers.
After the blaze was put out, the firemen examined the wiring.
If you have time, I wish you'd help me with my math.
Whether you like it or not, he's going with us.
Until we know what Al's going to do, we can't make any plans.

S-groups as sentence modifiers can occur at the end of the sentence too:

> He's going ⌐with⌐ us ⌐whether you like it or ⌐no⌐t
>
> **He's going with us, whether you like it or not.**

But this is a lot trickier to punctuate. This is also a position for S-groups as verb modifiers, and often the only difference is in the juncture. If double bar juncture occurs, the S-group modifies the sentence, and the pattern parts are as shown:

He's going with us ‖ whether you like it or not.
He's going with us / whether you like it or not.

But if single bar or no juncture occurs, the pattern parts are like this:

He / 's going with us whether you like it or not.

This second sentence means about the same thing as the first, but the emphasis is quite different.

Sometimes, however, the meaning is quite different too. If an S-group with *since* has double bar juncture before it, it modifies the sentence and gives the reason:

I don't like him, since he always makes fun of me.

But with single bar or no juncture it modifies the verb and tells the time:

I haven't liked him since he made fun of me that day.

It would be possible to give a complicated description of when S-groups have double bar juncture and when they don't. For instance, S-groups with *though* and *although* usually do; S-groups with *when* and *if* usually don't. But there are so many exceptions and fine distinctions that it's easier to go by the intonation.

Read these aloud and hear the double bar juncture:

He was not a bad fellow, although he had a nasty temper.
His family moved to Buffalo in 1948, because his father had been offered a job there.
I don't know why he did it, unless he thought it was funny.
I don't have much use for her, not after what she said about my sister.

Now read these. You should move into the S-group on a level pitch.

Don't come unless you want to.
I might help you when I get finished here.
They came in just as we were sitting down to supper.
He asked if we knew where Stanley Jones lived.

S-groups in which the subordinator is of the *who* type may be sentence modifiers or noun modifiers.* They are sentence modifiers if they are separated from the rest of the sentence by double bar juncture. This is always indicated in writing by commas:

Mr. ⌐Boog⌐le ╵who was very ⌐hung⌐ry ╵ ate seven ⌐ham⌐burgers

Mr. Boogle, who was very hungry, ate seven hamburgers.

Now compare that with this:

Any man who eats seven ⌐ham⌐burgers must be very ⌐hung⌐ry

Any man who eats seven hamburgers must be very hungry.

In the first example the S-group modifies the rest of the sentence; it adds to it the idea that Mr. Boogle was very hungry. In the second example the S-group is part of a noun cluster; it modifies *any man* and gives a particular meaning to *any man.* S-groups that modify sentences just add an idea to the sentence. S-groups that modify nouns identify or change or affect the meaning of the nouns in some way.

S-groups as sentence modifiers and S-groups as noun modifiers are kept separate not only by the junctures but also, usually, by various other signs and signals. Sometimes the signal is in the subordinator: *that* regularly introduces a noun modifier; *which* usually introduces a sentence modifier. Sometimes the signal is in a determiner or a proper noun or elsewhere in the sentence.

But there's no need to itemize all the signals or to memorize

---

* These are like the verb clusters discussed in Chapter 49. We could say that these S-groups of the *who* type with double-bar juncture don't modify anything but just add another fact to the one in the main pattern. But it seems simpler to call them sentence modifiers.

them. We all react to them more or less automatically. And there's always the juncture.

Read these aloud, noticing the rises of double bar juncture:

Charlie, who should have known better, ate his stew with his fingers.
Springfield, which is the capital of Illinois, was Stanley's home town.
Stanley lived in Springfield, which is the capital of Illinois.
My mother, to whom I showed the letter, wasn't very happy.
He knew better than to ask his teacher, who wasn't speaking to him.

Now read these. Notice that you go into the S-group on a level pitch.

The man who was washing the window said nothing.
He lived in a town that he hated.
All seniors who are taking part in the play will be excused from classes.
He didn't like to talk to women who were less than ten years old.

Sometimes the juncture is the only signal. Read these aloud:

The mechanic, who was looking at the distributor, said nothing.
The mechanic who was looking at the distributor said nothing.

What is the difference in meaning?

● **EXERCISE 52**

A. Write five sentences with S-groups as sentence modifiers. Make all the S-groups with subordinators of the *because* type, and put them all at the front of the sentence patterns they modify.

B. Write three more sentence modifiers with subordinators of the *because* type and put them at the end of the sentences. Make sure they are S-groups that will take the double bar junctures.

C. Write five sentences with *who* type S-groups as sentence modifiers.

D. Write five sentences with *who* type S-groups as noun modifiers.

E. Write sentences from the following formulas. Watch the junctures.

1. S 1 2 4 ‖ 1 2 D 1
2. D 1 2 D 1 ‖ S 1 2 4
3. D 1 2 D 1 S D 1 2 3
4. 1 ‖ S 2 3 ‖ 2 D 1
5. D 1 S 2 3 | 2 D 1
6. D 1 2 1 ‖ S 2 D 1
7. S D 1 2 4 ‖ 1 ‖ S 2 D 1 ‖ 2 3

1–noun   2–verb   3–adjective   4–adverb
D–determiner   S–subordinator

---

53 : Appositives

One other kind of modifier is regularly separated from the rest of the sentence by double bar juncture in speech and by commas in writing. This is something called an **appositive**. An appositive is most commonly a noun cluster. It occurs after another noun referring to the same thing or the same person.

In the following sentence the noun cluster *an old man with white hair* is an appositive. Note the pitch pattern:

> The ⌐jud⌐ge, an old man with white ⌐hair, spoke ⌐slow⌐ly

Notice that the pitch and junctures are the same as for an S-group or a verb cluster in this position:

> The ⌐jud⌐ge, who was an old ⌐man, spoke ⌐slow⌐ly

> The ⌐jud⌐ge, being an old ⌐man, spoke ⌐slow⌐ly

All three — the verb cluster, the S-group, and the appositive — are cut off from the main pattern by juncture, and all are punctuated in the same way:

> The judge, being an old man, spoke slowly.
> The judge, who was an old man, spoke slowly.
> The judge, an old man with white hair, spoke slowly.

Appositives can occur in various places in the sentence, after nouns in all sorts of function units.

> Charlie, the president of the class, spoke up.
> We decided to ask Charlie, the president of the class.
> That was Charlie, the president of the class.
> She came with Charlie, the president.
> She named Charlie, the president.

Notice that if we were to write the formula of the last sentence, it would appear to be this: 1^a 2 1^b D 1^b. But this is the formula for the object–complement construction. We can turn this formula back into a sentence and get this:

> **She named Charlie the president.**

This means that she appointed Charlie to be president, whereas the first one meant that Charlie is the president and she named him in connection with something else.

The difference is in the juncture. If we put in the double bar, *president* is an appositive:

> She named ⌈Char⌊lie, the ⌈pre⌋sident

But if we put in the single bar or no juncture, *president* is an object complement:

> She named Charlie the ⌈pre⌋sident

To distinguish these two, we must write two formulas with double bar juncture shown in one and not in the other:

> 1^a 2 1^b 1^b (The second 1^b is an object complement.)
> 1^a 2 1^b ‖ 1^b (The second 1^b is an appositive.)

This is just another example of the importance of the junctures. The sentence can change meaning entirely with a change of intonation. For this reason we will from now on always indicate double bar and double cross juncture in our formulas. When no juncture is shown, you can suppose that the formula stands for a sentence with single bar juncture or no juncture.

Here are some more examples of appositives.

His aunt, an old battle-ax, wouldn't let him go.

The car, a '38 Chevy, was badly battered.

We had to read *Macbeth*, a play by someone named Shakespeare.

The gift he brought, a box of stale chocolates, wasn't appreciated.

He has a little hideaway somewhere, a place that nobody else knows about.

He gave his brother a car, a 1950 Hudson.

He gave his brother, a fellow of seventeen, a new car.

Sometimes we use appositives that don't connect to any particular noun in the sentence they modify. Appositives of this kind sum up the whole idea of the modified sentence:

> He was flat broke, a fact of which none of us were aware.
>
> Charlie was hungry, a fairly common condition for him.

● **EXERCISE 53**

A. Write ten sentences with appositives. Read them aloud and try to notice the double bar junctures.

B. Write a pair of sentences on the model "She named Charlie the president" and "She named Charlie, the president." The verb will be something like *named, called, elected, chose.*

C. Write sentences from the following formulas.

1. D 1 ‖ D 3 1 ‖ 2 4 #
2. 1 2 P D 1 ‖ D 3 1 #
3. D 1 ‖ D 3 1 ‖ A 2 #
4. D 1 ‖ 2-ing D 1 ‖ 2 4 #
5. D 1 ‖ S 2 3 ‖ 2 4 #
6. D 1 ‖ D 1 P D 3 1 ‖ 2 V 3 #
7. D 1 2-ing D 1 2 4 #
8. D 1 S 2 3 2 4 #
9. S D 1 2 4 ‖ 1 2 D 1 #
10. S D 1 2 4 ‖ 1 ‖ D 3 1 ‖ 2 D 1 #
11. S D 1 2 4 ‖ 1 ‖ S 2 V 3 ‖ 2 D 1 #
12. 1 ‖ D 1 S 2 D 1 ‖ 2 D 1 #
13. 1 2 P 1 ‖ D 1 S 2 D 1 #
14. D 1ᵃ 2 D 1ᵇ ‖ D 1ᵇ ‖ D 3 1ᶜ #
15. D 1ᵃ 2 D 1ᵇ D 1ᶜ ‖ D 3 1ᶜ #

1—noun   2—verb   3—adjective   4—adverb

A—auxiliary   D—determiner   P—preposition   S—subordinator   V—intensifier

54: Review of punctuation

Obviously this book doesn't tell the whole story of English punctuation. There are many marks we haven't dealt with at all — dashes, colons, quotation marks, parentheses, brackets. You'll have to learn about these in two ways: by reading about them in handbooks of punctuation and by noticing what other writers do with them.

We have been concerned with three marks only: commas, semicolons, and periods. And we have been concerned with these only as they connect the patterns of sentences that we write.

We have made two distinctly different connections between the punctuation marks and the patterns of English sentences. First of all, we have seen some relations between punctuation marks and word groups and function units. We have seen that when two sentence patterns come together with nothing between them, we have a period or semicolon between the patterns. When a conjunction connects two patterns, we have a comma, a semicolon, or a period before the conjunction. When a sentence connector connects two patterns, we have a semicolon or a period before the sentence connector.

We have seen that we don't ordinarily use commas to separate the parts of noun clusters or verb clusters. We don't usually separate a noun cluster from a verb cluster to which it is tied as its subject. On the other hand, we usually do mark off certain kinds of sentence modifiers from the patterns they modify. When a verb cluster or an S-group or an appositive works against a sentence, it is separated from the sentence by a comma or commas.

The second connection we made was between punctuation marks and intonation. We saw that double cross juncture, a fall in pitch, is represented in writing by a period or a semicolon; double bar juncture, a rise in pitch, is represented by a comma;

single bar juncture, level pitch across a break in a sentence, is shown by no punctuation.

This connection between punctuation and intonation is especially important, because it will serve you as a guide when nothing else will. For example, we haven't said anything about whether you put commas after P-groups when they are sentence modifiers. Do you write this?

At the end of the day, we all felt very tired.

Or do you write this?

At the end of the day we all felt very tired.

We haven't said anything about this construction because there's no simple thing to say about it. Punctuation here depends on the type and length of the P-group, on the writing style of the writer, and on the reading habits of the people who are expected to read it. It would take a great many pages to cover all the possibilities.

The simplest way is to train your ear to hear double bar juncture. If you hear double bar juncture in the sentence, put in a comma. If not, leave the comma out.

Or put it this way. If you want the *reader* to hear double bar juncture, put in a comma. You may think that a reader doesn't hear anything unless he reads aloud. But actually he hears everything he reads, in a way; if he can't hear it, he has trouble reading it. Read this sentence:

I think Jones plays for Baltimore.

Now try this one:

I think Kryhljhnstp plays for Omkhurtqhnip.

Did you stumble on the second one? Yet, there would seem to be no reason to stumble. You can see that Kryhljhnstp is the name of a person, just like Jones, and that Omkhurtqhnip is the place he plays, like Baltimore. But while this might satisfy your eyes, it won't satisfy your throat. Your throat wants to make little movements corresponding to the sound, and when you come to Kryhljhnstp it doesn't know just what little movements to make.

This is what is called "subvocal reading." It's the tail end of the process through which human beings have learned to read. We can suppose that when our ancestors some thousands of years ago learned to write and to read writing, they pronounced the sounds aloud from the letters they saw. Then they learned to keep silent, but they still moved their lips as if they were forming the sounds. Now we have learned to read with the lips closed, but the throat and mouth still makes thousands of small movements — so small that we scarcely notice them — as the eye passes along the page. We might call it mouth memory. The mouth remembers the sounds as the eye falls on the letters.

The mouth remembers the intonation too. When the eye sees a comma, the mouth and throat tend toward the rise of double bar juncture, and the reader gets the message that double bar juncture signals. Suppose we see this sentence:

After studying Charlie went out to the ball game.

We're likely to read this wrong, thinking about a primary stress on *Charlie* with double bar juncture after *Charlie* instead of after *studying*. This would give us the idea that somebody studied Charlie. When we see that the sentence won't work out that way, we have to go back and start over. A comma will call up a double bar in its right place:

After studying, Charlie fell asleep.

So listen for the junctures and put in what you want the reader to hear. Say you're going to write:

Charlie was my best friend yet I didn't altogether trust him.

Do you want a pitch rise after *friend*, which will show the structure break but tend to tie the patterns together? Then you put in a comma:

Charlie was my best friend, yet I didn't altogether trust him.

Or do you want the reader to hear the fall of double cross juncture after *friend?* This will tend to separate the patterns and throw a little more weight on the second pattern:

Charlie was my best friend. Yet I didn't altogether trust him.

Here's one more bit of general advice. Lean toward less punctuation rather than toward more. The punctuation habits of writers and editors are changing slowly but steadily and in general in the direction of fewer commas. A passage printed two hundred years ago will look peppered compared to a similar passage printed today. The comma used to occur in many places where single bar juncture would occur in speech, and the semicolon used to indicate double bar juncture. Now the comma has in general moved out of single bar territory and regularly indicates double bar juncture. Meanwhile the semicolon has moved on to double cross areas.

This change reflects a change in reading style. People generally read faster than they used to, with less attention to minor sentence rhythms. The writer tries to help the reader by putting fewer breaks in the line. Often one doesn't even mark the double bar juncture when other signals make the pattern perfectly clear.

Another reason for the change in punctuation is that there is less reading aloud than there was a hundred years ago. When a novelist expected that people would read his books to each other around the fireside, he indicated more of the intonation for them. People don't read to each other much any more, and writers don't expect them to.

● EXERCISE 54

A. Read these sentences aloud, listening to the junctures. Then copy the sentences, using commas for double bar junctures, semicolons or periods for double cross, nothing for single bar.

1. I knew it was Martha | because I recognized the hat # **2.** I knew it was Martha ‖ although I didn't recognize the hat # **3.** I knew it was Martha ‖ but she had certainly changed # **4.** I knew it was Martha # but she had certainly changed # **5.** Going into the last turn ‖ Ed was leading | by several yards # **6.** Ed ‖ running a very fine race ‖ was leading by several yards # **7.** Ed was leading | at the turn | by several yards # however | Sam was coming up fast # **8.** Ed was leading by several yards | at the turn # Sam ‖ however ‖ was coming up fast # **9.** Anyone who wants a ticket | had better speak up # **10.** Agnes ‖ who didn't want a ticket ‖ kept still # **11.** Whistling a little tune | to keep his spirits up ‖ Scott entered the cave # **12.** Scott ‖ whistling a little tune | to keep his spirits up ‖ entered the cave # **13.** The package left by the postman | contained dried lizards # **14.** The package ‖ a big box tied with twine ‖ contained dried lizards # **15.** I went home to bed ‖ not having enough money | for the show # **16.** Not having enough money | for the show ‖ I went home to bed | and had a good sleep # **17.** He brushed his teeth ‖ combed his hair ‖ and put on his new suit # **18.** We can't both go # there isn't room | for two of us # **19.** Stanley wasn't afraid of the snake # having lived in India ‖ he knew all about cobras # **20.** The newcomer ‖ a tall ‖ handsome lad | wearing a leather jacket ‖ seemed very nice # nevertheless | we weren't at all sure | that we wanted him in the club #

B. Here are some sentences written without any punctuation. Read them over carefully. Then put in punctuation to correspond to the junctures that you hear.

1. After washing Alice sat down to the piano **2.** He answered very politely but everybody knew he was upset **3.** Peering through the window we thought we saw a man sitting by the fireplace **4.** After you finish the windows George you can start washing the walls **5.** The principal staring at me in horror backed away **6.** Papers written in ink are easier to read than papers written in pencil **7.** Stan ate a hamburger and a piece of pie and his dog barked enviously **8.** The new coach a former quarterback for Wisconsin was extremely popular **9.** Encountering a burglar in the dining room my mother a woman with nerves of iron laid him out with a poker **10.** While we were eating my brother got the hiccups. **11.** Inside the house looked rather nice but the outside was terrible. **12.** Stunned by what she had seen Mabel couldn't speak she just collapsed on the sofa and sobbed violently

Part Nine

SOME OTHER SENTENCE PATTERNS

55 : Statement patterns with *it*

We haven't by any means covered all the different patterns of English statements, and we won't cover them all. We mean just to look at the main lines, the basic patterns. But there is one basic pattern that we haven't yet touched. This is a pattern that begins with *it is* or *it was*, followed by a number of different structures. This is important because it is a high-frequency pattern. It occurs in a great many of our sentences.

One of the simplest forms of this pattern is a series of statements dealing with time or the weather. This is just *it* plus some form of the verb *be* plus a noun or adjective:

It's hot.	It is summer.
It was windy.	It's February.
It might be cool.	It was two minutes past six.

Sometimes *it* is followed by a verb other than *be*, but the reference is still to time or the weather.

It was raining.
It snowed for three days.
It seemed like January.

In another form of this pattern the *it is* or *it was* is followed by a noun cluster. This noun cluster is usually made up of a noun plus an S-group, like *Sam who found the money.*

> It was Sam who found the money.
> It was my father who objected.
> It's my kid brother that makes all the trouble.
> It was a time when nobody had enough to eat.

This construction has single bar juncture between the noun and the S-group ordinarily. If we have double bar juncture there, we get a different kind of construction:

> It was Sam, who found the money.

This means something like "The fellow you saw was Sam; he's the person who found the money." But "It was Sam who found the money" means something like "Sam (not Ed) was the one who found the money." The effect of this construction is to emphasize *Sam* or whatever follows *it was.*

A very common variety of this *it is* structure has an adjective and an S-group after the *it is.* The S-group usually begins with *that:*

> It was strange that he didn't mention it before.
> It's good that you had plenty of warning.
> It was too bad that you didn't get a chance to see Elvira.

Often we just leave out the *that:*

> It was strange he didn't mention it before.
> It's good you had plenty of warning.

Sometimes we have a verb cluster after the adjective. The verb in this cluster will be of the *to* type:

> It's hard to dislike Thompson.
> It was easy to see what would happen to him.
> It's impossible to please him.

You see that there is quite a lot of variety in this construction, but all the sentences have something in common. They all start with *it*, and the *it* doesn't mean anything in particular. This is different from the *it* in "I patted the dog, and *it* bit me." This *it* refers to *dog*. But the other *it* doesn't refer to anything. It's just a way of getting the sentence started.

We can think of this *it* as a pronoun if we like, but it is clearly a very special kind of pronoun. No other pronoun and no noun will substitute for it. Whether it is a pronoun or not, it is the subject of these sentences. You remember that a subject is the word that is tied to a verb. This *it* is tied to the verb, because it is always followed by the singular form, *was* or *is*. *Were* and *are* never occur in this structure, no matter what comes in the rest of the sentence. In this respect this structure differs from structure word *there*, which is not the subject.

Notice another thing about this *it* construction: it isn't punctuated. Double bar juncture doesn't occur in it, so there are no commas.

● EXERCISE 55

A. Write five sentences with the *it* construction described in this chapter. See if you can use several different varieties. Be sure that your sentences have no double bar juncture. If they do, you have a different pattern.

B. Write sentences from the following formulas.

1. it was 3
2. it's 3
3. it was 1
4. it was 1 S 2 4

5. it was 1 S 2 D 1
6. it's 3 S 1 2 4
7. it is 3 S D 1 2 D 1
8. it was 3 to 2 1

9. it was 3 to 2 S 1 2 D 1
10. it was 3 S D 1 2 to 2 D 1

1–noun   2–verb   3–adjective   4–adverb
D–determiner   S–subordinator

56: Verbs modifying other verbs

One of the most interesting developments in the patterns of English is the way in which we have come to change the meaning of verbs through modification. Most of this subject we have already been over. We have seen how verb clusters build up after the verb through the addition of adverbs, P-groups, and S-groups and also through the addition of various kinds of complements and objects. We have seen that the cluster can expand before the verb headword also. In this position we have seen that the auxiliaries and some adverbs pattern with the verb to change its meaning:

	A	A	A	2
He				went.
He			should	go.
He			might	go.
He			is	going.
He			has	gone.
He		should	have	gone.
He		might	be	going.
He	must	have	been	gone.
He	might	have	been	going.

	4	2
He	usually	went.
He	sometimes	went.
He	gladly	went.

But there's still another kind of modifier that will occur in front of verbs in the verb clusters. Other verbs will occur there. At first glance these other verbs seem to be just more auxiliaries. They appear to pattern like auxiliaries.

He **was** going.	He **got** going.
They **were** going.	He **kept** going.
I **am** going.	He **started** going.
He **is** going.	He **quit** going.

But actually there's a difference. The auxiliaries form a unit with the verb that is different from the unit formed by the verb modifiers and the verb, and they occur in patterns that the verb modifiers do not occur in. For instance, if we turn "He was going" into a question, we get "Was he going?" The subject and the auxiliary reverse. But we can't do that with "He kept going." We don't say "Kept he going?" Instead we put in a real auxiliary: "Did he keep going?"

Or we say "He wasn't going," but we don't say "He gotn't going." So *kept*, *got*, *started*, and *quit* are verbs all right. But they are also modifiers. They modify *going*, the headword in the verb cluster. Here are some more examples:

	MODIFIER	HEADWORD	
	2	**2**	
He	kept	moving.	
He	began	talking.	
He	ceased	fidgeting.	
He	continued	looking	at me.
He	quit	eating	when Sam came in.
He	went	fishing	every spring.
He	stopped	staring	at the mayor.

The headword in this structure can be a 2-ing verb, as in the examples above. Or it can be a *to* verb:

	MODIFIER		HEADWORD	
	2	**to**	**2**	
He	began	to	talk.	
He	continued	to	talk.	
He	likes	to	fish.	
He	wanted	to	see	the movie.
He	refused	to	give	me the money.
He	went	to	speak	to the mayor.

Between the modifier and the headword we have either single bar juncture or no juncture at all.

Sometimes we pile up two or three or even four modifiers of this sort before the headword:

> He wanted to stop **speaking**.
> He began to go **fishing**.
> He likes to keep **staring** at the mayor.
> He hated to keep stopping **speaking**.
> He wanted to begin to stop **smoking**.
> He likes to refuse to begin to stop **staring** at the mayor.

But as you see, the structure gets a little sticky when too many modifiers pile up.

So far as pattern parts go, verb clusters which contain other verbs as modifiers work just like any other verb clusters. You begin at the left and work in to the headword, then go to the right.

Let's cut this sentence as an example:

> He usually wanted to stop speaking his lines before the curtain came down.

The top pattern parts are the subject and the verb cluster:

> He / usually wanted to stop speaking his lines before the curtain came down.

The headword in the verb cluster is *speaking*. We begin on the left. *Usually* modifies everything else:

> usually / wanted to stop speaking his lines before the curtain came down

Wanted modifies what follows:

> wanted / to stop speaking his lines before the curtain came down

To patterns against the rest as follows:

to / stop speaking his lines before the curtain came down
stop / speaking his lines before the curtain came down

Now we have reached the headword. The S-group modifies *speaking his lines:*

speaking his lines / before the curtain came down

His lines is the object of the verb:

speaking / his lines

● **EXERCISE 56**

A. Write sentences from the following formulas.

1. 1 A 2-ing D 1
2. 1 A 2-ed D 1
3. 1 2 2-ing D 1
4. 1 A 2-ing D 1
5. 1 2 to 2 4
6. 1 A 2-ing to 2 4
7. 1 2 to 2 2-ing 4
8. 1 A 2 to 2 2-ing 4
9. S 1 2 to 2 4 ‖ 1 2 2-ing D 1
10. 1 A 2-ing to 2 S 1 2 to 2 4

B. Cut the following sentences into their pattern parts. You might want to look again at the sentence that is cut on pages 270–71.

1. He usually eats a steak. **2.** He ate a steak yesterday. **3.** He sometimes eats a steak for breakfast. **4.** He was eating a steak when we came in. **5.** He was beginning to eat a steak. **6.** He began eating a steak. **7.** He was happily picking some roses. **8.** He stopped picking the roses when it started to rain. **9.** He hated having to stop picking the roses. **10.** He had never quit hating having to stop picking the roses.

––––––––––

1–noun   2–verb   4–adverb
A–auxiliary   D–determiner   S–subordinator

57 : Question patterns

You may remember that we said a long way back that English has three main types of sentences: **statements, questions,** and **requests.** The difference between them is the different effect they tend to have on those who hear them. Questions tend to make the hearer say something in answer to the questions:

> **Have you seen Al?** (Hearer answers "Yes" or "No.")
> **Who was with him?** (Hearer answers "George.")

Requests tend to make the hearer do something:

> **Get into the boat.** (Hearer gets into the boat.)
> **Stick around awhile.** (Hearer sticks around.)

Statements just tend to make the hearer keep on listening.

So far we have been concerned almost entirely with statements. There are two reasons why. In the first place, most of the structures we have studied are the same in questions and requests as they are in statements. The same form classes occur, and most of the same structure groups. There are the same noun clusters and verb clusters, and the same pattern parts. We can study these for all three types by studying them in statements.

In the second place, statements are the most important of the three sentence types in the material we are likely to write. Statements are no more common in speech, but they make up the great bulk of what we put into themes and compositions and letters.

But speech is another story. In our daily living most of us spend a good deal of time asking questions and ordering people around, and it may be interesting to see how we do it.

There are several ways of showing that the sentence we are uttering is a question — that is, that we want an answer. One way is by changing the places of the subject and the verb — putting the subject after the verb instead of before it, as in statements. Compare the following examples:

STATEMENT	**She is** beautiful.		STATEMENT	**They were** here.
QUESTION	**Is she** beautiful?		QUESTION	**Were they** here?

Remember that the subject is the word in the sentence that is tied to the verb by some kind of agreement of forms. So long as the verb is some form of the verb *be*, the statement pattern can be made into a question by simple reversal of subject and verb. The reversal is then a question signal.

STATEMENT

	SUBJECT	VERB	
D	**1**⟷**2**		**3**
The	girl	was	happy.
The	girls	were	happy.
The	weather	was	bad.
His	answers	were	foolish.

QUESTION

VERB		SUBJECT	
2	**D**	**1**	**3**
Was	the	girl	happy?
Were	the	girls	happy?
Was	the	weather	bad?
Were	his	answers	foolish?

STATEMENT

	SUBJECT	VERB		
D	**1**⟷**2**		**D**	**1**
	Sam	is	the	boss.
That	tree	is	a	cypress.
His	father	was	a	carpenter.
The	jewels	were		gifts.

QUESTION

VERB		SUBJECT		
2	**D**	**1**	**D**	**1**
Is		Sam	the	boss?
Is	that	tree	a	cypress?
Was	his	father	a	carpenter?
Were	the	jewels		gifts?

When the verb is some other verb than *be*, we signal the question by using an auxiliary and reversing the subject and the auxiliary, like this:

STATEMENT

SUBJECT	VERB
1 ⟵⟶ 2	
Babies	cry.

QUESTION

AUXILIARY	SUBJECT	VERB
A ⟵⟶ 1		2
Do	babies	cry?
Must	babies	cry?
Can	babies	cry?

Here are some more examples:

STATEMENT

	SUBJECT	VERB	
	1 ⟵⟶ 2		
The	coach	lives	here.
His	mother	plays	the piano.
	Charlie	gave	up.
	Susie	went	by herself.

QUESTION

AUXILIARY		SUBJECT	VERB	
A ⟵⟶ 1			2	
Does	the	coach	live	here?
Can	his	mother	play	the piano?
Is		Charlie	giving	up?
Should		Susie	go	by herself?

There is one verb that will work either way in questions. This is the verb *have*. With *have* we can either simply reverse the verb and the subject, or we can use an auxiliary and reverse the auxiliary and the subject:

STATEMENT He has a father.
QUESTION Has he a father?
QUESTION Does he have a father?

But the first pattern — the simple reversal — is becoming rare with *have*. Probably your great grandchildren won't use it.

When the basic pattern is the one with structure word *there*, the word *there* is what reverses with the verb. The subject is already after the verb in the statement pattern.

STATEMENT

there	2 ⟵⟶ 1			
There	was	a	man	here.
There	were	some	men	here.
There	's	a	cake	in the oven.

QUESTION

2 ⟵⟶ 1	there			
Is	there ,	a	man	here?
Were	there	some	men	here?
Is	there	a	cake	in the oven?

It may strike you that there's another signal in these questions besides the reversal of the subject (or *there*) and the verb (or the auxiliary). What about the pitch? Well, the pitch is sometimes a signal of a question but more often not. Most people have the notion that the pitch rises for questions and falls for statements. But it isn't that simple. Pitch often falls in questions and sometimes rises in statements. It's sometimes a signal but not usually the chief signal.

The question "Is he going?" could be spoken with several pitch patterns, among them these:

Is he ⌐going   Is he ⌐go⌐ing

The first would be just a polite question. The second would be a rather insistent one, as if the questioner had asked the question before and not got a very satisfactory answer. In both of them the reversal rather than the pitch is the main question signal.

Notice that the first question ends with double bar juncture. This is fairly common at the end of questions. As we have seen, double cross is more common at the end of statements.

We do sometimes, however, ask questions in which pitch is the only question signal. This happens when we use statement word order but put double bar juncture at the end. The double bar signals a question:

STATEMENT   John is ⌐he⌐re   STATEMENT   You are ⌐go⌐ing

QUESTION   John is ⌐here   QUESTION   You are ⌐going

It is very common in conversation to leave out the verb or auxiliary in questions of this sort:

John ⌐here   You ⌐going

● EXERCISE 57

A. Turn the following statements into questions. Notice what happens to the subjects, verbs, and auxiliaries.

1. He was here. **2.** He was helping his father. **3.** They had seen the movie. **4.** Sam is sad. **5.** That's a mongoose. **6.** Angela went home early. **7.** The milk sometimes comes in the afternoon. **8.** I should see a doctor. **9.** Charlie had a pretty good day at bat. **10.** The fellow who came in was asking me questions.

B. Can you think of any other pitch patterns to use on "Is he going?" How would they change the meaning or emphasis?

C. Write sentences from the following formulas.

1. 1↔2 3	**7.** D 1ᵃ↔2 D 1ᵃ
2. 2↔1 3	**8.** 2 D 1ᵃ D 1ᵃ
3. D 1↔2 4	**9.** A D 1ᵃ 2-ing D 1ᵇ
4. 2 D 1 4	**10.** there 2 D 1 P D 1
5. 1↔A 2-ing P D 1	**11.** 2 there D 1 4
6. A D 1 2-ing P D 1	**12.** A D 1ᵃ 2 D 1ᵇ D 1ᶜ

1—noun   2—verb   3—adjective   4—adverb
A—auxiliary   D—determiner   P—preposition

58 : Question words

Another way to ask a question is to use a **question word.** A question word is a structure word that signals that the pattern is a question — that is, that it should be answered. Compare these two sentences:

She helped him.
Who helped him?

You will recognize that these are different kinds of sentences. The first is a statement, and the second is a question. If you hear the first, you say "Oh" or "She did?" or perhaps you just nod your head. But if you hear the second, you say "Sheila" or "Sam" or "Some of the girls." In other words, you answer the second but not the first.

Now the only difference between these two sentences is the difference between *she* and *who*. There is ordinarily no difference in intonation. In both the pitch would most commonly be like this:

Therefore, since the two sentences are really different and since the only difference is that one has *who* and the other has *she*, there must be a real difference between *who* and *she*. There is. *She* is a pronoun; it appears in noun positions without changing the basic structure of the sentence. *Who* is a question word. It appears in noun positions, but it *does* change the basic structure of the sentence, making it a question.

There are nine question words in common use in English. They are *who, whom, whose, what, which, when, where, how,* and *why*. All of these have other uses too. They are question words only when they signal that the sentence is a question. (If they don't signal that, they are subordinators.)

Notice the use of question words in the following sentences.

Notice that if we replace the question word with some other word, we no longer have a question but a statement:

Who came? (question)   He came. (statement)
What hurts? (question)   It hurts. (statement)
Which was the winner? (question)   Sam was the winner. (statement)
Whose got lost? (question)   Mine got lost. (statement)
When is the man there? (question)   That is the man there. (statement)
How is the patient? (question)   Edna is the patient. (statement)
Whose father came in? (question)   My father came in. (statement)

Notice that in the last example the question word is in the determiner position. But it's not a determiner; it's a question word.

When we want to indicate question words in formulas, we'll give them the symbol Q:

Q	2
Who	came?
Which	came?
What	hurts?

Q	2	D	1
Which	was	the	winner?
Where	is	my	hat?
How	is	the	patient?

Sometimes we signal a question in two ways at once: by using a question word and also by reversing the subject and verb. But this reversal takes place only when the verb is *be*.

		VERB		SUBJECT
Q		2	D	1
Where		is	the	cat?
Where		are	the	cats?
How		is	the	patient?
How		are	the	patients?
Who		was	the	winner?
Who		were	the	winners?

With verbs other than *be* we use an auxiliary and reverse the subject and the auxiliary.

	AUXILIARY		SUBJECT	
Q	**A**	**D**	**1**	**2**
What	is	the	boy	doing?
What	are	the	boys	doing?
When	is	his	mother	leaving?
When	will	his	mother	leave?
What	could		Charlie	do?
Why	did		he	wait?
Whom	is	the	lawyer	accusing?

When there is no reversal, and when the verb is not *be*, we may say that the question word is itself the subject. In such sentences the question word will always be *who, whose, which,* or *what:*

Q	**2**	
Who	came?	
What	hurts?	
Which	broke?	
Whose	broke?	
What	gives	him that idea?
What	gives	them that idea?
Who	killed	cock robin?

Sometimes a question word occurs after a preposition. Here the question word will be *whom, whose, which,* or *what:*

P	**Q**	
With	whom	did he come?
With	what	did he hit her?

The questions that have question words as the signal are different from those that have just reversal of subject and verb. The reversal questions are a kind that can be answered with *yes* or *no* or some equivalent. We can call them *yes–no* questions:

QUESTION	Is he here?	ANSWER	Yes.
QUESTION	Did he want it?	ANSWER	No.
QUESTION	Are any of them going?	ANSWER	Probably not.

But the questions with question words cannot be answered with *yes* or *no*. We answer them by saying a noun, a verb, an adjective, an adverb, or perhaps a word group:

QUESTION   Who came in?
ANSWER   Charlie.

QUESTION   What are you doing?
ANSWER   Working.

QUESTION   How is she getting along?
ANSWER   Pretty well.

QUESTION   Why did you hit him?
ANSWER   Because he made a crack about my necktie.

There is another way of asking a *yes–no* question besides reversing the subject and the verb. This is to utter the sentence as if it were a statement, then to add something like *didn't he*, or *can't they*, or *shouldn't I* at the end:

He can come with us, can't he?
Your father likes me, doesn't he?
I should hear from him pretty soon, shouldn't I?

Notice the form of this **question marker** at the end of the sentence. It consists of an auxiliary plus *n't* plus a pronoun that repeats the subject. The *n't* is a weakened form of *not*, and it is in a class by itself. Nothing patterns like it. If we want to indicate it in a formula, we'll use the symbol **N**.

	A	**N**	**1**
He can come with us,	can	't	he?
He started it	did	n't	he?
Charlie is going,	is	n't	he?

Notice that at the end of the main pattern we have double bar juncture in speech, and in writing a comma.

The auxiliary that occurs depends on what goes before. If the main pattern contains an auxiliary, then that auxiliary is repeated in the question marker.

The girls **were** going, **weren't** they?
Sam **might** do it, **mightn't** he?
They **have** gone, **haven't** they?

If the main pattern doesn't contain an auxiliary and the verb is *be* or *have*, we just repeat the verb in the trailer, as this construction might be called:

The girls **were** here, **weren't** they?
The pie **was** good, **wasn't** it?
He **has** the money, **hasn't** he?

If the main pattern doesn't contain an auxiliary and the verb is anything but *be* or *have*, we use *don't*, *doesn't*, or *didn't* in the trailer:

Charlie **left, didn't** he?
She **looks** better, **doesn't** she?
They **raise** parrots, **don't** they?

● **EXERCISE 58**

A. The following sentences are all statements. Turn each one into a question in three different ways.

EXAMPLE   Charlie is here
        (1) Is Charlie here?
        (2) Charlie is here, isn't he?
        (3) Who is here?
            Why is Charlie here?
            When is Charlie here?

Notice that questions 1 and 2 are *yes–no* questions and the questions in 3 are not.

1. He was sick. **2.** They were feeling better. **3.** They felt better. **4.** Your mother is a good cook. **5.** Your mother makes good pies. **6.** There's a doctor in the house. **7.** He fixed the car himself. **8.** Alice knows how to change a tire.

B. Write sentences from the following formulas.

1. 1 2 3

2. Q 2 3

3. 2 1 3

4. Q 2 D 1

5. Q A D 1 2

6. Q A D 1ª 2 D 1ᵇ

7. 2 there D 1 P D 1

8. Q 2 there D 1 P D 1

9. P Q A D 1 2-ing

10. 1 2 3 ‖ A N 1

11. 1ª A 2 D 1ᵇ ‖ A N 1ª

12. D 1ª 2 D 1ᵇ ‖ A N 1ª

1–noun   2–verb   3–adjective
A–auxiliary   D–determiner   N–n't   P–preposition
Q–question word

---

59 : Request patterns

The third and last main type of sentence is the request. A request sentence is a sentence which tends to make the hearer do something:

> Close the window.   (Hearer closes the window.)
> Sit down.   (Hearer sits down.)
> Go to bed.   (Hearer goes to bed.)

The request pattern is the simplest of all the sentence patterns. It consists basically of just the simple form of a verb, without any subject. There may be nouns in the sentence, but they will not be tied to the verb and so will not be subjects of the verb.

The verb of the request can expand into a verb cluster. All the kinds of verb clusters occur here as they do in the statement patterns we studied earlier. Here are some:

2	4	2L	3	2	D	1
Stop.		Be	good.	Stop	that	racket.
Hurry.		Be	patient.	Watch	that	squirrel.
Come	here.	Keep	quiet.	Watch	those	squirrels.
Walk	quietly.	Look	sharp.			
Sleep	well.					

2L	D	1
Be	a	man.
Be		men.
Be	my	helper.

2	P	D	1
Stay	in	the	house.
Walk	on	your	hands.
Go	to		bed.

2	D	1ᵃ	D	1ᵇ
Give	the	man	his	money.
Write		me	a	letter.

4	2	D	1ᵃ	D	1ᵃ
Never	call	a	man	a	fool.
	Consider		me	your	friend.

Sometimes we vary the request patterns by using either *please* or *let's* in front of them. *Please* and *let's* are structure words which signal that the following sentence is a request sentence.

please	**2**	
Please	stop.	
Please	come	here.
Please	come	to the office.
Please	help	me with my homework.
Please	pay	the man his money.
Please	be	patient.
Please	stop	that racket.

let's	**2**	
Let's	stop.	
Let's	help	Al with his homework.
Let's	pay	the man his money.
Let's	be	patient.
Let's	put	some wheels on the car.
Let's	get	a place down in front.

Notice that, though *please* and *let's* are both request signals, they are different kinds of request signals. *Please* signals that the hearer is to do the action. *Let's* signals that both the hearer and the speaker are to do the action:

> **Please go quietly.   (Hearer goes quietly.)**
> **Let's go quietly.   (Hearer and speaker both go quietly.)**
>
> **Please help the men.   (Hearer helps them.)**
> **Let's help the men.   (Hearer and speaker both help them.)**

Please and *let's* have both developed from verbs, and these forms still occur as verbs sometimes. For example, *please* is a verb in "That will please Mother." Here we could substitute various verbs without changing the pattern: "That will annoy Mother," "That will satisfy Mother," and so on.

But none of these words will substitute for *please* in "Please go away." Here *please* is unique for some speakers. Some other speakers use *kindly* in the same way:

> **Please go away.**
> **Kindly go away.**

We can see that *please* is a request signal if we put it into a sentence like "Will you come this afternoon." Without *please* this might be ambiguous. It might be taken as either a question or a request. But if we put in *please*, it is a clear request:

> **Will you please come this afternoon.**

The structure word *let's* developed from *let* plus *us*. Sometimes this combination is still used in such a way that *let* is a verb and *us* is a pronoun: "Let us help you." Here we could put in other verbs in place of *let:* "Make us help you," "Watch us help you," "Permit us to help you," and so on.

But no verbs will substitute for *let* in "Let's go over and see Charlie." Here *let's* is just a way of including both speaker and hearer in the action proposed. *Go* and *see* are the verbs of the sentence, and *let's* is in a class by itself.

● **EXERCISE 59**

A. Turn each of the following statement patterns first into a question and then into a request.

EXAMPLE   He's going to the store.

Is he going to the store?
Who's going to the store?
When is he going to the store?

Go to the store.
Please go to the store.
Let's go to the store.

1. He was waiting for a bus. **2.** He bought the baby a small alligator. **3.** You're the boss here. **4.** He had the car fixed. **5.** We should elect Al. **6.** He didn't call me a liar. **7.** They kept going until they reached the highway. **8.** He isn't afraid of anything.

B. Write sentences from the following formulas. In order to keep question patterns separate from request patterns, all tied (subject-verb) constructions are marked here with a double arrow (↔). If the double arrow isn't shown between a noun and a verb, the noun isn't the subject of the verb.

1. D 1↔2 4

2. 2 D 1 4

3. 2 D 1 4

4. please 2 D 1 4

5. let's 2 P D 1

6. D 1ᵃ↔2 D 1ᵇ D 1ᶜ

7. please 2 1ᵃ D 1ᵇ

8. A↔1ᵃ 2 1ᵇ D 1ᶜ

9. 1ᵃ↔A N 2 D 1ᵇ

10. A N 2 3

11. 2 there D 1 P D 1

12. let's 2 P D 1 S D 1↔2 4

1–noun   2–verb   3–adjective   4–adverb
A–auxiliary   D–determiner   N–n't   P–preposition   S–subordinator

Part Ten

60: Form classes

Well, we haven't by any means said all there is to say about the patterns of English. We could easily go on through a dozen books the size of this one, uncovering new structures and arrangements, new forms and features. There's no end to the complications of a living language.

But we've seen enough to get a general notion of what English is like. We've traced out the main lines. If you've survived this far, you ought to have a pretty good idea of what the stuff is that you use when you talk to your friends or write English compositions or yell at an umpire.

It's time now to look back and try to see it as a whole.

English sentence patterns are made up of several different features working together in complicated ways. On one level we have sounds — vowels and consonants. There are thirty-three of them, nine vowels and twenty-four consonants, and when we write, we try to represent these sounds with the twenty-six letters of the alphabet. As we've seen, our English spelling doesn't represent English sounds very well, but insofar as the letters stand for anything they stand for sounds.

The vowels and consonants combine to form words, and the words fall into different groups according to their form and the positions they occupy in patterns. We have two main kinds of word groups: form classes and structure groups. The great bulk of the words in our vocabularies pattern as members of the form classes. Only a couple of hundred are distributed in the structure groups.

Certain arrangements of the form classes give us the half-dozen or so basic sentence patterns. These basic patterns can all be expanded through modification. Any noun may expand into a noun cluster, any verb into a verb cluster. Adjectives and adverbs can be the nuclei of adjective and adverb clusters.

A sentence pattern — whether simple or expanded — can be made part of another pattern through the operation of a subordinator. Two patterns can be combined by a conjunction or a sentence connector. It is in this process of modification and combination that the structure words play their part in the patterns of English.

Looking through the structure of English sentences, we see various units that cannot be linked up with any single class of words or single kind of structure. These we call function units, and we have noticed such function units as subjects, objects, noun modifiers, verb modifiers, sentence modifiers. These are not word classes because all kinds of words occur in them. A subject is most often a noun or a pronoun, but it might also be a verb or verb cluster or an adjective or an S-group or even a P-group. But even though function units are not word classes, they are always clearly marked in a clear sentence. We always know whether a word is a subject or a linking-verb complement or a modifier or something else.

The whole complex of the English sentence is composed of pairs of structures. These we have called pattern parts. As a whole the sentence has two pattern parts, each working as a unit against the other. Each of these parts has two parts, each of these two, and so on down to the word unit. We have seen that when we cut a sentence into its pattern parts, we are constantly separating out a few frequently recurring structures: noun clusters, verb clusters, P-groups, and S-groups. Even very complicated sentences are seen to consist of a few familiar patterns repeated and combined in different ways.

Over the whole business lies intonation: pitch, stress, and juncture. These play a very important part in English patterns. They mark out sentences, tie pattern parts together, separate word classes sometimes, signal sentence modifiers, and keep the whole course of the pattern straight. In writing, we try to reflect something of the intonation through punctuation.

We will now take a look at these features in review, and we'll begin with form classes.

FORM CLASSES

English has four **form classes,** which we call **nouns, verbs, adjectives,** and **adverbs.** They are very large classes. Any good speaker of English commands tens of thousands of nouns and thousands of verbs, adjectives, and adverbs. These are *classes* because each one occurs in a certain set of positions in English patterns. They are *form* classes because they are signaled by features of form, mostly suffixes and prefixes.

It would take a very long time to describe all the form features of any one of the form classes. But each class has one prominent feature that can be quickly noticed.

The obvious form feature of **nouns** (1) is the plural ending: *boys, men, witches, mice, oxen,* contrasted with *boy, man, witch, mouse, ox.* The regular ending is /s/, /z/, or /əz/, depending on the sound structure of the singular form: /kæts/, /bɔyz/, /wicəz/. In writing, this is always *s* or *es: cats, boys, witches.*

The great majority of noun plurals have this regular ending. The others — like *men, mice, oxen, alumni* — are irregular, and the child learning the language has to learn them one by one and discover that they are special. But all the plural endings — regular and irregular — are alike in that they are features of nouns; they all give the noun the meaning "more than one."

The nouns with plural endings may be thought of as the hard core of the noun class. Words like *indignation, chaos, Charlie* don't usually have plural endings. We call these words nouns simply because in general they pattern like the words that form plurals.

Another feature of nouns is what is called the possessive form: *boy's, man's, witch's, mouse's, ox's.* In speech the possessive is exactly like the plural form except that there aren't any irregular possessives. Thus /bɔyz/ is the speech form for either *boys* or *boy's.* In writing we use the apostrophe before the *s* for the possessive but not for the plural. If you have trouble keeping possessives and plurals separate in writing, you might remember that if the *s* doesn't signify more than one, the form is a possessive and should be written with an apostrophe.

A complication comes in when we make a plural noun possessive. Then we put the apostrophe after the *s: the boys' mother.* This is a writing signal only. Notice that these would sound exactly alike in speech:

the boy's mother   the boys' mother

The hearer must have some other way of knowing whether the speaker means one boy or more. With irregular plurals, however, there is a distinction:

the man's mother   the men's mother

The central form feature of the **verb** (2) class is the past tense form. Again we have one regular form and several irregular forms. The regular past tense form is the set of endings /t/, /d/, and /əd/. We choose one or the other automatically, depending on the sound structure of the verb: /piykt/, /siymd/, /endəd/. We spell nearly all of these with *ed: peeked, seemed, ended.*

Something like two hundred English verbs have irregular forms of one kind or another for the past tense — *told, brought, wrote, fell, bent, got, set,* and so on. When we learn English, we learn the regular pattern as a pattern; but we learn the irregular forms one by one.

Verbs are different from the other form classes in that their central form feature — the past tense — runs all the way through the class. Not all nouns form plurals, but all verbs can form a past tense in some way or other.

Another possibility that all verbs have is the possibility of ending in *ing: peeking, seeming, ending.* This form occurs when the verb is used with the auxiliary *be* and also commonly when the verb is used as a modifier or in other function units.

All verbs can take the past tense form or the *ing* form, but not all words with these forms are verbs. In the course of the development of the language there has been a tendency for some of these words to move into the adjective class. Thus *charming* is now usually an adjective, as in "She's a very charming girl," where it patterns like *beautiful* or *sad.* Of course, we can still use it as a verb, as in "She was charming a snake."

The hard core of the **adjective** (3) class is the group of words that take the endings *er* and *est* to give the meanings "more" and "most." Such forms are *braver, bravest; quicker, quickest; sharper, sharpest.* An adjective like *brave* is sometimes called the **positive** form; one like *braver* is called the **comparative** form; and one like *bravest* is the **superlative** form. These words are adjectives, and other words that pattern like them are also adjectives.

The adjectives that take *er* and *est* are mostly one-syllable words, although quite a few two-syllable adjectives and a few three-syllable adjectives take them too: *happier, unhappiest.* Other adjectives express these meanings with *more* and *most: more beautiful, most beautiful.* We don't ordinarily use the two forms on the same word. That is, we don't say "more braver."

Nearly all adjectives also pattern with *very* and other intensifiers: *very brave, very beautiful.*

The most conspicuous form feature of **adverbs** (4) is the *ly* ending added to an adjective base: *bravely, happily, quickly, beautifully.* Not all words with *ly* are adverbs. If you add *ly* to a noun base, you get an adjective: *costly, queenly, lovely.* But the great mass of *ly* words are adverbs, because nearly all adjectives can be turned into adverbs by the addition of *ly*, whereas only a few nouns add *ly* to form adjectives.

Words without *ly* that pattern in general like *bravely, happily, beautifully* are called adverbs too. There are two chief groups in addition to the *ly* group. One is a set of words like *seldom, sometimes, often, never, ever, once, twice.* The other is a larger group including *away, up, in, sideways,* and several dozen others. These are adverbs when they pattern with verbs: *went away, went up, went in, went sideways.* *

We have observed that there is a good deal of shifting around of the membership of the form classes. A word will turn up now as a noun and again as a verb. A word will be an adjective in one pattern and an adverb in another. But in all good sentences the form classes are always marked by a complicated system of signals. If you actually can't tell whether a word is a noun or a verb, a noun or an adjective, an adjective or an adverb, a verb or an adjective, then you can't understand the sentence.

● **EXERCISE 60**

A. To what class — noun, verb, adjective, or adverb — does each of the following words belong? Frame sentences to prove your answer. Each word patterns in just one class, except in very unusual usages.

1. foolish	**8.** gardenia	**14.** circular	**20.** formerly
2. strength	**9.** suitcase	**15.** dungeon	**21.** reveal
3. miserable	**10.** realize	**16.** friendly	**22.** bird
4. loudly	**11.** vicious	**17.** boastful	**23.** tripe
5. write	**12.** frequently	**18.** forget	**24.** hesitate
6. quicken	**13.** ladder	**19.** farther	**25.** reasonable
7. lengthwise			

* An interesting contrast can be seen in the sentences "She went in" and "That's the house she lived in." In the first sentence the *in* has strong stress, but in the second it has weak stress. Probably only the first *in* should be called an adverb. The second can be considered a special use of a preposition. Notice also the contrast between "Lean out the window" and "Clean out the desk." In the first, the pattern parts are: "Lean / out the window." *Out* is the preposition in a P-group. But in the second, the pattern parts are "Clean out / the desk." *Desk* is the object of *clean out,* and *out* is an adverb patterning with *clean.*

B. These words commonly occur in more than one class. Which classes? Frame sentences to show their usage.

1. wall	**5.** walk	**9.** phone	**13.** down
2. hard	**6.** map	**10.** phoney	**14.** worry
3. well	**7.** quiet	**11.** early	**15.** private
4. interesting	**8.** smell	**12.** grip	**16.** word

C. Write the plurals of these nouns.

1. book	**7.** tree	**13.** toe
2. pass	**8.** button	**14.** tomato
3. woman	**9.** knife	**15.** piano
4. plug	**10.** half	**16.** hitch
5. mouse	**11.** ox	**17.** louse
6. sheep	**12.** child	**18.** tooth

D. Which of these nouns don't ordinarily have plurals?

1. bed	**6.** triviality	**11.** pleasure
2. honesty	**7.** anger	**12.** mud
3. lawn	**8.** size	**13.** mutton
4. gravel	**9.** gold	**14.** wisdom
5. surprise	**10.** happiness	

E. Write the past tense forms of these verbs.

1. sell	**8.** shut	**15.** make	**22.** send
2. fall	**9.** fly	**16.** do	**23.** begin
3. scream	**10.** speak	**17.** slap	**24.** come
4. mean	**11.** shout	**18.** sit	**25.** hope
5. hit	**12.** end	**19.** lead	**26.** water
6. talk	**13.** bend	**20.** cry	**27.** leave
7. bring	**14.** quit	**21.** drive	**28.** anchor

F. To which of these adjectives would it be natural for you to add *er* and *est?* With which would you be more likely to use *more* and *most?*

1. happy	**6.** low	**11.** certain
2. sad	**7.** hopeful	**12.** suitable
3. beautiful	**8.** decent	**13.** kind
4. courageous	**9.** interesting	**14.** flashy
5. long	**10.** honest	**15.** stubborn

61 : Structure groups

We can say how many form classes there are in English: four. But we can't say how many groups of structure words there are. The number we identify would depend on how complete we wanted our description of the language to be and also on how fine and detailed a description we wanted to make. What we have done here is to pick out the important groups that operate in the most common patterns of written English.

The structure groups differ in several ways from the form classes. The most obvious difference is size. Whereas the form classes are very large, with thousands and thousands of items in them, the structure groups are very small. The largest of them has something like seventy items. Some of them have only one item.

Another difference is that the structure words have no features of form to mark them in our sentences. The form classes may be marked by features like plural endings or tense endings or suffixes and prefixes of various kinds. But the structure words don't have these. We have shown this to be true by substituting nonsense words for the form classes and seeing that we can do this and still understand the structure of the sentence. But when we put in nonsense words in place of the structure words, the structure of the sentence disappears.

A third difference is that the basic patterns of English consist of a few arrangements of the form classes: "Birds sing," "Birds are beautiful," "Birds eat worms," and so on. The structure words come into play mostly when these basic patterns expand: "Most of the birds that I've seen are very beautiful when they manage to keep themselves clean."

Some of the structure groups have special connections with certain form classes. The distinctive feature of **determiners** (D) is that they pattern in a special way with nouns. Such words as *the, a, my, every, our* regularly mark the beginning of a noun cluster. They serve as signals that nouns are coming. Sometimes the noun follows immediately: *the hat, a rabbit, my brother*. But the space between the determiner and the noun can open up, and all sorts of other noun modifiers can come in after the determiner: *the silly hat, a cute little lettuce-nibbling cottontail rabbit.*

Words like *some, both, each, these* are sometimes determiners and sometimes pronouns. They are determiners when they operate like *the*, opening a noun cluster: "These rabbits get on my nerves" or "These little cottontail rabbits get on my nerves." They are pronouns when they occur in the place of the noun cluster: "These get on my nerves."

Many words occur only as **pronouns** (1) and never as determiners: *he, me, anything, mine, everyone*, etc. These occur in noun positions. They don't mark the beginning of noun clusters; that is, instead of signaling that a noun is coming, as determiners do, they take the place of a noun or a noun cluster.

Prepositions (P) also pattern with nouns but in a different way. They form units with following nouns or noun clusters, standing before the determiner if there is one: *with the rabbit, on his silly hat, under the table, after dinner*. Preposition groups are very frequent in English patterns. We have seen the unit **P 1** or **P D 1** occurring over and over again.

Auxiliaries (A) pattern with verbs. There are three types of auxiliaries. One includes such words as *may, can, will, do, might, should;* these pattern with the simple form of verbs, like *go, watch, help, see, return*. Forms of the auxiliary *be* (*am, is, are, was, were*) pattern with *ing* verbs, like *going, watching, helping, seeing, returning*. Forms of the auxiliary *be* and the auxiliary *have* pattern with past forms of verbs, like *gone, watched, helped, seen, returned*. Auxiliaries change the meaning of verbs in various ways. Some indicate time. Some add such meanings as possibility or necessity. Some show that the action is going on or relate it in time to some other action.

Intensifiers (V) pattern with adjectives and adverbs. We use the symbol V from the word *very*, which is one of the most common

intensifiers. Others are *rather, more, most, quite, somewhat, fairly.*
Not all speakers use the same intensifiers. For example, some
speakers use *plenty* and *real* as intensifiers, and others don't.

Then we have three structure groups used to combine patterns
in various ways. These are the **conjunctions,** the **sentence connectors,** and the **subordinators.**

Conjunctions (C) are words that pattern like *and.* Sometimes
they connect parts of patterns:

The boys and the girls talked and played.

Sometimes they connect whole patterns:

The boys talked, and the girls played.

In writing we usually have a comma before a conjunction when
it connects whole patterns. Or we might have a semicolon or a
period. We don't usually have any punctuation before the conjunction when it connects parts of patterns. Common conjunctions are *and, but, or, nor, for, yet, so,* though some of these words
have other uses too.

Sentence connectors (T) are words that pattern like *therefore.*
These usually connect whole patterns and usually have a semicolon or a period before them. Unlike conjunctions, sentence
connectors can move around in the second of the two patterns
they connect. That is, we can say either "Charlie was sleepy;
therefore he went to bed" or "Charlie was sleepy; he therefore
went to bed."

Subordinators (S) are words that pattern like *because.* They
stand in front of sentence patterns and make them part of
larger structures. Unlike conjunctions or sentence connectors,
they can join two patterns while standing in front of both of
them. That is, we can say either "Charlie went to bed because
he was sleepy" or "Because he was sleepy, Charlie went to
bed."

A different kind of subordinator is a word like *who* in "The
man who went to bed was Charlie." This also makes a sentence

pattern part of a larger structure, but it is itself part of the pattern it subordinates.

A special group of structure words are the **question words** (**Q**), words which signal that the sentence is a question. Such words are *who* in "Who is he?" or *where* in "Where is he?" Forms commonly used as question words in English are *who, whom, whose, what, which, where, when, how,* and *why.*

The other structure words that we have noticed pattern uniquely. That is, each one is in a class by itself. A very important one is structure word *there,* which occurs in such sentences as "There is a man here." This is important because it figures in a basic statement pattern which has become very common in English.

Other special words are *please, let's,* and *not. Please* and *let's* signal different kinds of request sentences: "Please go" and "Let's go." *Not* makes sentence patterns negative: "He is not here." It most commonly occurs in the variant form that we spell *n't*: "He isn't here." *Not* is special because of the way it combines with auxiliaries and verbs and the way it is used in questions: "Isn't he here?"

There are many other structure groups that we haven't noticed. We use a special set of words to attract attention. An example is *say* in "Say, Charlie was just looking for you." Another set of words signals a response to some statement. Such a one is *why* in "Why, I don't think he meant that." *Hello* and *good-by* pattern specially, as do *yes* and *no,* and *okay,* which is different from *yes,* and many others. It would take a very long time to give a full description of the structure words of English.

● EXERCISE 61

A. Rewrite the sentence below using nonsense words in place of the form classes. Try to mark the nonsense words with suffixes so that the structure will be clear.

When the courageous sailor waved his hand and left, the girl who had been talking to him wept bitterly.

B. Now write the sentence again, keeping the original form-class words but putting nonsense words in place of the structure words. What happens to the sentence meaning?

C. The following words have just one structural use in ordinary English. Make sentences to show their use, and say what structure group they belong to.

1. every	**3.** or	**5.** because	**7.** nevertheless
2. with	**4.** my	**6.** if	**8.** let's

D. The following words pattern sometimes in one group and sometimes in another. Frame sentences to show their different possibilities. Some occur in the form classes.

1. some	**4.** before	**7.** both
2. when	**5.** each	**8.** but
3. that	**6.** please	**9.** though

---

62 : Basic patterns and function units

Nearly all the complicated structures that make up our English sentences can be seen as variations of a very few basic patterns. This is one of the things that explain how we can learn our language and use it as easily as we do. We are not dealing with new structures all the time. We are just making changes in old ones.

BASIC PATTERNS

It would be as hard to say what all the basic patterns of English are as it would be to say what all the structure groups are. Something depends on how detailed and complete the description is to be. But certain common patterns stand out prominently.

One is simply a noun tied to a verb:

$$1 \longleftrightarrow 2$$

Birds	sing.
Charlie	sings.

Another is a noun tied to a verb with an adjective following:

$$1 \longleftrightarrow 2 \qquad 3$$

Birds	are	happy.
Al	is	happy.

The verb in this pattern is what we have called a linking verb.

When we have a noun after the verb, we may have either of two patterns, depending on whether the verb is a linking verb or not. If it is a linking verb, the two nouns will refer to the same person or thing. The verbs that commonly link nouns in this way in American English are *be* and *become:*

$$1^a \longleftrightarrow 2 \qquad 1^a$$

Pigeons	are		birds.
Al	became	my	friend.

Other verbs signal that the two nouns refer to different people or different things. This gives us another basic pattern:

$$1^a \longleftrightarrow 2 \qquad 1^b$$

Robins	like		worms.
Al	hates	my	friend.

When we have two nouns after the verb, we again get different patterns according to whether the second two nouns refer to the same person or thing or not. If they do, we get a construction like this:

$$1^a \longleftrightarrow 2 \qquad 1^b \qquad 1^b$$

Robins	consider	worms		candy.
Al	called	Stan	a	hero.

If they refer to different persons or things, we get this basic pattern:

1ᵃ ⟷ 2		1ᵇ		1ᶜ
People	feed	pigeons		crumbs.
Al	gave	Stan	a	medal.

The signal which distinguishes these last two patterns is the verb. Some verbs signal that the two following nouns refer to different persons or things: *gave, feed, send, tell,* etc. Other verbs signal that the two following nouns refer to the same person or thing: *consider, think, appoint, elect.* Some verbs, like *call,* appear in both patterns. With these, ambiguity is always possible, as in "The Sultan called me a slave." This might mean (1) "He said I was a slave" or (2) "He summoned a slave to wait on me." Another basic pattern involves the structure word *there.* This is followed by a verb — usually *be* — then a noun tied to the verb and then some other construction, like an adverb or a P-group:

there	2	D	1	4
There	is	a	man	here.
There	are	some	men	here.

All of these basic patterns can be expanded into much longer constructions:

Birds sing.
Birds sing sweetly.
The birds sing sweetly.
The birds sing very sweetly.
The little birds sing very sweetly.
The little birds are singing very sweetly.
The little birds are still singing very sweetly.
The little birds in the tree are still singing very sweetly.

But all of these are basically the same pattern: "Birds sing." Any of the other basic patterns could be expanded in similar ways.

FUNCTION UNITS

The various positions occupied by the nouns in these basic patterns are what we have called **function units**. Function units are not word classes. Other kinds of words besides nouns can occur in them and often do.

In the basic patterns the noun that is tied to the verb is called the **subject**. The noun and verb are tied in the sense that the form of one depends upon the form of the other. We say "Birds sing" but "The bird sings." In most statement patterns the subject comes before the verb. But in the *there* pattern the verb comes first. The verb comes first also in similar patterns which begin with certain adverbs, like "Seldom were the men happy."

The noun after the linking verb in the pattern 1^a **2** 1^a is called a **linking-verb complement**. In the pattern 1^a **2** 1^b the second noun is an **object**. In 1^a **2** 1^b 1^b the noun after the verb is an **object**, and the last noun is an **object complement**. In 1^a **2** 1^b 1^c the 1^b is an **indirect object**, and the 1^c is an **object**.

Remember that these function units are not word classes. We illustrate them with nouns, because it's easy to do so, but many other structures occur in them. Here is some of the variety in the subject unit:

Pigeons eat worms.   (simple noun)
The little pigeons that live around here eat worms.   (noun cluster)
He is the boss.   (pronoun)
Swimming is a lot of fun.   (simple verb)
Splashing around in the lake is a lot of fun.   (verb cluster)
What he wants to do will cost plenty.   (S-group)
Who came in?   (question word)

Function units of a somewhat different sort are the **modifiers**. We have noticed three in particular: **noun modifiers, verb modifiers,** and **sentence modifiers**. All of these have a great deal of variety.

The most common modifiers of nouns are of course the determiners. Probably next most common are adjectives and other nouns. When adjectives and nouns modify other nouns, we tell the two kinds of modifiers apart not only by the form contrasts that distinguish adjectives from nouns but also, usually, by the stress. In *old house* the louder stress would come on *house;* in *town house* it would come on *town.*

Various kinds of verbs also occur as noun modifiers: *barking dog, reading room, scalded finger.* Notice that the first two of these would be distinguished by stress. Adverbs frequently modify nouns, coming after the noun: *the people here.* P-groups and S-groups are other common noun modifiers.

Verbs are most commonly modified by adverbs of three different types: *go away, go quietly, go often.* P-groups and S-groups are also very common: *go to the store, go if you can.* Certain nouns modify verbs: *go next Wednesday, go that way.* These are the nouns that we have called *th* nouns, because their meanings are similar to the meanings of *then, thus,* or *there.* Auxiliaries modify verbs, as determiners do nouns, and in addition verbs modify other verbs, as in *keep going* or *keep trying to go.*

Sentence modifiers are most likely to be word groups, with P-groups and S-groups as the most common. Verb clusters also occur as sentence modifiers, as in "Diving into the pool, Alice caught the seal." Sentence modifiers often come before the pattern they modify, and when they do, they are marked as sentence modifiers by position. When they come in the middle or at the end of the pattern, intonation (or punctuation in writing) becomes a more important signal. "Alice caught the seal, diving into the pool" and "Alice caught the seal diving into the pool" don't mean the same thing. *Diving into the pool* is a sentence modifier in the first but a noun modifier in the second.

There are several other function units that we haven't gone into much because they don't play so important a part in sentence patterns. One such unit is the adjective modifier. Adjectives are most commonly modified by intensifiers: *very sad.* But they can also be modified by adverbs, *quietly sick;* by P-groups, *ready for anything;* by S-groups, *taller than you are;* by nouns, *skin deep;* by verbs, *boiling hot;* and by other adjectives, *icy cold.*

● **EXERCISE 62**

A. Write sentences to illustrate each of the basic sentence patterns listed in this chapter.

B. Write four sentences using a different kind of structure as the subject in each one. For example, you might use a noun, a noun cluster, a pronoun, a verb, a verb cluster, or an S-group. If you think hard enough, you might even manage an adverb or a P-group.

C. Write four sentences using a different kind of structure as an object in each one.

D. Illustrate the different kinds of noun modifiers by writing clusters in which the noun *man* is the headword.

E. Illustrate the different kinds of verb modifiers by writing clusters in which the verb *walk* is the headword.

---

63 : Pattern parts

One of the things we have to know when we hear or read a sentence is what goes with what. Another way of saying this is to say that we have to know what the **pattern parts** are. Think of an English sentence as a series of levels. On each level there are two parts, one part working against the other.

Mostly, English structure goes by twos. There are some structures — particularly series of words — in which there are more than two parts. But to keep things simple we can limit our study to two-part levels. This will give a satisfactory idea of the way sentences build up.

PATTERN PARTS OF WHOLE SENTENCES

The top level is the whole sentence. The pattern parts on this level are the sentence modifier, if there is one, working against the rest of the sentence:

> After he milked the cows / he took a little nap.
> Diving into the pool / Alice caught the seal.
> Alice caught the seal / diving into the pool.
> Fortunately / Charlie knew how to change a tire.

If there is no sentence modifier, the pattern consists of the subject as one part and the verb or verb cluster as the other. As we have seen, the subject is most often a noun, or noun cluster or pronoun, but it doesn't have to be:

> Charlie / changed the tire.
> A man who happened along / changed the tire.
> What he does with it / is his own business.
> He / 's going to give my brother a job.
> Driving in heavy traffic / is very tiring.

PATTERN PARTS OF NOUN CLUSTERS

Noun clusters and verb clusters have their own kinds of build-up. In a noun cluster the pattern consists of the last modifier after the noun as one part and the rest of the pattern as the other. That is, the last modifier modifies everything else:

> a handsome young man with a tire wrench / who happened along
> some trees on his farm / that were in full blossom

Then the next modifier toward the headword modifies everything in front of it:

> a handsome young man / with a tire wrench
> some trees / on his farm

The first modifier on the left of the headword modifies everything after it up to the headword. The second modifies everything after it, and so on:

> a handsome young man / with a tire wrench
> a / handsome young man
> handsome / young man
> young / man

Of course we must know whether the word is a modifier of the noun or is patterning with one of the other modifiers. *A very handsome young used car salesman* would be grouped this way:

> a / very handsome young used car salesman
> very handsome / young used car salesman
> young / used car salesman
> used car / salesman

PATTERN PARTS OF VERB CLUSTERS

The build-up of a verb cluster is in a sense the opposite of that of a noun cluster. The modifiers *before* the headword modify everything that follows:

> often / walked to the store in the rain when he felt good

Then the last modifier on to the right of the headword modifies the rest, and then the next, and so on up to the headword:

> walked to the store in the rain / when he felt good
> walked to the store / in the rain
> walked / to the store

Auxiliaries and objects and all the other paraphernalia that occur in verb clusters behave just like modifiers so far as pattern parts are concerned:

> sometimes / answered the phone cheerfully
> answered the phone / cheerfully
> answered / the phone

> must / have been telling everybody in town my business
> have / been telling everybody in town my business
> been / telling everybody in town my business
> telling everybody in town / my business
> telling / everybody in town

PATTERN PARTS OF S-GROUPS

The pattern parts of an S-group are the subordinator as one part and the sentence pattern as the rest. The subordinator works against the pattern, subordinating it to some other structure:

> because / he liked to walk to the store
> if / a man with a tire wrench comes along
> that / he was going with us

Subordinators of the *who* type are slightly different, but the principle is the same:

> who / liked to walk to the store
> that / we met on the road
> whom / he wanted us to meet
> to whom / he had never been introduced.

PATTERN PARTS OF P-GROUPS

The pattern parts of a P-group are the preposition as one part and the rest as the other. The rest is likely to be a noun or pronoun or a noun cluster, but it doesn't have to be:

> with / Charlie
> from / a friend
> to / a friend of mine
> by / a fellow I knew in Kansas
> for / having talked back to a policeman

Notice that in the last example the preposition is patterning with a verb cluster. We can now go on and cut the cluster and observe that the parts are just what they would be for any verb cluster:

> having / talked back to a policeman
> talked back / to a policeman
> talked / back

These different structures — noun clusters, verb clusters,

P-groups, S-groups — occur in all sorts of function units. But wherever they occur, their pattern parts are always the same, always work together in the same way.

Once again we have hit only the high spots. But this is the general idea and shows the principle on which the language operates. Generally it goes by twos. Probably you can take other patterns and figure out the parts for yourself. For example, the pattern "There are some men here" consists of two parts — *there* as one and the rest as the other. *There* gets the whole thing started; *are some men here*, with the verb coming before the subject, works like a verb cluster:

> There / are some men here
> are some men / here
> are / some men

● **EXERCISE 63**

A. What are the two top parts of the following sentences?

1. Because he loved art, Steve visited the museum. **2.** The people in the rear were shoving. **3.** In the meantime the doctor had lost his stethoscope. **4.** Alice caught the seal, diving into the pool. **5.** Alice caught the seal diving into the pool.

B. What are the two top parts of the following noun clusters?

1. a boy who came in later **2.** the young fellow in the blue suit **3.** the young fellow in the blue suit who came in later **4.** a rather shy college professor **5.** rather shy college professors

C. What are the two top parts of the following verb clusters?

1. moved into the house in the nick of time **2.** moved into the house on the corner **3.** seldom did what he was told **4.** might help us with the dishes **5.** acted up like a wild man when he couldn't have his way

D. What are the two top parts of the following P-groups and S-groups?

1. with his old mother **2.** when the rain started **3.** after the dinner that we had last night **4.** by answering cheerfully whenever anyone spoke to him **5.** for the old man who comes around when we need vegetables

E. Cut the following sentences to show all of their pattern parts. The best way is to keep working down on the left until you get to single words, then do the same thing on the right.

EXAMPLE

When she got there the cupboard in the hall was bare.
When she got there / the cupboard in the hall was bare.
When / she got there
    she / got there
       got / there
           the cupboard in the hall / was bare
           the cupboard / in the hall
           the / cupboard
                in / the hall
                the / hall
                    was / bare

1. After the furniture was moved out, the house seemed very large. **2.** A friend of mine once walked all the way across Kansas in two months. **3.** The young gentlemen in the first row who were throwing spitballs at the actors were thrown out by a husky usher who had just served a hitch in the Marine Corps.

64: The underlying sound

People who speak English are among the most literate people in the world. Nearly all of us can read and write, and nearly all of us have been reading and writing since we were five or six or seven years old. Scarcely a day goes by that we don't let our eyes pass over letters on paper, unless we go into the wilderness on a vacation. And even there we're likely to bring along a loaf of bread with writing on the wrapper or a can of beans with writing on the label.

This is good of course. This is civilization. It lets us send our thoughts over long distances or know what our ancestors did or give advice to people not yet born. It lets us get things done and makes the world prosper. But it has one odd effect. It makes it very hard for us to understand what language is.

Literate people, with letters passing constantly before their eyes, tend to confuse the letters with the language they stand for. Ask them how many sounds there are in the word *they* and and they are likely to answer "Four — three consonants and one vowel." But actually there are just three sounds in this word: a single consonant at the beginning, made with the tongue between the teeth; a vowel made with the tongue midway between high and low in the mouth and bunched forward; and an upward glide made by moving the tongue from the position of the vowel in *bet* to that of the vowel in *bit*.

Writing is one of the great accomplishments of the human race, but writing isn't language. Writing is just a set of marks that we make on paper to call to our minds what goes on in our mouths when we speak. Even when we read a dead language, a language no longer spoken, like Latin, the letters and words suggest to us first a series of sounds and only after that the deeds and ideas that the sounds convey.

We have seen that the connection between speech and writing is not always a close and clear connection. One reason is that writing always lags behind speech. We tend to write more as our grandfathers or our great-great-great-grandfathers spoke than as we speak. This is more so in some languages than in others, and it is particularly so in English. The *gh* in *brought*, for example, stands for a sound that hasn't been pronounced for something like five hundred years. The spelling of *brought* doesn't any longer make us think of this sound. The word as a whole makes us think of the sound we actually make: /brɔt/. If this should change and people should come to say /brat/ or /brut/, then the spelling *brought* will make them think of those sounds.

One thing that everybody notices about English is that it is very hard to spell. This is because of the great lag between speech and writing. The spelling is frozen, and the speech keeps drifting away from it. As it drifts the connection between the letters and the sounds they call up becomes more and more complicated. The spelling *ough* is a very clumsy and peculiar spelling for the vowel sound in the word *brought*.

Some day the spelling may be changed so that it will show the sounds more simply and directly. This will happen when the sounds have drifted so far from the present spelling that the gap between them has become too great to put up with. But it probably won't happen in the twentieth century and probably not in the twenty-first either.

If the spelling were to be reformed right now, it would look something like this.

"If ðə spelıŋ wər tə biy rifɔrmd rayt naw, it wud luk səmpθiŋ layk ðis."

This is phonemic spelling. It reflects the thirty-three phonemes of modern English and reflects them directly, with just one letter to one sound. Naturally a change of this sort would have its stresses and strains. It would look funny, and it would take a lot of getting used to. Also it would cut us off from all the writing of the past. We'd have to take special instruction to be able to read Shakespeare and Dickens. On the other hand, because of the close connection with the sound, it would be much easier to learn than the present system. Children would spend much less time learning to read and write.

Here's another interesting thing. If our spelling were changed to something like that shown above, we'd want to freeze it again immediately. Bad though it is, our present writing system has one good feature: it's the same for everybody. We don't actually want people to write as they talk because they talk too differently. We want just one way of spelling words; then we can understand other people's writing no matter how they pronounce their words. If we decided to change *right* and *now* to *rayt* and *naw*, then they would have to be *rayt* and *naw* for every-body, even though some people say /rat/ and /næw/.

Even if the spelling were changed, the language would keep on drifting of course, and sounds and spelling would start to grow apart again. Then five hundred years later the spelling could be changed again.

One difference between speech and writing is that speech has many more signals in it than writing has. We can express our meanings much more efficiently and with less chance of being misunderstood when we talk than when we write. Also we can express many more shades of meaning and ways of feeling about the meaning. This is because our writing system doesn't show intonation, or at least doesn't show very much of it.

You will remember that intonation is a complex of three features. The first is **stress,** which is the relative loudness or soft-ness with which we say the syllables. The second is **pitch,** which is the relative speed of vibration of the sounds. The third is **juncture,** the way in which we end or break different stretches of sound. We have four contrasting stresses, four contrasting pitch levels, and four different junctures.

One indication of the efficient working of intonation is that it is much easier to dig up two-meaning structures in writing than it is in speech. "That's a smoking room" is ambiguous in writing. It could mean a room where smoking is permitted or a room that is on fire. But these meanings would be clearly separated in speech by the stress. We would have primary stress on the first syllable of *smoking* for the first meaning and primary stress on *room* for the other.

Or consider how many different meanings we can give to a simple utterance like "He's going to school" just by changing the intonation. We can show surprise or astonishment or anger or disbelief or insistence or questioning or mockery or various other emotions just by changing the intonation. Or we can even say it with an intonation that will make it a plain statement of fact.

Not much of our intonation shows in our writing, but some of it does, particularly the junctures. The connection between punctuation and the junctures is not exact, any more than the connection between letters and sounds is exact. But by and large the period suggests the fall of double cross juncture, and by and large the comma suggests the rise of double bar.

Intonation is always a part of language. You can't speak without speaking loudly or softly or in between, and the voice always vibrates, fast or slow. But different languages make different uses of intonation. The Chinese, for example, use pitch to distinguish between different words, much as we use the individual sounds. One use that English has made of intonation is to separate patterns, breaking them off sharply one from another. This has helped us develop the concept of the sentence and shows up in our writing in our use of periods and capital letters.

Important as intonation is, it is only very recently that we have begun to understand it and to explain how it works. Like so much of our language, it is so close to us and so deep in us that it is hard to stand back and understand what it does.

There is nothing closer to us than our native language. It is as close as our bodies and our minds. In a way our language *is* our mind and our memory. All our childhood experience, all our knowledge of the world is reflected in the words we use and the way we use them. We look at the universe as the patterns of our language teach us to look at it, and we can never see it any other way except by learning another language.

To know the language of a people is to know that people. To know one's own language is to know one's self. There is no more important study.

Index